SCAPEGOATS

SCAPEGOATS

SCAPEGOATS

THIRTEEN VICTIMS OF MILITARY INJUSTICE

MICHAEL SCOTT

Foreword by Magnus Linklater

First published 2013 by Elliott and Thompson Limited
27 John Street, London WC1N 2BX
www.eandtbooks.com

ISBN: 978-1-908739-68-1

9 8 7 6 5 4 3 2 1

A CIP catalogue record for this book is available from the British Library.

Printed and bound in the UK by T. J. International Ltd., Padstow

Typeset by Marie Doherty

'And he shall take the two goats, and present them before the Lord at the door of the tabernacle of the congregation. And Aaron shall cast lots upon the two goats; one lot for the Lord, and the other lot for the scapegoat. And Aaron shall bring the goat on which the Lord's lot fell, and offer him for a sin offering. But the goat, on which the lot fell to be the scapegoat, shall be presented alive before the Lord, to make atonement with him, and to let him go for a scapegoat into the wilderness.'

Leviticus 16:7–10

By the same author

(With David Rooney)
In Love and War: The Lives of General Sir Harry and Lady Smith

CONTENTS

FOREWORD

by Magnus Linklater

General Mike Scott is well placed to write about military scapegoats – he might so easily have become one himself. As commanding officer of the 2nd Battalion Scots Guards in the Falklands War, he was in charge of the assault on the heights of Mount Tumbledown on the night of June 13/14, 1982. It was to be an attack conducted uphill in pitch dark and freezing weather, against experienced Argentine marines, dug into well-defended positions. As General Scott himself concedes in the course of this book, 'There is an old military maxim that has stood the test of innumerable engagements: the odds favour the defender 3:1.'

He would have been well aware of that. He would also have known that, in the hours before the battle, he had twice questioned the orders he had been given, and twice succeeded in getting them changed. If, therefore, things had gone wrong, he would not only have borne the blame, his superiors could, legitimately, have pointed out that he was uniquely responsible for what had ensued. And Tumbledown was a close-run thing. Pinned down under sustained enemy bombardment, with dawn approaching, the battalion might well have had to withdraw, sustaining casualties as it pulled back. Instead it launched a bayonet attack, and, after fierce hand-to-hand fighting, took the last bastion that stood between British troops and the islands' capital, Port Stanley.

General Scott's absorbing account of military disasters, and those who were blamed for them, is full of knife-edge engagements like this – and the consequences that flowed from them. They are, in his hands, peculiarly fascinating, because he looks at them with a soldier's eye. He points out how easily, in the 'fog of war', things might have gone another way, but he can also stand back to analyse why they went wrong, and then distil from them the evidence that points to those who were ultimately responsible.

Scapegoats are usually sought when reputations are at stake, and they tend to be found among the ranks of those who are closest to the action when disaster strikes. Not only are they the ones least capable of answering back, they are there, on the front line, smoking gun in hand, while everyone else runs for cover.

In almost every case that the author examines, however, he finds that the muddled orders, poor communications, failed intelligence, weak strategy or even cowardice of those in overall command were more often responsible for the outcome than those charged with carrying out the orders – though not always, of course, because General Scott is honest, too, about the failings of soldiers and the circumstances in which they operate. Grand strategy, he points out, may as easily be undermined by the actualities of war – tiredness, hunger, fear, lack of sleep, weather – as by poor decision-making or unclear objectives. The fatal blowing up of the bridge at Sittang in Burma in February 1942 might have been avoided if the officer who ordered it had not been suffering from painful sores in his backside. Would Gettysburg have been lost if General Lee, in command of the Confederate forces, had been a bit more outgoing and communicative, and his right-hand man General Longstreet less taciturn on the morning of the attack? The luckless Admiral Byng might not have faced a firing squad for failing to rescue a British stronghold in the Mediterranean if the wind had held up at the crucial moment.

The themes running through this book are as relevant in today's theatres of war as they were in the campaigns and actions that General Scott describes. Time and again we find political or military leaders failing to connect with those whose responsibility it is to deliver the strategy. Chains of command are weak or non-existent; orders are imprecise or muddled; even experienced statesmen and generals, insulated from the realities of the front, can make catastrophic mistakes. And when the worst happens, their instinct is almost always to blame those further down the line.

General Scott is refreshingly brisk in his assessments of character. The governor of Gibraltar in Byng's day is dismissed as 'a useless soldier … obstructive, deceitful and pathetic'. General Sir Redvers Buller, commander-in-chief in the Second Boer War, is 'a superb major, a mediocre colonel and an abysmally poor general'. General Wavell, responsible for the Burma campaign in the Second World War, was 'not an easy man to understand and interpret, with his interminable silences', while his 'extraordinary out-of-touch demands and querulous telegrams' contributed, in Scott's view, to British setbacks against the Japanese.

He finds among this catalogue of disasters heroes, ill served by their superiors, who battle against great odds and then are blamed for what transpires: Brigadier George Taylor, 'a straightforward, uncomplicated man with a love of soldiering and a deep respect for his men', who was summarily dismissed in order to placate American allies after winning a stunning victory in Korea; Colonel Charles Bevan, a decent family man who killed himself after being made a scapegoat by Wellington for a setback in the Peninsula War; and Lieutenant General Roméo Dallaire, the hero of Rwanda, who attempted to avert a massacre and was abandoned by a supine United Nations which refused to give him the troops he needed.

Each inglorious episode is addressed by General Scott with the experience drawn from thirty-five years of soldiering. He weighs the circumstances, assesses the characters of those involved, then leaves the reader to form his or her opinion as to who should bear the final responsibility.

In the course of this unsparing account, we learn more about the military mind and the pity of war than we do in many a more conventional narrative. This is history from the inside – flawed, confused, frequently dysfunctional – which reminds us, nevertheless, that at the heart of great events are human beings whose fate is determined by forces over which they have little or no control.

ACKNOWLEDGEMENTS

The book covers a very wide spectrum of nationality, time, place and activity, so the help I had went much wider than, perhaps, I would have received for a single subject. Everyone has their pet scapegoat! A number of suggestions, therefore, would have happily qualified but I have tried to identify the most prominent, while spreading the time frame and country of origin.

I am indebted to Charles Messenger for his continual encouragement and suggestions. He suggested Dupleix, in particular, as a possible scapegoat although one, perhaps, more let down by his government, and cast adrift, rather than fitting the criteria. Philip Bambury redesigned the initial synopsis of the book to gather more succinctly the haywire of my thoughts. John Kiszely pointed me in the direction of Brigadier Taylor and David Elazar, and Randall Nicol, with his abiding interest in the First World War, was kind enough to scan the chapter on Corporal Short.

However, where I really started was with the descendants of Admiral Byng: the charming and ever-helpful Sarah Saunders-Davies and Thane Byng, introduced by Viscount Torrington, as direct a relative as can be in that convoluted family. I was privileged to be allowed into Wrotham Park by the Hon. Robert Byng where, with Felicity Wright's help, I took photographs which I have their permission to print, together with the front of the park itself. Nigel Pascoe QC, one of my heroes from the Bar and author of the play *To Encourage the Others: The Court Martial and Example of Admiral John Byng*, supported me in my 'third career'. I hope the chapter helps their drive to have the good admiral exonerated.

Viscount Slim sent me his copy of *DEKHO! Journal of the Burma Star Association* and introduced me to John Randle, one of the outstanding leaders during the Sittang Bridge disaster. The latter had little time for Jackie Smyth, a very understandable view from someone who saw his own troops decimated and stranded on the Japanese bank of the river. I hope, however, to have restored some balance to the story and was grateful for the views of Jackie's grandson, Sir Tim Smyth, now a doctor in Australia, and for his permission to use the photograph. Didey Graham, secretary of the Victoria and George Cross Association, helped to add colour to Jackie's later life.

I had lengthy and highly informative exchanges of emails with Julian Putkowski when writing the chapter on Corporal Short. Julian was one of the main drivers of the 'Shot at Dawn' movement, which resulted in the pardon for all those executed for alleged cowardice and desertion in the First World War. We did not always reach the same conclusions, but I was grateful for the time he took out of his very busy life.

Following a very interesting battlefield tour of the Peninsula Campaign run by Dick Tennant for the British Commission for Military History, I decided to include Charles Bevan who was the obvious scapegoat for the French escape from Almeida. Both Dick and Andy Grainger kindly carried out the 'red ink corrections' on my draft and gave me their approval. I was most grateful for Dick's permission to use his photographs.

Of the chapters that rely on readers to reach their own decision, the one on Brigadier Taylor stands out. It was the most difficult one to see why he had been so treated. I am indebted to Beverly Hutchinson in Officers' Records in Glasgow, who discovered the deliberations of the Army Council in the case, and to Leonie Seely, George Taylor's daughter, for allowing me access to the documents and to use his photograph. Hew Pike's father's papers, sadly, failed to reveal anything, but I was grateful for Hew's interest. Tony Cran, the Intelligence Officer of 1 KOSB at the time, was as helpful as he could be, but admitted that, from his level, the machinations of those higher up were beyond his pay scale! Robin Davies, in Australia, was very interested as he is writing the story of the Battle of Maryang San, but neither of us could throw any more light on the situation than I have done.

My old friend from Sandhurst days (The Sovereign's Company 1959), Joe West, helpfully commented on the Longstreet chapter. Coming from someone who gained the highest points ever recorded in the specialised subject on *Mastermind* (American Civil War), this was value indeed. Ed Coss, Associate Professor of Military History US Army Command and General Staff College, introduced me to Josh Howard, one of America's experts on the Civil War, who was kind enough to read the final draft and gave me invaluable advice and encouragement. I was also in correspondence with Susan Rosenvold of the Longstreet Society in America, which tries to reduce the damage done to the 'Old Warhorse'.

I owe a huge debt to Hanoch Bartov, a close friend of David Elazar's. We had a number of email and telephone exchanges and he honoured me with an inscribed copy of his book, *Dado, 48 Years and 20 Days.* I return the compliment with a copy of this one in the hope that I have done his old friend the justification he deserves. Yair, David Elazar's son, was also enormously helpful and allowed me to publish the letter from his father to Golda Meir on his resignation. It was elegantly translated by Ildi in Tel Aviv.

My one living scapegoat is, of course, Senator Roméo Dallaire. He is not actually a scapegoat, although he would have been if the United Nations could have engineered it. A victim of the perfidy and apathy of the Security Council, he is a hero to many, including me, and it was very valuable therefore to have his approval and comments on Chapter 13.

I am most grateful to Barbara Taylor for the elegance of the maps from my often spidery drafts and a variety of sources. An enormous thanks must go to my publishers Lorne Forsyth, Olivia Bays and Jennie Condell who put in a great deal of hard work and gave me endless ideas, help and encouragement. They are an outstanding team.

Finally, Magnus Linklater wrote a typically thoughtful and penetrating foreword, which was a great honour.

INTRODUCTION

At all costs avoid blame. Such is the creed of dictators and politicians, tycoons and company chairmen, media celebrities and spin doctors the world over. Identify a suitable scapegoat and make them take the blame. The idea that 'it must be someone else's fault' is a sad principle of a modern world. Today we see this in Cabinet leaks, kiss-and-tell tabloid exposures, Tweeting, super-injunctions and Wikileaks, but the tactics used to deflect the finger of blame or, better still, bury the knife in someone else's back, have never changed. To hold someone else accountable allows people to move on and avoid responsibility for the immediate past. Finding a scapegoat provides a relief and release for everyone except the victim. The urgency to do this is often out of step with the proper speed of justice. History crawls with the tales of those who have been wrongly castigated by people in a rush to find a culprit, any culprit, as soon as possible. Only later, sometimes much later, when the real truth comes out, is the scapegoat exonerated. For others, the mud sticks forever.

But what about men at war? Often those with the most to lose are the military scapegoats. The penalties for errors of judgement, the responsibility for avoidable casualties or the blame for the loss of national prestige can be devastating. This book is about them.

Exposed here are the real stories that allow the reader to make a balanced judgement on history's fairness to the individual. Military scapegoats can be found across the ranks and throughout the world and, although the officers, as commanders, bear responsibility for much of what went on, this has been no bar to those lower down being blamed. This book covers ranks from general to lance corporal, a US Navy captain and a civilian marquis; about half are British and the remainder American, French, Israeli and Canadian. It is arguable that they were all scapegoats, and they have been chosen to reflect that, regardless of nationality or status. Each chapter stands on its own; they are presented not chronologically, but in an order that will contrast the differences between the individuals and their stories.

In military history, the man himself is so often more interesting than the military industrial base, equipment, balance of forces, obstacles, firepower and the like. This is not to say that the latter were not vital to the outcome of any major campaign; of course, they were. However, the fascination is not only the interaction between commanders at all levels and the troops under their command, but also their own qualities in times, invariably, of extreme stress. What were the effects of illness, tiredness and exhaustion, fear and anxiety? Field Marshal Earl Wavell wrote to Sir Basil Liddell Hart: 'If I had time and anything like your ability to study war, I think I should concentrate almost entirely on the "actualities" of war – the effects of tiredness, hunger, fear, lack of sleep, weather. ... The principles of strategy and tactics and the logistics of war are really absurdly simple: it is the actualities that make war so complicated and so difficult.' For the men under them, George MacDonald Fraser put it so aptly in his superb *Quartered Safe Out Here*, 'With all military histories, it is necessary to remember that war is not a matter of maps with red and blue arrows and oblongs, but of weary, thirsty men with sore feet and aching shoulders wondering where they are.' This is to say nothing of elements well beyond individual control. Were these the demons that tipped the scales into an irrecoverable situation where the man carried all the weight, became the scapegoat and took all the blame?

'Scapegoat' in the old biblical sense one might think highly convenient: load all one's sins onto someone else, expel him into the desert and start with a clean slate. Fine, unless the scapegoat returns, having survived the desert, and poses some uncomfortable questions or, by his very presence, constitutes a threat. Brigadier Jackie Smyth, who was blamed for the Sittang Bridge disaster of 1942, and was highly critical of the official historian's subsequent coverage of the operation, is a prime example. The best scapegoat was, clearly, a dead one. Admiral Byng, executed on the quarterdeck of the *Monarch* in 1757 for failing to engage the enemy, and Lance Corporal Short, for inciting mutiny in Étaples in 1917, happily for their detractors, fitted the bill.

To most, a scapegoat is someone who has been unfairly accused or has taken the blame for something that has gone wrong. However, it is not always as simple as that. People have been blamed or vilified not necessarily in order to cover up someone else's ineptitude but, often, through pure envy and jealousy.

Professor Norman Dixon, in *On the Psychology of Military Incompetence*, elaborates on the process:

> This process [the discovery of scapegoats], to be efficient, must white-wash the true culprits (and their friends) while effectively muzzling those who might be in a position to question this action. This muzzling is a subtle process, the main inducement to silence being the unspoken threat that any attempt to undo the 'scapegoating' might put the undoers in jeopardy. Secondly, it must 'discover' scapegoats who are not only plausible 'causes' but also unable to answer back. Thirdly, it must impute to the scapegoats undesirable behaviour *different* from that which actually brought about the necessity of finding a scapegoat. By so doing it distracts attention from the real reason for the disaster and therefore from the real culprits.

So, even more complicated. One might call this person the 'non-scapegoat'; in other words, the individual who is allowed to go unpunished because to do so would expose others. Was General Sir Redvers Buller in 1900 such? Or was he quite justifiably to blame for Spion Kop and the weak message to the besieged in Ladysmith? Lieutenant General Sir Charles Warren was certainly partly responsible and Buller ensured he was made the scapegoat. Astonishingly, nothing happens to Buller until considerably later when he is 'compelled' to resign over a speech he made.

An unpleasant aspect of scapegoating is the undue haste in which the action is taken – the 'quick fix' – and how very indicative this is of the vulnerability the accusers must feel. The luckless Captain Carey, ostensibly in charge of the patrol on which the French Prince Imperial was killed by the Zulus in 1879, was court-martialled and cashiered within ten days of the event. Lord Chelmsford, the commander-in-chief, had just suffered humiliating defeat at Isandlwana and, having had his reputation saved by courageous soldiers at Rorke's Drift, clearly did not want any blame attached to him for the Prince's death.

The French marquis, Dupleix, Clive's opposite number in India in 1754, may be a name vaguely known but, since he was virtually cast out by his own country and died in penury and obscurity, it is unlikely. Few will know of Charles Bevan, a battalion commander in the Peninsula War. He so enraged Wellington after the French escaped from Almeida in 1811 that Bevan ultimately took his own life, preferring not to live with the disgrace.

David Elazar, the real hero of the Yom Kippur War in 1973, was forced to resign in the wake of the Agranat Commission. Later, the Israeli people would not tolerate it, and Golda Meir, who should have supported him, and her government, including Moshe Dayan, were removed from office. Elazar died, a broken man, aged 50.

Substantial rivers have always been military obstacles, even with today's sophisticated crossing equipment. An opposed river crossing almost beats breaching a minefield for one of the least attractive operations in the soldier's book. So capturing a bridge intact is a jewel worth every effort. Likewise, successfully defending it is as valuable. The opportunities for blame to be levelled when things go very publicly wrong are legion. The Sittang Bridge in Burma in 1942 was blown when much of the 17th Indian Division was left on the eastern, Japanese side of the river. Brigadier Jackie Smyth was unjustly accused of 'losing Burma' by this action. However, like many events in these stories, it was not quite as simple as that.

On 29 July 1945, the USS *Indianapolis*, under command of Captain Charles McVay, was torpedoed by a Japanese submarine in the Pacific. The ship sank with the loss of more than 800 crew. McVay was court-martialled and convicted of hazarding his ship. Yet why was he in waters known still to contain enemy submarines without being warned? What had happened to the intelligence assessments? Who knew of the dangers but allowed the ship to sail, unprotected? How convenient to let the unfortunate captain shoulder the blame.

A sacrifice to the gods of appeasement produces the occasional scapegoat. To preserve the cooperation of allies or the integrity of a formation, it becomes necessary to single out an individual to blame for a disaster. In Korea in 1951, the newly formed 28th British Commonwealth Brigade went into action. A very experienced Second World War battalion commander with two DSOs, Brigadier George Taylor, commanded it. Operation Commando was a success albeit after a very difficult protracted battle involving British, Australian and New Zealand troops. For many, the large, jocular Taylor was a popular leader, particularly among the Australians. However, stirrings among some of his British commanding officers and fairly open hostility from the New Zealanders led to his being peremptorily replaced. The cohesion of the international formation could not be risked.

The battle of Gettysburg was the most significant defeat for the Confederates in the American Civil War. Although it was not the final engagement, it marked the beginning of the end. For the South, their hero, General Robert E. Lee, had failed. How could this happen? There must be a reason for it. It was impossible, in Confederate eyes, for this man to have been outmanoeuvred and out-fought by General Meade. He must have been let down. How and by whom? The finger of disappointed ex-Confederates, promoters of the 'Lost Cause', pointed at Longstreet, one of Lee's corps commanders – the man who had argued with his leader, was allegedly late on the second day and then responsible for not supporting Pickett's breakthrough – surely, a cast-iron scapegoat.

Captain Alfred Dreyfus was a Jew. Convicted of high treason in 1894, he was sent to Devil's Island and not exonerated until 1906. The case was a complete fabrication, motivated by military paranoia, political opportunism and personal greed. Contrary to popular misconception, the French military hierarchy was not racially institutionalised, although, reflecting the standards of the day, it had its fair share of those who took no trouble to conceal their dislike of Jews. Nevertheless, it was highly convenient to blame a Jew and the newspapers were quick to whip the public up into a frenzy of anti-Semitic hysteria, making him the scapegoat and letting him carry all the blame for whatever ills Jews were seen to be causing the country.

The final chapter is about General Roméo Dallaire and his mission for the United Nations in Rwanda during the massacres of 1994. A man of outstanding moral and physical courage, who faced unbelievable carnage on an hourly basis, he never gave up trying to persuade the UN where their responsibilities lay and would never desert 'his' Rwandans. The Belgians, and no doubt others, would have made him a scapegoat for their own utter inadequacies, but could not do so. He certainly felt as such in the aftermath when they court-martialled one of his best officers. He is included, therefore, not as a scapegoat who fits the criteria, but as an example of what happens to a man when he is deserted, in effect, by the international consortium and abandoned to fight his own battles on their behalf.

The stories in this book are of people, many of whom, on the whole, faced appallingly difficult, life-threatening decisions that affected themselves, their men and their responsibilities. A few do not come out of it very well; some unfairly took the blame; others accepted what happened to them with varying degrees of grace. The judgement of whether they were really scapegoats or deserved their fate, ultimately, must rest with the reader. Before being too critical, armchair warriors should recall what Joseph Conrad wrote in *An Outcast of the Islands*: 'It is only those who do nothing that make no mistakes.' He was not entirely right; of course, mistakes are often made by people prevaricating or failing to grip a situation. Earlier, Marshal Turenne had put it better, saying, 'Show me a general who has made no mistakes and you speak of a general who has seldom waged war.' Finally, before weighing in with the benefit of hindsight, we should note what Professor Sir Herbert Butterfield wrote in *George III, Lord North and the People 1779–80*: 'One of the perpetual optical illusions of historical study is the impression that all would be well if men had only done "the other thing".' Quite.

ONE

Captain Jahleel Brenton Carey

The Killing of the Prince Imperial

June 1879

As scapegoats go, Captain Carey's story is arguably the prime example of how blame can be pushed down from above onto one who did not deserve it.

If Shakespeare had been alive in 1879, he would surely have written *The Tragedy of the Prince Imperial*. The tale had all the components he loved so much: high-born players, passion, battle, courage, death, failure and cover-up. He would not have had to invent anything, although he might have written the ending in brighter colours.

Eighty years later, officer cadets in the Sovereign's Company at the Royal Military Academy, Sandhurst, looking out of the window could see a statue of the Prince Imperial (see plate III) gazing out over the playing fields and lake. With the indolence and arrogance of youth, they paid it little attention except on high days and holidays when the statue was adorned with inappropriate articles or daubed with paint. They knew little of the Prince and cared even less. A study of the Anglo-Zulu War was usually confined to Stanley Baker's and Michael Caine's parts as Chard and Bromhead winning VCs at Rorke's Drift in the film *Zulu*.

So why the statue of this Frenchman? What was he doing in the British Army not that long after the French, the old enemy, had been so soundly beaten in 1815 and, more recently, by the Prussians? How and why had he met his end in a relatively unknown war a long way from home? What military incompetence and social unease had led to his death – and where had the blame been subsequently spread to absolve those responsible?

The origins of the Anglo-Zulu War, like many other wars, were simple, but the fighting – bloody, difficult and lasting much longer than anticipated – and the conclusion and extraction were much more complicated than planned. Disraeli's government had reluctantly supported the war, without expressly authorising it. As ever, there was increasing exasperation with escalating costs and the length of the campaign.

Europe's seafaring nations had a strong interest in the Cape as it provided the ideal base for ships sailing between the Atlantic and Indian Oceans. South Africa was a convenient and benign staging post for ships rounding the Cape. The Dutch were the first settlers but, in the seventeenth century, had made little effort to colonise further inland and were content merely to grow enough crops and manage water systems to provide for the various fleets. Amid the turmoil of the Napoleonic Wars, the British, nervous of French expansion and influence, seized the Cape by force. By the early 1800s, the Dutch settlers, augmented by other refugees such as the Huguenots and unprepared to accept the shackles of British administration, pushed inland to set up their own largely farming communities. In the 1830s, the Great Trek, as it became known, was relatively haphazard and raised tensions and animosity with the local tribes through whose territory it crossed and on which the Boers settled. British authority was left, effectively, on the coast in an uneasy relationship with the settlers. From 1820 onwards, the British had encouraged large numbers of people to settle in the Eastern Cape and this increased demand for expansion into what many thought, incorrectly, were the empty lands of the Veldt. In Natal, north and east of the Cape, the legendary Zulu chief, Shaka, established a powerful warlike tribe which, inevitably, came into conflict with the Boers. The British formally colonised Natal in 1843, pushing the settlers even further inland. Uneasy local treaties were formed with the Zulus and other tribes. The latter sometimes took the opportunity to break from the Zulu yoke and side with the British. In essence, the British kept a presence in South Africa because of the sea route. There was very little wealth to be extracted from the colony and the government in Whitehall merely desired a quiet and uncomplicated life with South Africa.

This changed dramatically in 1867 with the discovery of diamonds at Kimberley. At once, British eyes opened to visions of unbelievable wealth and profit. A loose confederation of the various states, such as the Transvaal and Orange Free State, under British rule suddenly became attractive and, in 1877, this was declared in Pretoria, to the disgust and confusion of the Boers. It was not difficult to see that, in addition to alienating the Dutch, the British were going to go head to head with the Zulus in their northern Natal kingdoms. A confrontation with the new king, Cetshwayo, was inevitable. The British administration in South Africa anticipated a quick success with a modern army against spear-carrying savages, followed by a leisurely peace in which to sort out the difficulties. As history has so often demonstrated, it does not always work like that. After the British issued a deliberately unacceptable ultimatum to the Zulus in December 1878, the Anglo-Zulu War began in January 1879.

The British commander for this swift action was Lieutenant General Lord Chelmsford. He was a professional soldier with experience in the Crimea, the Indian Mutiny and Abyssinia in 1868. Despite that, he was not an innovative military thinker and, as generals are sometimes criticised for doing, he tended to fight today's battles with the last war's tactics. Having overcome the weak Xhosa tribes relatively easily, he was overconfident when dealing with the Zulus. Chelmsford failed to gather sufficient intelligence on the Zulus' modus operandi, their strengths or whereabouts. He had to rely on an inadequate, and indifferently trained, force of a mixture of British soldiers, volunteer horsemen and locally raised native militia. Coupling these defects with a severe misjudgement of his own and a superbly and courageously orchestrated Zulu attack, the result was the disaster at Isandlwana where 1,300 of Chelmsford's men were killed, a third of his effective force. The outstanding defence of Rorke's Drift immediately following this defeat was probably the only thing that saved Chelmsford from dismissal. The effect at home was devastating and Chelmsford was frantically reinforced with virtually all that he asked for. Among these reinforcements appeared Louis Napoléon Bonaparte and Lieutenant Jahleel Brenton Carey of the 98th Regiment of Foot.

Napoléon Eugène Louis Jean Joseph, the Prince Imperial of France, was born in Paris on 16 March 1856. He was the son of Napoleon III, emperor of France, the third son of Louis Bonaparte, king of Holland in the time of his brother, the great emperor Napoleon Bonaparte. The prince's mother was Eugénie Marie de Guzman, younger daughter of the Spanish Count de Montijo and his Scottish wife, Donna Maria Kirkpatrick. As both his parents spoke English well and his nurse was English, it was not difficult for him to acquire the language fluently. When he was 14, the Franco-Prussian War broke out and, on 19 July 1870, dressed in the uniform of a *sous-lieutenant*, he rode out with his father, who was to take personal command of the French forces. On 2 August, he had his first experience of battle at the skirmish of Saarbrücken. The war, however, was short-lived and Napoleon III surrendered to the Prussians on 2 September. The emperor was taken prisoner of war and Eugénie and Louis sought sanctuary in England. Napoleon was soon released by the Prussians and joined his wife and son at Chislehurst in Kent where they were befriended by Queen Victoria. Given Prince Albert's natural antipathy to the Bonapartes (he was a Coburg) and British Francophobia, this was difficult to understand, particularly as Victoria still firmly endorsed the views of her husband, although he had been dead for eighteen years. One can only put it down to Victoria's very firm views on the sanctity of the European monarchies, whose crowned, or nearly crowned, heads were, in many cases, her relations. Many people regarded Napoleon III at best as a lightweight fop, and at worst, an inadequate upstart, but, nevertheless, there were those who had some sympathy for his predicament.

In 1872, to his great delight, Louis became an officer cadet at the Royal Military Academy, Woolwich. Woolwich then trained officers for the Royal Artillery and Royal Engineers, while Sandhurst trained the cavalry and infantry. Napoleon Bonaparte himself had started life in the artillery, so what could be more appropriate for his great-nephew? Louis was extrovert and energetic and engaged in outlandish bouts of skylarking and showing off. Was this to compensate for his rackety upbringing and very uncertain and ambiguous future? With no actual commission in the British Army, despite his education at Woolwich, he could not command troops nor fill a post on the staff. What was he to do? The Establishment had made a serious problem for itself. He must have carried considerable psychological baggage. Dr Adrian Greaves, the historian and consultant clinical psychologist, clearly explains:

> I believe Louis was destined from birth to become a neurotic extrovert. At first sight, this might indicate him to be a gregarious, flamboyant risk-taker keen to impress. He may well have appeared to everyone as such but in psychological terms, he had serious and destructive psychological problems…An extrovert is one who 'shows out' behaviour in order to make up for under-arousal, usually as a child. Children who are controlled or repressed, frequently because they have suffered the controlling influence of the parental 'learning curve' need, in teens and onwards, to express themselves to make up this deficiency. It is common for adventurers and 'high flyers' to come from strict families and many are the first born; subsequent siblings are more relaxed as their parents settle into parenthood.
>
> The Prince Imperial certainly fits the criteria for classification as both a neurotic and an extrovert. His parents reared and educated him with one role in mind, to become the future Emperor of France. Sadly for Louis, exile to England severely curtailed this process leaving him a victim and with every need to re-prove himself. It is no wonder that he employed his inner childhood tactics of showing off to gain credibility.

Was this the reality behind his application to the commander-in-chief, the Duke of Cambridge, to serve in South Africa? It cannot have been through any 'political' thoughts of his own, which, if anywhere, would have directed him towards his own country's interests in Austria and the Balkans. No, it was clearly a desire to prove himself, coupled with his romantic nature and sense of destiny. He needed to taste his own 'whiff of grapeshot'. The Anglo-Zulu War contained the required spice of danger with, for him, no international complications. But for the Commander-in-Chief, what was the Prince Imperial actually going to *do*? Perhaps some nice little sinecure could be arranged, tucked away in Chelmsford's headquarters, well out of harm's way? With the tacit approval of Queen Victoria, the Duke overcame Disraeli's refusal to allow the Prince to go with the understanding that the boy was to be there in a private capacity with no official standing. Disraeli was apoplectic but Cambridge had slipped it past the Queen and rid himself of a minor, but potentially major, irritation. The Duke wrote to Sir Bartle Frere, the high commissioner in South Africa:

> I am anxious to make you acquainted with the Prince Imperial, who is about to proceed to Natal by tomorrow's packet to see as much as he can of the coming campaign in Zululand in the capacity of a spectator. He was anxious to serve in our army having been a cadet at Woolwich, but the government did not think that this could be sanctioned; but no objection is made to his going out on his own account, and I am permitted to introduce him to you and to Lord Chelmsford in the hope, and with my personal request, that you will give him every help in your power to enable him to see what he can. I have written to Chelmsford in the same effect. He is a charming young man, full of spirit and energy, speaking English admirably, and the more you see of him, the more you will like him. He has many young friends in the artillery, and so I doubt not, with your and Chelmsford's kind assistance, will get through well enough.

This was the first of the buck-passing exercises, which were going to be so useful later.

The Prince reached Durban on 31 March 1879 and, accompanying Lord Chelmsford, moved with the headquarters to Pietermaritzburg. On 8 May, Chelmsford reached Utrecht and the Prince was placed under Colonel Harrison, the assistant quartermaster general (AQMG) who was responsible for the administration of the command. Far from being tucked away as the Duke of Cambridge wished, however, Louis was allowed out on patrol.

We must now turn to the other main player in the drama, Lieutenant Jahleel Brenton Carey. He was born in Leicestershire on 18 July 1847, the son of a parson. Interestingly, he was educated for much of his early life in France. He could, of course, speak fluent French and had adopted many French mannerisms and perceptions, which was subsequently to his advantage in his relationship with the Prince Imperial. On graduation from Sandhurst, he was commissioned into the West India Regiment, at the time serving in Sierra Leone. 'Colonial' regiments such as these were unpopular in military circles and lacked cachet and sophistication. However, officers could live on their pay while others in 'smarter' regiments, based at home, required a private income. Foreign service, such as with Carey's regiment and those regiments of the Indian Army, also provided a good quality of life and the opportunity for advancement through distinguished service in 'small wars'.

Such a small war occurred in 1867 in Honduras, to which Carey's battalion had been sent to deal with friction between the settlers engaged in logging and the local population. In one action, a British patrol under Major Mackay was badly ambushed, which resulted in a rout for the security forces. Major Mackay was duly censured but Carey, who had been instrumental in covering the withdrawal of the unlucky force, emerged with a good deal of credit. There appeared to be no doubt as to his personal courage. Carey had clearly adopted a professional approach to his career which, in some circles, was disdained by those who thought they could succeed by mere amateurism.

Carey returned to England in 1870 suffering from the debilitating effects of service in the fever-ridden swamps of Central America, married and settled down to a solid career. Particularly devastating for him, though, was when he was placed on 'half-pay'. This was a sort of semi-redundancy whereby the government could reduce the officer corps but maintain a hold over them for future expansion if needed. To someone of Carey's financial means and newly married this was a real blow. However, with the onset of the Franco-Prussian War, he volunteered for service with the English Ambulance. Speaking French, he emerged with a decoration for 'his conduct in the relief of French wounded'. With this behind him he was able to obtain a commission in the 81st Regiment of Foot, with a subsequent transfer into the 98th, then stationed in the West Indies, his familiar haunt.

In 1878, he passed the Staff College course well and quickly volunteered for service in South Africa. He travelled out with a draft of reinforcements on the SS *Clyde*. As bad luck would have it, the *Clyde* was holed on a sandbar 3 miles offshore, unpleasantly close to where the SS *Birkenhead* had famously gone down in February 1852. Carey, together with the other officers, organised the disembarkment from the sinking ship and set up camp ashore. Not one man was lost and after their speedy rescue by HMS *Tamar*, the officer in command, Colonel Davies, formally mentioned Carey in dispatches for his outstanding conduct. This did nothing but good for his self-confidence.

What sort of man was he? His courage was proven, his ambition properly in evidence and his professionalism well developed. He was tactically experienced and battle inoculated in Honduras and the Franco-Prussian War. With a steady family background and an unusual education in France, he was clearly an asset in anyone's unit or headquarters. He was conscientious, hard-working and probably rather dull for the more extrovert younger officers. Working in a headquarters, at whatever level, is not much fun for an officer who prefers to soldier with his men, and for both Carey, with his front-line experience, and Louis, a young man thirsting after adventure and the opportunity to prove himself, Chelmsford's camp must have seemed boring and restrictive.

It is also important to realise how the two would have related to one another. Carey, with his French upbringing would have, naturally, been an attraction for the Prince, and his combat experience a subject of admiration. For Carey, the Prince represented a completely different world and, in those Victorian times when social divisions, even within classes, were strictly maintained, Louis might have come from another planet. Although, of course, the Prince was not a commissioned officer, Carey would have been very careful not to give him strict or peremptory orders. To a certain extent they would have been thrown together in the headquarters, with Carey being Colonel Harrison's number two as deputy assistant quartermaster general (DAQMG), and Louis a sort of extra aide-de-camp (ADC) for whom there could be no proper job.

Part of Carey's responsibility was to carry out reconnaissance for future campsites and, in the absence of reliable maps, find safe routes capable of taking the ox-drawn wagons. This work involved making sketches and hand-drawn mapping, which both he and the Prince were relatively good at. With varying degrees of success, Louis was allowed to accompany some of these patrols.

Louis, however, was rash and impetuous and there were a number of instances when he rushed off on a reckless frolic of his own, to the annoyance of the patrol commanders and not least danger to himself. People like Captain Bettington, an experienced commander of irregular Natal Horse, whose men – scruffy and ill-disciplined compared to conventional British cavalry, but, nevertheless, highly versed in soldiering in the Veldt – had little time for him and regarded him as a dangerous nuisance. Soldiers, on the whole, like their young officers to show a certain amount of 'form', but not to the extent that it leads them into danger or they have to go and pull them out of trouble. Ian Knight in his masterly *With His Face to the Foe* quotes Colonel Buller voicing concerns about the Prince to Lord Chelmsford, who ordered Harrison to ensure the Prince did not leave camp without a proper escort. This he put in writing. (Harrison's *Recollections of a Life in the British Army* was not published until 1908, by which time, presumably, memories had faded and the temptation to put a gloss on the more difficult occurrences of June 1879 must have been irresistible.)

By 30 May 1879, Chelmsford was ready to push forward; routes had been recced, cavalry protective screen deployed and the first night's campsite had been selected. Intelligence, such as it was, suggested that the Zulus would not oppose the advance until well after the second night's bivouac. So, when Louis badgered Harrison to be allowed to leave camp and take out a patrol, the latter anticipated little danger and, as Carey agreed to accompany the patrol to verify some of his earlier sketches, Harrison was reassured that the Prince would be safe under his supervision. Clearly, there was no real need for this additional patrol, and whether Harrison merely wanted to be temporarily rid of the tiresome Prince when he had much work to do, or whether he just wanted to be pleasant to the young man, can only be guessed. He therefore agreed and, allegedly, put in writing orders (which were never found) containing the proviso that the patrol was to be protected by a suitable escort. It was unclear who was actually in command of the patrol: Louis could not be, as he held no rank, and Carey was merely 'accompanying' the patrol to verify his previous sketches, so perhaps it was thought the escort commander, possibly Captain Bettington, would be in command?

Accordingly, Carey approached the brigade major of the Cavalry
Brigade to order an escort from Bettington's Horse and the Natal Native
Horse. Six men were detailed from Bettington's troop and Carey was
told to put in an order for the rest of the escort (the Basuto auxiliary
element) to their commander, Captain Shepstone. There was then a
muddle. Carey merely left the order with Shepstone for the Basutos and
hurried on. By the time the Basutos had fallen in, Carey and the rest of
the patrol, including a friendly Zulu guide, had left. Carey sent a message
to Captain Shepstone to have his men meet them at a forward rendezvous and left with the impatient Prince. Whether there was an inference
that Captain Shepstone would accompany his Basutos, and therefore
possibly command the patrol, can only be conjecture. Bettington's men
were experienced soldiers and included a sergeant and a corporal. Carey,
no doubt, had full confidence in them and happily expected to be joined
shortly by the rest of the escort.

The rendezvous for the Basutos coincided with the position for the
division's first night's camp. While Carey and Louis were waiting there,
Colonel Harrison and Captain Grenfell appeared, in order to mark out
the areas for the various components of the division. Harrison reinforced
his instructions to Carey and the Prince that they were not to proceed
without the Basuto escort, then left. Grenfell, having completed his tasks,
agreed to accompany Carey and Louis for part of the way. Maybe this,
and the Prince's increasing dominance of the patrol, persuaded Carey
to allow the small force to push on without waiting for the Basutos. It
is not difficult to see the self-confident and impatient Louis asserting
himself with Carey and the soldiers. He had been used, all his life, to
deference, even from senior army officers, and Carey would have been
highly conscious of this. Additionally, right or wrong, Carey did not see
himself as the commander of the patrol. That is not what he volunteered
for. He was, in his own eyes, merely there to amend his sketches. With
hindsight, one might wonder how he could have possibly thought this,
knowing full well the Prince had no rank and could not possibly be put
in command. Had Colonel Harrison's orders been properly given out,
which they may have been, the 'command' paragraph would have been
mandatory and abundantly clear. It is difficult to imagine that there was
any option other than Carey commanding the patrol in the absence of

any other officer. But in the turmoil before the patrol left, did Harrison actually issue the order?

Grenfell accompanied the patrol for about 7 or 8 miles and then left to return to the main camp, saying cheerfully, 'Take care of yourself, Prince, and don't get shot.' Louis responded, pointing to Carey, 'Oh no! He will take very good care that nothing happens to me.'

A while later, they came upon an unoccupied small collection of about eight or ten huts (kraal) and various cattle pens and decided to take a break, unsaddle the horses and let them have a roll and graze on some of the nearby mealies (maize). While it was quickly apparent that there were no Zulus occupying the kraal, there was thick grass growing up to 5 or 6 feet high and a dried-up water course, a donga, providing a very obvious concealed approach towards the kraal. Despite Carey's experience, and that of the Bettington's Horse NCOs, none of this was 'cleared' by even the most cursory close-in patrol around the area. No sentries were posted – not even a single lookout – and no order was given to load weapons (apparently the latter were carried unloaded when men were mounted). One wonders what the sergeant thought he was doing? His job, when the officer is busying himself with map reading, planning or putting his orders together, is to bustle about dealing with standard basic procedures: posting sentries, producing a roster, designating alarm positions, loading weapons with safety catches applied and pointing out the emergency rendezvous. Only then can a brew-up take place. This is not making a judgement by today's standards; these procedures were firmly in place in those days and had been for many years before.

The Prince and Carey sat around chatting in the hot sun. At about half past three, Carey suggested saddling up and moving on. After a brief delay, with reluctance the Prince agreed and the patrol started to round up the hobbled horses. As they were doing so, their native guide reported seeing a Zulu down by the main river. This does not appear, though, to have caused particular alarm; he could merely have been a local herdsman. Saddling up proceeded, and by about four o'clock the Prince (note, not Carey) gave the order to mount.

At that moment they were attacked by a force of about forty to fifty Zulus who had crept up unobserved through the long grass and the dead ground of the donga. They appeared about 20 yards away before opening fire. These Zulus were a harassing group of enemy whose job it was to act separately from the main body and pick off small parties of British when the opportunity arose. Fit young men, they would have relished their independent and special role. There was a volley of shots from the Zulus which, while not very accurate, came as such a profound shock to the members of the patrol that immediate panic set in. Carey was already in the saddle and others had varying success in mounting as the terrified horses bolted. The Prince was in severe trouble. He had not been able to mount his horse but was running alongside, grasping a stirrup leather or part of the saddle. At some point, his grip broke. The last anyone saw of him, he was running along the donga closely pursued by about a dozen Zulus. Carey and Troopers Cochrane and Le Tocq scrambled their horses over the donga and were joined by Corporal Grubb and Sergeant Willis. Trooper Abel had been brought down with a shot and there was no sign of Trooper Rogers or the native guide.

Carey had completely lost any control if, indeed, he had any in the first place. He paused to look round at the pursuing Zulus and realised the Prince had not made it. The patrol was too spread out and beyond effective voice range to rally even if, by doing so, they could have resisted the attackers. What weapons they had left with them were unloaded in any case. There was, at that point, no question of being able to save those who had not made their escape. Had they tried to do so, there is no doubt that they would all have been killed. Eventually, they managed to regroup and the pursuers gave up the chase. The full realisation of the appalling tragedy started to become apparent. There was only one option: to return to the main camp and bear the consequences.

As the news of the Prince's death spread, a shock wave was felt throughout the army and, subsequently, at home. On 9 June, Chelmsford sent an immediate telegram to the Secretary of State for War in England:

Prince Imperial under orders of AQMG recced on 1 June road to camping ground of 2 June accompanied by Lt Carey DAQMG and 6 white men and 'friendly Zulus'. Halted and off-saddled about 10 miles from this camp. As the Prince gave the order to mount a volley was fired from the long grass around the Kraals. Prince Imperial and 2 troopers reported missing. Lt Carey escaped and reached this camp after dark. I myself not aware that Prince had been detailed for this duty.

One can already sense the speedy raising of an umbrella in the last sentence.

With the loss of Isandlwana, a defeat from which he never properly recovered, and now this, Chelmsford sank into deep despair. Colonel Harrison could also feel a cold chill running up his spine. The Prince was *his* responsibility. He had it *in writing* from the General. How was this going to be handled without them both going down?

While there were those who were quick, and justifiably so, to criticise Carey, there were also those who, perhaps considering the situation a little more deeply, thought, 'What would I have done in similar circumstances?' Certainly, among the survivors of Isandlwana, there would have been a number who might not have considered themselves to have been entirely covered with glory. There was an uncomfortable feeling that Carey was being lined up as a scapegoat. An immediate Court of Inquiry was held and the *prima facie* evidence was wholly damning against Carey: he could say little to justify the fact that the patrol had bolted; the troopers with him were quick to say Carey was first to run; there was no attempt to hoist up onto the survivors' horses those who failed to mount; and Carey was unable to absolve himself from responsibility for commanding the patrol. The court had no alternative but to recommend Carey be tried by General Court Martial on a charge of 'misbehaviour before the enemy'. He was promptly removed from his appointment as DAQMG on Harrison's staff. There were those who might have considered this to be punishment enough and, possibly, under normal circumstances this would have been a distinct possibility; ambushes happened and there were casualties and not everyone behaved exactly as others thought they should, but they were not court-martialled. But these were not ordinary circumstances; the heir to the French Empire had been killed. What would have happened if Prince Harry had been on a reconnaissance with the Americans in Afghanistan, ambushed by the Taleban, killed and deserted by members of the patrol?

Carey's court martial began on 12 June, eleven days after the Prince's death. In the midst of serious campaigning, it is difficult to understand how proper arrangements could be made and a court of experienced

officers assembled, let alone the prosecution and defence be given enough
time to prepare their cases. The speed with which this happened raises the
inevitable suspicion that there was an anxiety to have Carey firmly nailed
before anyone else could be held to blame. It is not surprising, therefore,
that the proceedings would end in embarrassment and come to haunt
the hierarchy to such an extent that the record would be barred from the
public in the National Archives at Kew, not for a standard thirty years,
as normal for secret and sensitive documents, but for a hundred years.
Not until 1979 were people allowed access; by then everyone involved
was safely dead.

The court opened with a colonel as president and four other officers. In attendance was a major as officiating judge advocate. Names
were read out but there is no record of the members being sworn.
Carey was charged that: 'He having misbehaved before the enemy on
the 1st June 1879 when in command of an escort in attendance on His
Imperial Highness Prince Napoleon, who was making a reconnaissance
in Zululand, having when the said Prince and escort were attacked by
the enemy galloped away, not having attempted to rally the said escort,
or otherwise defend the said Prince.' Carey pleaded not guilty and the
prosecutor, Captain Brander, then outlined the case for the prosecution
– he would call witnesses to show a map of the action and where the
bodies were found, and the survivors to cover precautions taken and the
subsequent behaviour of the prisoner. He would also call the AQMG,
Colonel Harrison, to prove Lieutenant Carey was in command of the
whole party. Finally, he would call evidence to show the cause of death.

Carey decided to defend himself. Nowadays this would be considered unwise but he may have felt sufficiently self-confident to answer
the charges or, in the time available, been unable to identify someone to
defend him. Long before the days of the Army Legal Service, it might
have been difficult to find someone of the calibre required or even someone with sufficient sympathy for Carey that he would be prepared to
risk others' opprobrium in allying himself with such an obvious loser.

The map markings were shown, and agreed. Then Captain Molyneux,
an ADC to General Chelmsford who was on the expedition to recover the
Prince's body, was asked what position the Prince held on the General's
staff. Molyneux proved vague, as well he might. The fact was that the

Prince held no position, nor could he. No one really knew what he was doing there apart from the General, who had been told to host him by his commander-in-chief in Whitehall. While this might have helped Carey's case in that the Prince had no business to be anywhere near the patrol, it certainly did not assist when he was trying to convince the court that the Prince was in command of the party. He had no rank, he was not an officer and was not even in the British Army.

The thread of Carey's defence, apart from the angle that the Prince was in charge of the patrol, was: what could anyone have done under the circumstances other than what they did, which was to run?

'Was there any chance of success if we had recrossed the donga to try to save the Prince [i.e. pulled up, reorganised and returned to the attack]?'

'No ... if a man fell from his horse, he had no chance at all,' maintained Carey.

Le Tocq was next. 'Yes, the Prince ordered us to mount.'

'Who was in charge of the escort?'

'The Prince,' said Le Tocq, a Channel Islander, who comes out of it better than most. His evidence was strong. 'The Prince asked if we were ready and we said yes. And he said to mount.'

Then it was Cochrane's turn. He was an 'old soldier' with sixteen years' previous service in the Royal Artillery. He had seen the Prince running in the donga with fourteen or so Zulus after him.

'Could we have rallied?' asked Carey.

'No.'

'Could we have done anything?'

'No. We only had three carbines. We could do nothing except gallop away. We would have all been killed had we stayed. We could do nothing to save the Prince.'

'Who was in command?'

'I don't know. I think the Prince gave the commands.'

Colonel Harrison was then called to give crucial evidence as to who was in charge of the patrol. He had given Carey no orders about command of the patrol. He maintained that the senior 'combatant' officer must assume command in accordance with Queen's Regulations. He did not know who was the senior combatant officer, not having seen the escort before it started, and therefore, not knowing whether an officer would accompany it when Lieutenant Carey volunteered to go on the duty, to best of his belief, he said, 'I was glad he had volunteered because he could look after the Prince.' If Carey had not gone he should have requested another officer of the staff to go for that purpose. He went on to say if the Prince had been senior to Carey he would naturally have been in command, unless there had been another officer senior to him with the escort. He could not say if an officer performing reconnaissance duties should be in command of an escort over another officer who is similarly employed. He never said Lieutenant Carey was in command of the escort. What he said was that the senior combatant officer must command troops on any duty by virtue of Queen's Regulations. He maintained he treated the Prince just like any other officer.

Harrison was clearly nettled and defensive. He must have known that the Prince was simply not allowed to command at all. He admitted the Prince was on a reconnaissance to find a campsite for the second night of the advance. The Prince should not have been entrusted with an unsupervised job; Carey had another task (verifying his earlier sketches) and, in theory anyway, was not there to monitor the Prince's work. The General had specifically told Harrison to look after the Prince properly. Not even knowing who was in charge of this little operation, and, perhaps, relying on someone else turning up, was hardly doing that. Carey was in charge, purely because he was the *only* combatant officer in the party. Harrison, though he never, it seems, gave any specific orders, escapes because of that. Sadly, Carey did not have a professional lawyer. One such would have had Harrison significantly embarrassed.

Captain Bettington then gave his men a good report, saying they were his most trustworthy soldiers. He clearly did not think it necessary to comment on the fact that the NCOs had not taken standard protective measures when they were halted at the kraal. Had they done so – particularly, Sergeant Willis – the story may have been very different.

Carey then put forward his defence. It was closely argued, based on the evidence of the survivors and the reality of being able to do no more than he did. At no point, whether in camp or when they met later, had Colonel Harrison ordered him to be in charge of the patrol. He always thought he was junior to the Prince. However, that was irrelevant at the 'moment of attack'. It was unquestionably his duty to rescue the

Prince. He heard the Prince give the order to prepare to mount, then mount, and he assumed that the Prince had done so, having seen the others doing so. In the melee there was a hut between him and where he thought the Prince was; it was therefore difficult to see. Even when he had slowed his horse to a walk having crossed the donga, his group was widely separated. Willis's and Grubb's horses were 'knocked up' and were not able to join him until later. The possibility of being able to rally and return to the fray, with only three men armed with rifles and the 'fagged' horses, was out of the question. The others unanimously substantiated this. Carey finished by effectively asking the members of the court what they would have done in his place. There were a number of written testimonials in his favour, from various officers, produced to the court.

The prosecutor really had little to do except repeat his accusation that of course Carey was in charge. He went on to pick holes in the witnesses' statements and remind the court that these witnesses were defending themselves and it suited their case to exaggerate their difficulties. He maintained that there was not 'the slightest attempt to rally or defend the Prince' and he failed to see 'that *anything* was done'.

On 17 June 1879, the court found Lieutenant Carey guilty and sentenced him to be cashiered (dismissed from the army with disgrace).

In forwarding the papers to Lord Chelmsford, Colonel Glyn, the president of the court martial, made the following points in Carey's favour:

1. That the Prisoner was out for the second time only with the Prince Imperial and for the first time as the senior officer and did not appear to realise that he was in that position.
2. That the Prisoner was employed on duty independent of that of taking charge of the Prince.
3. The weakness of the escort, that it was composed of men not under the same discipline as soldiers and they were not under one of their own officers.
4. That the Prisoner was evidently under the impression that the Prince Imperial held some military status and was the senior officer.
5. The Prisoner's length of service and the high character he bears as testified to by several superior officers.

When Lord Chelmsford passed the papers to the adjutant general for submission to the field marshal commander-in-chief for the Queen's decision, he based a plea for mercy on the fact that Carey was not wanting in courage but had lost his head in the heat of the moment. So, with no doubt an enormous sigh of relief from all those involved in the case in South Africa, Carey was dispatched, in disgrace, to the United Kingdom. The Queen, as the Confirming Authority, still had to see the papers, be given advice and make a decision. So Carey was in limbo until that happened.

Carey arrived back in England on 20 August but was kept aboard the ship in which he had travelled until told of the Queen's decision. No doubt to his surprise, he was not treated to the opprobrium that he might have expected. Even the army was divided rather than being wholly against him, which he had expected. There was considerable discussion and speculation in the press, and a series of exchanges of letters in *The Times*, the *Army and Navy Gazette*, the *United Service Gazette*, the *Morning Post* and the *Western Daily Mercury*.

So that Queen Victoria, the Confirming Authority, could reach a balanced and legally sound decision, the judge advocate general's department was tasked, as normal, to produce advice, rather in the same way that the UK's Attorney General nowadays might advise the Cabinet. Deputy Judge Advocate General James O'Dowd wrote an opinion. There were really two main points. The first was the technicality of the failure of the court to record the swearing in of the members. If the court had *not* been sworn, then quite simply, the proceedings were null and void.

His second point was more important in that it related to the quality of the evidence to support the charge of 'misbehaviour in the face of the enemy'. Was there sufficient evidence to support that 'escaping as quickly as possible' reached the threshold of guilty and was there a 'failure to rally or defend the Prince'?. In both cases he decided that it did not. He maintained that, in the second case, it came nowhere near, and in the first, although there was a slight chance, the main preponderance of evidence was against it.

There was considerable in-fighting and tension between the army and the government as to who had the final say in discipline matters. It was uncomfortable for everyone and the Queen herself was dissatisfied:

'The Queen regrets the charges laid and the imperfect evidence adduced should have led to what the Queen considers a very unsatisfactory conclusion. Her Majesty cannot help expressing the wish that a more perfect investigation had been made into all the circumstances preceding, during, and subsequent to the unhappy event which led to the trial.'

Carey, by now a captain (he had been promoted a few days before the patrol but news of it had not reached South Africa), was told of the decision but was dissatisfied with the 'non-confirmation' rather than an acquittal. He subsequently made some unwise statements to the press and even sought to approach Princess Eugénie, the Prince's mother, who, sensibly, refused to see him. He was posted back to his regiment, the 98th, then serving in Malta. While on garrison duties with his regiment later in India, Captain Jahleel Brenton Carey died of peritonitis on 22 February 1883.

That Carey was a scapegoat is clearly without contradiction – even his contemporaries realised that. Had the Prince not been killed on the patrol, only Troopers Abel and Rogers, Carey would have had an official rebuke and an entry on his conduct sheets at worst, or a severe interview with his commanding officer (Colonel Harrison) at best. The reality is that the Prince, a foreigner, a non-combatant and not a member of the British Army, should never have been there at all – not on the patrol or, indeed, even in South Africa. The Duke of Cambridge, the commander-in-chief, was to blame for sending him there in the first place. The Prince was a tiresome embarrassment. He had been trained at Woolwich but could not be commissioned, so now what to do with him? Send him off to dear old Chelmsford. Chelmsford had quite enough problems as it was; a broken man after Isandlwana, he needed to restore his reputation. (Buller remarked, 'I hope I may often meet Chelmsford again as a friend but I trust I may never serve under him again as a General.') The killing of the Prince must have sounded his death knell. Fix Carey was the neatest solution.

Colonel Harrison had much to lose. He was the man ultimately given responsibility for the Prince, but, busy and overworked himself, it slid from his grasp. Ultimately, it did his career no harm, as he ended it as a general. Lower down the ladder there must have been others who slept uneasily during the court martial. What instructions and briefing did Bettington give to his men? Did they just lurch off on the patrol as yet another boring fatigue? Under whose command were they? Had they rehearsed their drills, their action on meeting the enemy, their quick reaction techniques to protect the Prince? What orders had Sergeant Willis given for protection and emergency action during halts, in particular, at the kraal? Where had Captain Shepstone and his Basutos gone when they failed to turn up? Why did they make no effort to catch up with the patrol?

This was altogether a sad affair, which rocked society in England and France at the time, destroyed the life of an engaging and lively young man, scion of the Bonaparte dynasty, and ruined the career of an experienced and steady officer.

Carey's court martial was never confirmed and therefore, legally and effectively, was null and void. Nevertheless, he was never found *not guilty* and exonerated. We must look to the next chapter to find a man who was exonerated, but too late to save him.

TWO

Captain Charles McVay

The Sinking of the USS Indianapolis

July 1945

On Wednesday, 6 November 1968, Captain Charles McVay III, former captain of the USS *Indianapolis*, took his service revolver and shot himself in the head outside his house. He died a few hours later. For him this was the tragic end to the sinking of his ship, the loss of more than 800 men and his subsequent court martial. But by the efforts and dedication of the surviving members of his crew, he was eventually awarded a posthumous presidential exoneration.

In the Pacific, by the spring of 1945 the war with Japan was nearing its final stages. On 1 April, following the recapture of the Philippines and the capture of Iwo Jima, United States forces landed on Okinawa. Heavy fighting ashore continued until 21 June, when organised resistance ceased. The Pacific Fleet was, throughout, in full support of the landings and fighting. However, this was at considerable cost. The damage was suffered mainly by destroyers and their escorts. These ships, which acted as guard ships for the main force, were the principal targets for kamikaze attack. The demand on this class of ship together with the drain on effectiveness by necessary repairs meant that, despite being reinforced from the North Pacific and Atlantic, priorities had to be made. Available escorts could only be used in the most exposed areas, and on tasks where they would contribute most to the safety of those lying off Japan and the troop-carrying ships. Other ships had to sail unescorted in the more remote areas.

During July the situation was being stabilised around Okinawa, and direct attacks on Japan itself by both carrier task forces and shore-based air forces were taking place, in anticipation of the forthcoming invasion. By the end of the month, the carrier task forces were delivering very heavy attacks, destroying many Japanese aircraft and practically eliminating the Japanese surface ships in their home ports. The Pacific Fleet was deliberately increasing the pressure on Japan in order to bring the war to an end and to drive the Japanese into submission without the necessity of a costly invasion. USS *Indianapolis* was to play a vital part in this operation.

Her captain, Charles McVay, was the son and grandson of Charles McVays, thus becoming the third. His father, an admiral, had distinguished himself in the Spanish–American War and commanded three battleships in the First World War. A difficult and forceful man, he was determined that his son should follow his success. His truculent behaviour was partially responsible for the break-up of his son's marriage – Charles III divorced his wife, Kinau, in 1936. Sadly, the insensitivity and cruelty inherited from his father meant that he, in turn, treated his two sons with apathy and disinterest. Perhaps this was the price Charles McVay III paid for what was, potentially, an outstanding career in the navy. He served with distinction as Chief of the Joint Intelligence Committee of the Combined Chiefs of Staff in Washington and his active service record was exemplary. He had been decorated with the Silver Star as executive officer in the cruiser USS *Cleveland* in the Solomon Islands campaign. He had taken part in the landings in North Africa and then, in November 1944, took over command of the USS *Indianapolis*. He immediately raised standards and morale among the crew. Although somewhat aloof, he was highly respected and trusted by his men. He led the ship through the invasion of Iwo Jima, then the bombardment of Okinawa in the spring of 1945, during which his anti-aircraft guns shot down seven enemy planes before the ship was struck by a kamikaze on 31 March, inflicting heavy casualties and penetrating the ship's hull. With considerable skill, McVay returned the ship safely to Mare Island in California for repairs.

On 12 July, McVay received orders for a top secret mission. Unknown to him at the time, this was to carry essential parts of an atomic bomb, ultimately destined for Hiroshima. He was to sail for Tinian in the Mariana Islands, via Pearl Harbor, and offload his special cargo there.

Setting sail from San Francisco on 16 July, the ship arrived at Tinian and deposited its cargo on 26 July without incident. On reaching Guam the following morning, McVay replenished the ship and was further ordered to Leyte in the Philippines to join the task force in preparation for the invasion of Japan, with a route and arrival estimate of 11 a.m. on Tuesday, 31 July at an average speed of over 15 knots. He was not told of any specific submarine threat. Indeed, the *Indianapolis* was not equipped for anti-submarine warfare. It had no depth charges or sonar equipment. Escorting ships were not available and, in any case, the threat did not warrant it. The passage was merely routine, with no special instructions.

On Sunday night, 29 July, the ship had been zigzagging – an evasive movement making the vessel, supposedly, a difficult target for torpedoes fired from submarines – up until dark. Thereafter, as the moonlight was only intermittent and often obscured by cloud, it was considered safe to proceed normally. At approximately five minutes after midnight the ship suffered two violent explosions. Arriving on the bridge, McVay could not see anything through the dark and smoke. He asked the officer of the watch if he had had any information. He said he had lost all communications and had tried to stop the engines but had no idea whether his order had been received by the engine room. All other communication systems appeared to have been lost.

Another officer appeared on the bridge to tell McVay the ship was going down rapidly bow-first and asked, did he want to give the order to abandon ship? He demurred, saying that there seemed to be only about a 3-degree list. They had been through this sort of damage before, and were able to control it quite easily, so were not too perturbed. However, within another two or three minutes, the executive officer, Commander Flynn, McVay's second in command, appeared and said, 'We are definitely going down and I suggest that we abandon ship.' Knowing Flynn well and having great regard for his ability and judgement, McVay agreed and said, 'Pass the word to abandon ship.'

Although this order had to be passed verbally, an experienced crew who had been in battle before would sense when something was badly wrong and go to their action stations without being told, so McVay was confident the crew would react. His next concern was whether the distress message had gone out. He had asked Commander Janney, the navigator, when he first went on the bridge to make certain that he sent the signal. Janney went down below and that was the last that was seen of him. Knowing that it was absolutely essential that someone be notified where the ship was, since it was unescorted, McVay made his own way to the radio room.

As he did so, the ship listed 25 degrees to starboard. People started to slide down the decks as he went down to the signal bridge. As he reached it, the ship listed another 40 or 45 degrees, then 90 degrees. He then made his way to the stern of the ship, walking on her side before being sucked into the water by a wave caused by the rapid sinking of the bow. Looking above him, to his horror, he saw the propellers and thought his end was imminent. He swam rapidly away from the descending blades and felt hot oil gushing over him and, with that, the ship was gone. In his own words:

> The sea at this time was rather confused. There had been storms up north and I was buffeted about quite a bit. We had a long, heavy, ground swell, the wind was from the southwest and force about two. We could still see nothing. It was still dark and I could hear people yelling for help. Something bumped into me, it was a potato crate and I got astride of that with some more debris which I had under my right arm and I considered myself pretty well off and in a few minutes, a few seconds later I would say, two life rafts came by. They apparently had been released from the ship when she went down, or had been torn loose as one was on top of the other. I crawled on these two life rafts. I couldn't find any paddles or anything whatsoever on them, and I yelled back at the people who I heard yell and we picked up three others, pulled them on the raft. That was all that we saw, or all that we heard. There were two of them, two youngsters, that were pretty well filled up with salt water and oil and I placed them on one of the rafts by themselves, and a quartermaster by the name of Alert and I took the other raft. We secured the two rafts together, and nothing that I remember happened that night. I guess everybody was pretty well exhausted. These two boys that were on the other raft didn't move all night and I thought probably they had died, but they pulled through perfectly all right, about 36 hours later.

At dawn the next morning, McVay found himself with three rafts, which were hitched together, and nine people. They discovered some cans of water, emergency food and a flare pistol with twelve cartridges. There were two paddles but all the first aid kit and matches had been soaked with water or contaminated by oil. They spotted two other rafts some way away and heard yelling but were too exhausted to make their way over to them. At this stage, McVay thought they were probably the only survivors of the ship, totalling some twenty-five to thirty. Rationing out the food and water, he reckoned his group could last about ten days.

On the Tuesday, they paddled over to the raft they had seen recently and joined it to theirs. Taking four and a half hours, it completely exhausted them. They had terrible blisters on their hands and it was quite evident that every abrasion and cut was going to develop into a very nasty saltwater ulcer. Additionally, fuel oil getting into eyes caused a great deal of pain and discomfort. Paradoxically, though, the coverage of fuel oil protected them to some extent from sunburn, and, finding some canvas, they cut it up into rudimentary sunhats. From time to time they saw planes and signalled to them, by day with a mirror and by night with the flares, but, clearly, the planes were flying too high and were not searching for them. But it seemed to them that they could not possibly be missed.

At midday on Thursday, they spotted planes circling well to the south of them and, at night, some ships' searchlights, so they reckoned there must be survivors found there but worried that they were too far north now to be rescued. On that assumption, McVay reduced the rations to half. However, on Friday planes were seen much closer and, to their joy, two ships were seen approaching their position. His group were picked up by USS *Ringness* and the raft further away by the other ship at about 10.30 a.m., having been in the sea for 107 hours. They had not been spotted by planes but by the ships' radars. An empty metal ammunition box they had with them acted as a radar reflector and, although only detected at a range of about 4,000 yards, it was enough to register a blip on a ship's screen.

McVay now discovered that there was a large group of survivors, about 10 miles to the south, who had existed in the water for four days, purely in their lifebelts, with some even having to share. Not surprisingly, this group suffered the most. Some hallucinated, swimming away from the group convinced that the ship had not sunk or there was an island close by, and were never seen again. Many simply died from exhaustion, just gave up the will to live or went mad from drinking seawater. There were those who were willing to sacrifice themselves for others, those who were just too stupefied to do anything and those who merely put themselves first. Sharks abounded and took anyone they could but some men even survived shark bites and lived to show off their scars. They owed their eventual rescue to the pilot of a Ventura patrol bomber. He was on a regular routine reconnaissance from his base when he went back into the plane to fix a radio aerial. Ordinarily, the radio operator would do it, but he was busy and as the pilot did so, he happened to glance down towards the water and saw a large oil slick. He then decreased his altitude and followed the oil slick for a number of miles, when he sighted the group of what he thought were about thirty survivors. He did not know that they were survivors from the *Indianapolis*. He did not even know the *Indianapolis* was missing. This was about 11.25 a.m. on Thursday, 2 August. He dropped a transmitter, lifeboat and emergency beacon. Then, an hour later, he sighted another group of survivors and sent a message, 'Send rescue, 11 degrees 54 minutes North, 133 degrees 47 minutes East, 150 survivors in lifeboat and jackets. Dropped red ramrod.' They were saved.

Once he had fed and rested on his rescue ship, McVay's thoughts inevitably turned to his own position:

> You have rather peculiar thoughts that go through your mind. I thought that, well, it may be embarrassing if I'm the only one left, or at least if I, as a Captain, am left and my ship is gone. But, I decided that I would attempt to save myself. I must admit that I had the thought that it would have been much easier if I go down, I won't have to face what I know is coming after this. But, something stronger within me decided that, spurred me to get out of the way, at least to attempt to save myself. And, on the raft, of course, I had a great many hours to think of the disaster and I knew of some of the people I had lost.

He tortured himself with the thought that they had not been able to send out the SOS signal before the ship sank, hence the long delay before being rescued. Going over it again and again in his mind, he convinced himself that, indeed, they had done so but could not understand how a message sent on the emergency frequency, which was always monitored by four receivers in the area, had not got through.

In the end, 316 men from a crew of 1,196 survived.

On 6 August 1945, the atomic bomb was dropped on Hiroshima and, on the 9th, on Nagasaki. The war with Japan was effectively over. So what was the navy to do about the loss of USS *Indianapolis*? There would have been a temptation to sweep the matter under the carpet and lose it in the euphoria of conquest. What good would be done, at this stage, to hang out dirty washing? The war had ended, was there any point in establishing lessons from the disaster when there were going to be no more naval engagements? On the other hand, there were mothers, wives, fathers, brothers and sisters of more than 800 men who would, understandably, require not only an explanation but the punishment of any culprits. What about the honour of the navy? A loss of this magnitude could not be ignored. What about the positions and reputations of people who might feel themselves uncomfortably close to the events? A speedy inquiry to establish blame, punish the guilty, as far down the ranks as possible, and move on, seemed to be the answer.

Commander-in-Chief Pacific Fleet, Admiral Chester Nimitz, convened an inquiry in Guam. In Washington, Secretary of the Navy James Forrestal and Chief of Naval Operations, Admiral Ernest King, had their own worries and were determined that the navy's name would be cleared. If this was to be at the expense of the captain of the *Indianapolis*, then so be it. There would certainly be others in the frame, perhaps even Nimitz himself, for not ensuring that procedures for reporting the non-arrivals of ships were sound. Nimitz was a fair man. He had actually been court-martialled for running his ship aground in his early years so he knew the anxiety and stress this caused. He therefore took a cautious and deliberate attitude, leaning heavily on the advice of his staff. The inquiry opened on 13 August and Japan surrendered on the 15th. On the same day, a classic good time to bury bad news, the navy publicly announced the loss of the USS *Indianapolis*.

The inquiry bounced to and fro, with the shore-based witnesses, those who had failed to warn McVay of the submarine threat and those who failed to register the non-arrival of the ship, trying to minimise their responsibility. McVay, to a lesser extent, was asked why he hadn't zig-zagged and why he had not ordered the ship to be abandoned earlier. While hardly optimistic, McVay, nevertheless, did not expect more than some level of admonition. After all, the navy had lost some 700 ships in the war and no captain had been court-martialled, so why him? Therefore, it was to his horror that the judge recommended that he should not only receive a letter of reprimand but also be tried by court martial for inefficiently performing his duties and endangering his crew's lives through negligence.

It was Nimitz's turn to be concerned. He did not agree with the rec-ommendation of the inquiry. He accepted that McVay may have made an error of judgement but not that he was not guilty of the negligence that would justify charges being brought at a court martial. In Nimitz's view, it could be said that McVay should have zigzagged; nevertheless, this was not a *mandatory* order and was up to the captain's discretion, so there was ample room for a reasonable defence to this charge. However, as Nimitz could be blamed himself, he did not want to appear to be slid-ing away from responsibility by failing to allow the case to be exposed to court martial. He wrote to the judge advocate general of the navy, refusing to agree with the recommendation of the inquiry, saying that the failure to zigzag was an error of judgement, which merely rated a letter of reprimand rather than a court martial. Admiral King was alarmed by this and saw the good name of the navy sinking in this scandal. (It has been suggested, although without good evidence, that King was driven by vindictiveness. Earlier in his career, he had suffered at the hands of McVay's father. Did he see this as an opportunity for revenge?)

Uncomfortably, relations of those who died were already making their voices heard, and some of them were loud and powerful. While McVay could be blamed for not zigzagging, the delay in searching for his ship, which was nothing to do with him, was going to be a diffi-cult hurdle. If McVay was court-martialled, he could be blamed for the actual loss of the ship, keeping the bereaved and the press off the backs of the naval hierarchy, and the rest swept away with some relatively junior knuckle-rapping. Therefore, King advised Forrestal to have McVay court-martialled despite Nimitz's misgivings. Forrestal still wavered. Perhaps it would be better to institute further inquiries? But what would happen if these further inquiries found even less evidence against McVay? If there was no court martial and no captain to blame, would the heat be then turned on him and the naval chiefs? The politician's self-protection system started to kick in. Albeit, to be fair, with considerable reluctance, Forrestal agreed to a court martial without further delay.

Before going further, it is worth recalling, before the froth of legal argument clouds the issues, what actually went wrong.

- *Was McVay properly warned of the threat?* The official press release of the navy dated 23 February 1946 reported:

  On July 27, Captain C. B. McVay, III, U.S.N., commanding offi-cer of the Indianapolis, visited the Office of the Port Director, Guam in connection with his routing to Leyte. Later that day the Navigator of the Indianapolis also visited the Port Director's office to obtain the Routing Instructions and discuss their details. Information of possible enemy submarines along the route was contained in the routing instructions and was discussed with the Navigator. The route over which the Indianapolis was to travel, which was the only direct route between Guam and Leyte, and was the route regularly assigned vessels making passage between these islands, was considered within the acceptable risk limit for combatant vessels. Circuitous routes were available from Guam to Leyte, but no special apprehension was felt regard-ing the use of the direct route by the Indianapolis and no other route was considered. The speed of advance of the Indianapolis (15.7 knots) was set by Captain McVay and was based upon his desire to arrive off the entrance to Leyte Gulf at daylight on July 31 in order to conduct antiaircraft practice prior to his entering the Gulf. To have arrived a day earlier would have required a speed of advance of about 24 knots. No special consideration was given [to] the possibility of delaying the departure of the ship from Guam in order to enable her to proceed in company with other vessels, since the route assigned was not thought by the Port Director to be unduly hazardous.

Although naval intelligence knew of four Japanese submarines in the area, from ULTRA sources, one of which was most likely to have sunk the USS *Underhill* on 24 July, it was not considered sufficiently threatening to adjust McVay's route or give him an escort. An error of judgement on the part of the intelligence people?

- *Why did he not zigzag?* It was at his discretion. He had zigzagged in daylight but once darkness fell and the moon was overcast, he deemed it unnecessary. Evidence later, from the Japanese submarine captain who sunk the ship, maintained that zigzagging would have made no difference in any case.

- *If the distress signal went out, why was it not acted on?* McVay tried to find out whether it had been sent but was too late. In fact, it had. The SOS was received by three operators in the Leyte area but was ignored when there was no response to their authentication queries. Did it not occur to them that the ship was now incapable of responding? The Japanese success signal was also intercepted in Guam but, with no coordinates, it was of no use. There was an enormous amount of radio traffic intercept and it was merely put down to Japanese exaggeration and deception.

- *Should McVay have ordered the ship to be abandoned earlier?* This might have saved more lives by allowing crew to board life rafts in time, rather than having to jump into the sea merely with life jackets. McVay was not initially aware of the full extent of the damage. He was an experienced officer and knew that a premature abandonment would have been likely to result in casualties, as well as unnecessarily losing the ship. It was his professional judgement when to give the order.

- *Why did the rescue take so long?* The *Indianapolis* was due at Leyte at 11 a.m. on Tuesday, 31 July. The rules were – no doubt to preserve security – that 'arrival reports shall not be made for combatant ships'. Fine, but does that absolve port staff from being *aware* of a combatant ship's arrival or, in this case, its absence, when they knew it was due? However, fighting ships were under operational command rather than administrative port authorities and could be redirected to other tasks before ever reaching the intended port. It was unlikely that the port officer would be informed of any change. So, even if he had noted the absence of a ship, he would not have been under any duty to report it. It was not his problem. Clearly, the link between operational and administrative elements of the command structure was fragile. But what about the operational commanders? Why did they not know where the ship was? Did they merely assume it had arrived, as ordered, in Leyte? *Indianapolis* was due to join Vice Admiral Oldendorf's task force in the Okinawa area prior to the invasion of Japan. However, before that, the ship was to report to Rear Admiral McCormick for refresher training at Leyte. McCormick knew when the ship was coming, but not why. Oldendorf knew where the ship was going, but not when. Thoroughly inadequate message passing and lack of attention to detail meant that the proper information completely slipped between the floorboards. So, in essence, the *Indianapolis* was never missed at Leyte and no enquiries were made and, of course, no search instigated.

The trial was due to start on 3 December 1945 at the Washington Navy Yard. McVay was notified but not told what specific charges would be brought against him. The reason was simple: the navy had not yet been able to make up its mind what he could be charged with. Four days before the trial began, this document was issued:

To: Captain Thomas J. Ryan, Jr., U.S. Navy
         Judge Advocate, General Court Martial, Navy Yard, Washington, D.C.

Subject: Charges and specifications in case of Captain Charles B. McVay, III, U.S. Navy

1. The above-named officer will be tried before the general court martial of which you are judge advocate, upon the following charges

and specifications. You will notify the president of the court accordingly, inform the accused of the date set for his trial, and summon all witnesses, both for the prosecution and the defense.

CHARGE I
THROUGH NEGLIGENCE SUFFERING A VESSEL OF
THE NAVY TO BE HAZARDED
Specification

In that Charles B. McVay, III, Captain, U.S. Navy, while so serving in command of the USS *Indianapolis*, making passage singly, without escort, from Guam, Marianas Islands, to Leyte, Philippine Islands, through an area in which enemy submarines might be encountered, did, during good visibility after moonrise on 29 July, 1945, at or about 10:30 p.m., minus nine and one-half zone time, neglect and fail to exercise proper care and attention to the safety of said vessel in that he neglected and failed, then and thereafter, to cause a zigzag course to be steered, and he, the said McVay, through said negligence, did suffer the said USS *Indianapolis* to be hazarded; the United States then being in a state of war.

CHARGE II
CULPABLE INEFFICIENCY IN
THE PERFORMANCE OF DUTY
Specification

In that Charles B. McVay, III, Captain, U.S. Navy, while so serving in command of the USS *Indianapolis*, making passage from Guam, Marianas Islands, to Leyte, Philippine Islands, having been informed at or about 12:30 a.m., minus nine and one-half zone time, on 30 July 1945, that said vessel was badly damaged and in sinking condition, did then and there fail to issue and see effected such timely orders as were necessary to cause said vessel to be abandoned, as it was his duty to do, by reason of which inefficiency many persons on board perished with the sinking of said vessel; the United States then being in a state of war.

JAMES FORRESTAL

McVay's defending officer was selected for him: a naval officer with minimal legal qualifications, named Captain John Cady. The prosecutor, the brilliant Captain Thomas Ryan, was about as good as the navy could get. They were determined not to lose this case.

The prosecution opened the case with the officer who had given McVay his route from Guam to Leyte and confirmed that the journey was routine with no abnormal threat. This, of course, bolstered McVay's view that zigzagging would be discretionary at best. Next, the officer of the watch at the time McVay turned in, testified that there was no moon, it was a very dark night and visibility was variable to very poor. He did not feel the need to call the captain as there was no significant change in visibility during his watch. He was aware of the general submarine threat but this was no different to other times in the war. He did not hear the order to abandon ship but this did not mean it had not been given. In his view the crew had sufficient time to prepare to leave the ship. Another good witness for McVay.

The engineering officer was next and the prosecutor attempted to show that McVay had not made enough effort to communicate with the engine room after the attack. It was clear the officer had properly come up on deck to see the captain as communications were down. He did not, at the time of leaving the engine room, consider the damage was bad enough to initiate an abandon ship order himself. Next came the medical officer, Commander Lewis Haynes, a staunch supporter of McVay and one of the people who comes out of this story with an outstanding reputation. Ryan could not dent him and he finishes, typically as many other of the crew, by saying that he would be honoured and pleased to serve again under Captain McVay.

Four more witnesses followed with varying recollections with regard to visibility, and whether they actually heard the 'abandon ship' order. This certainly did not reach the 'beyond reasonable doubt' test of evidence. Two more officers from the Guam routing agency were then examined on the submarine threat and the need for escorts or a zigzagging procedure. They had little to add to what they had already said. The prosecution then called Glynn Robert 'Donc' Donaho. Donaho was a naval officer widely known for his outstanding exploits as a submarine commander during the war, for which he received the Navy Cross four times, and the Silver and Bronze Stars twice each. Clearly, Donaho's technical expertise in submarine operations was going to weigh heavily with the court. There is an old adage that a good lawyer knows the answer to the question he is going to ask before the witness answers it. Ryan slipped up badly in this case because Donaho made it quite clear that against modern submarines, which had fire-control equipment, high-speed torpedoes and a well-trained control party, zigzagging would be ineffective. Furthermore, Donaho added that he would expect a ship, conventionally, to zigzag and, if it did not, he would find it off-putting. This was not what Ryan wanted to hear.

McVay was called. He repeated the instructions he had given about zigzagging and confirmed the orders covering the abandon ship.

Then came probably one of the most extraordinary witnesses to appear before a court martial: Commander Mochitsura Hashimoto, the Japanese commander of the submarine *I-58* that sank the USS *Indianapolis*. Hashimoto was born in Kyoto, the younger son of a Shinto priest. In 1927 he joined the Imperial Japanese Navy. Later, he volunteered for the submarine service and served on destroyers before entering the Navy Torpedo School in 1939. He was selected for submarine training the following year, and joined the submarine *I-24* in 1941. At the outbreak of the war, Lieutenant Hashimoto was the torpedo officer on the submarine *I-24*. This was the boat that launched a midget-submarine at Pearl Harbor. Hashimoto subsequently saw action in many Pacific operations, being promoted to lieutenant commander in 1944. Later in the war, Hashimoto was given command of the *I-58*. For a man of Hashimoto's background and Japanese codes and ethics, to be summoned to give evidence at the court martial of the captain of an enemy ship he had sunk must have seemed quite extraordinary. His first thought, not unnaturally, was that, somehow, he was going to be involved in a charge of war crimes. (He had counted himself quite lucky he was not actually a prisoner of war.) He was relieved to be told that this was not so and he was merely to appear as a witness to give his account of the sinking. McVay was equally perplexed; it was difficult to understand how the prosecution could call this witness – a man who had been responsible for the death of more than 800 Americans?

The prosecution's case, of course, was to get Hashimoto to say that the ship was not zigzagging, therefore it was easier to hit. However, Hashimoto's answers on both the weather conditions and whether the *Indianapolis* was actually zigzagging were ambiguous. The weather and light were variable; the ship made movements but was not noticeably zigzagging. Hashimoto was, however, very specific that had the ship zigzagged, it would have made no difference to his attack. Effectively, he was confirming Donaho's expert opinion. This was not good for the prosecution although, given the nervousness of having such an alien witness, the defence, perhaps, made less of it than they might. It was some relief, therefore, to both sides when Hashimoto was stood down.

In closing, Ryan hammered home the prosecution case of the failure to zigzag and give a timely order to abandon ship. The defence reminded the court of Donaho's expert statement and Hashimoto's confirmation that zigzagging made no real difference. Perhaps Cady failed to make enough of the fact that zigzagging was *discretionary* and the lack of doing so might be construed as an error of judgement but not an offence. He stressed that the essence of the abandon ship instruction, while it could not be formally given out due to the circumstances, was, nevertheless, effective and acted upon. The fact that so many men died was not the captain's fault but lay with the inability of the command system to realise the ship was missing and send out rescue parties earlier.

The court considered its verdict. It found McVay not guilty of the second charge, that of not giving a timely order to abandon ship, but guilty of negligence on the first, the failure to zigzag. He was sentenced to lose one hundred numbers in his temporary grade of captain and one hundred numbers in his permanent grade of commander. In recognition of his outstanding service, the court recommended him to the clemency of the reviewing authority.

Indeed, in 1946, McVay's sentence was remitted by Forrestal and he was restored to full duty. However, as Nimitz was at pains to point out, the *sentence* was remitted, not the *conviction*. The naval staff, nevertheless, was in a quandary. Relations of those who died still clamoured for heads to roll, particularly further up the ranks. Egged on by the press, there was a suspicion that McVay was a scapegoat for those who should have warned him about the submarine threat and those who failed to note the ship was missing. Was it enough merely to reprimand some of the lower ranks, which had already happened as a result of the earlier inquiry, or should they go further? There were a number of names in the frame:

- *Failure to warn of the threat*
  Admiral Murray
  Commodore Carter
  Commodore Gillette
  Captain Naquin

- *Failure to report ship's absence*
  Captain Granum
  Lt Comdr Sancho
  Lt Gibson

- *Failure to investigate the Japanese report*
  Captain Layton
  Captain Smedberg

- *Failure to find out why ship was overdue*
  Admiral McCormick

- *Failure to find out when ship was due*
  Admiral Oldendorf

- *Issuing ambiguous orders re reporting*
  Admiral Nimitz
  Admiral King

Clearly this was going to get out of hand, and Forrestal was not prepared to have his admirals censured. On 23 February 1946, the Navy Department issued a 'Narrative of the circumstances of the loss of the USS *Indianapolis*.' It concluded with this:

The following disciplinary action has been taken in connection with the loss of the *Indianapolis*: Captain Charles B. McVay, III, U.S.N., has been brought to trial by General Court Martial. He was acquitted of failure to give timely orders to abandon ship. He was found guilty of negligence in not causing a zigzag to be steered.

He was sentenced to lose one hundred numbers in his temporary grade of Captain and also in his permanent grade of Commander. The Court and also the Commander in Chief, United States Fleet recommended clemency. The Secretary of the Navy has approved these recommendations, remitted the sentence, and restored Captain McVay to duty. The Secretary of the Navy has given Commodore N.C. Gillette, U.S.N., a Letter of Reprimand, which will become part of his permanent official record. The Secretary of the Navy has given Captain A.M. Granum, U.S.N., a Letter of Reprimand, which will become part of his permanent official record. The Commander in Chief, Pacific Fleet has given Lieutenant Commander Jules C. Sancho, U.S.N.R., a Letter of Admonition, which will become part of his permanent official record. The Commander in Chief, Pacific Fleet has given Lieutenant Stuart B. Gibson, U.S.N.R., a Letter of Reprimand, which will become part of his permanent official record.

As far as the navy was concerned, the case was now closed. McVay had a congenial shore posting to New Orleans. The navy, of course, would not dare to give him another ship. He retired in 1949, aged 50, being promoted to rear admiral on his last day in service. In December 1946, the letters of censure against the others were quietly withdrawn and the sad Forrestal committed suicide in 1949.

But it was nothing like the end for McVay's loyal crew and family. They were determined he should be exonerated. It really began with the first survivors' reunion in 1960, which occurred thereafter every five years. Led by former Marine Private First Class Giles McCoy, the USS Indianapolis Survivors Organization, as it was now called, gained in strength and influence. Not surprisingly, the navy wanted little to do with it. A submission for a Presidential Unit Citation for the ship received unhelpful responses from both President Ford's administration in 1975 and, again, from President Reagan's in 1980. A request by McVay's family to have the court martial expunged or a posthumous pardon met equal resistance. In 1991, after considerable pressure, the navy announced it would re-examine the records and forward the findings to a congressional subcommittee. The writer Dan Kurzman, with his masterly book, *Fatal Voyage*, became, à la Zola, an articulate spokesman for the organisation. The navy fought its own corner with members of Congress and, in 1992, a committee recommended that McVay's court martial should not be reopened, no further review should be initiated and the court martial proceedings should not be reconsidered. This was supported by next of kin of some of those who died, who could see McVay only as a villain.

The House of Representatives, however, forwarded the following Resolution on 28 April 1999:

SECTION 1. SENSE OF CONGRESS CONCERNING THE COURT-MARTIAL CONVICTION OF CHARLES BUTLER MCVAY, III.

It is the sense of Congress that—

(1) the court-martial charges against then-Captain Charles Butler McVay III, United States Navy, arising from the sinking of the U.S.S. INDIANAPOLIS (CA-35) on July 30, 1945, while under his command were not morally sustainable;

(2) Captain McVay's conviction was a miscarriage of justice that led to his unjust humiliation and damage to his naval career; and

(3) the American people should now recognize Captain McVay's lack of culpability for the tragic loss of the U.S.S. INDIANAPOLIS and the lives of the men who died as a result of her sinking.

SEC. 2. SENSE OF CONGRESS CONCERNING PRESIDENTIAL UNIT CITATION FOR FINAL CREW OF THE U.S.S. INDIANAPOLIS.

(a) Sense of Congress. — It is the sense of Congress that the President should award a Presidential Unit Citation to the final crew of the U.S.S. INDIANAPOLIS (CA-35) in recognition of the courage and fortitude displayed by the members of that crew in the face of tremendous hardship and adversity after their ship was torpedoed and sunk on July 30, 1945.

(b) Waiver of Time Limitation. — A citation described in subsection (a) may be awarded without regard to any provision of law or regulation prescribing a time limitation that is otherwise applicable with respect to recommendation for, or the award of, such a citation.

Then, in September, the US Senate Armed Services Committee assembled to hear the case for McVay. The argument ran that if it was accepted that the court martial was appropriate then others should have faced charges. However, right or wrong, the court martial, having been held purely to try McVay, then reached the wrong verdict. It could not find him guilty of not zigzagging his ship, because the decision to do so was his alone. He was not under mandatory orders to do so. Perhaps he might have exhibited an error of judgement but that was not an offence punishable under court martial. It was difficult for his supporters to understand why naval authorities and Congressional subcommittees could not accept that. Even his old enemy, now a Shinto priest, went to his defence with a letter to John Warner, the chairman of the committee, on 24 November 1999:

I hear that your national legislature is considering resolutions which would clear the name of the late Charles Butler McVay III, captain of the USS Indianapolis which was sunk on July 30, 1945, by torpedoes fired from the submarine which was under my command. I do not understand why Captain McVay was court-martialed. I do not understand why he was convicted on the charge of hazarding his ship by failing to zigzag because I would have been able to launch a successful torpedo attack against his ship whether it had been zigzagging or not. I have met many of your brave men who survived the sinking of the Indianapolis. I would like to join with them in urging that your national legislature clear their captain's name. Our peoples have forgiven each other for that terrible war and its consequences. Perhaps it is time your peoples to [sic] forgave Captain McVay for the humiliation of his unjust conviction.

On 11 October 2000, McVay was technically cleared of guilt. Legislation was passed in Washington and signed by President Clinton expressing the sense of Congress that McVay's record should now reflect he be exonerated for the loss of USS *Indianapolis* and for the death of her crew who were lost. Sadly, this did not actually remove the conviction from McVay's record; nor would a presidential pardon. A pardon simply annuls punishment, but it does not clear the conviction or the stain of guilt from the person's record. Then in July 2001, the Navy Department announced in the National Defense Authorization Act of 2001 that McVay's record had been amended to clear him for the loss of USS *Indianapolis*, and the loss of those who perished as a result of her sinking. The stigma of a scapegoat was, at last, properly removed.

For McVay, of course, all this came too late. He never recovered from the weight of responsibility of losing more than 800 of his men. After leaving the navy, he was reasonably employed but was still harassed by vitriolic letters from the bereaved. In 1961, his second wife Louise died from cancer. Life looked even bleaker until he met up again with an old girlfriend, Vivian Smith, whom he speedily married. It was, though, not happy and the new Mrs McVay failed to fill the gap in his life and help him confront his demons. To the great sadness of his old crew and supporters, the end came on that snowy day in 1968.

Another naval officer who died – albeit before a firing squad, in 1757 – and did not deserve this fate, was Admiral John Byng, whom we meet in the next chapter.

THREE

Admiral John Byng

'Pour encourager les autres'

March 1757

'At twelve the Admiral was shot upon the quarter-deck,' recorded the log of HMS *Monarch* moored in Portsmouth Harbour.

On 14 March 1757, John Byng, an Admiral of the Blue, died with courage and composure before a Marine firing squad. The trial and execution of Admiral Byng was one of the more disgraceful miscarriages of justice in the annals of the Royal Navy even by the standards of the time. Byng was the luckless scapegoat for the inadequacy of the navy and its commanders, a vacillating and neurotic British government and a mob, whipped to a frenzy by political pamphleteers.

By 1756, the War of the Austrian Succession (1740–48) was still very much in the public consciousness and had planted the seeds for what was now to become the Seven Years War. The civilised world was in a state of anxiety and tension verging on paranoia. The War of the Austrian Succession began when Maria Theresa succeeded her father, the Holy Roman Emperor Charles VI, to the vast Hapsburg possessions in Europe, and the Treaty of Aix-la-Chapelle in October 1748 drew matters to an uneasy close.

The simmering enmity between Prussia and Austria had never really dissipated and the alliances forged after the War of the Austrian Succession were, again, thrown into disarray in 1756. In January, Britain and Prussia formed an alliance against the two old enemies, France and Austria. Conflict began in the autumn of that year with the invasion and defeat of Saxony at the hands of Frederick II of Prussia. Britain's worries were compounded by colonial rivalries with France and Spain, which had begun in 1754 in America over control of the Ohio valley.

Governance and leadership in Britain at the time was fragile. Cabinet was rent by petty quarrels, jealousies and rivalries. In March 1754, the Duke of Newcastle had assumed the leadership of the Whig party as first minister. Although facing the difficulty of controlling his ministry from the House of Lords, he had had long experience in government and was reasonably adept at handling the difficult George II. He was not a bad organiser, and had a good deal of common sense and integrity, unusual for the times. However, although his drawbacks were relatively minor, they were very obvious. He was perpetually in a state of anxiety and overexcitement. He also had great difficulty in concealing a substantial lack of self-confidence that led to public ridicule and mockery. In the House of Commons, Pitt and Fox were men of real stature, drive and political ruthlessness. Lurking in the wings was the redoubtable Duke of Cumberland, intent on making mischief. Admiral Lord Anson, an experienced and practical sailor, was First Lord of the Admiralty.

In May 1755, a small fleet under Admiral Boscawen was dispatched into the Atlantic to prevent the French reinforcing their troops in Canada and America. With France and Britain still technically at peace, this was a high-risk strategy. Boscawen's orders from the Admiralty were half-hearted and deliberately vague. In the event, he captured a mere two ships instead of the whole squadron that Newcastle had hoped for. The French, understandably, were indignant and rumours suggested that they were planning to invade England. There was a good deal of information being gathered but little of real substance. However, well-sourced intelligence was coming from the Mediterranean, particularly concerning the assembly of men and ships in Toulon. The objectives were obvious: Gibraltar and Minorca.

For controlling shipping movement in the Mediterranean from Gibraltar to the important ports in Italy, Greece and the Levant, Minorca was the ideal naval base. It had been a British possession since 1708. He who could hold Minorca for his fleet, could control the exits from the ports of Toulon and Marseilles, and the Spanish from Barcelona, as well as reinforcing Gibraltar when necessary. The threat alone of a strong and efficient fleet based there would be enough in itself. Land forces on the island, without naval support, would not be as effective because they could be denied reinforcement and resupply, and eventually starved out or picked off at will.

Minorca had a perfect natural harbour adjacent to the capital of Mahon, on the eastern side of the island, for basing the fleet. This harbour was well protected by the strongly built Fort St Philip. By 1756, however, the defences had been neglected and there were doubts as to its strength against an assault by land. The garrison itself had been allowed to dwindle. The commander was the 82-year-old Lieutenant General Blakeney. In theory, there were four regiments (about 2,860 men) to defend the island but of these, an unbelievable forty-one officers were on leave in England, including all four of the regimental commanding officers, and the governor of the island and fort.

Administrative corruption, financial abuse and embezzlement in the British Navy at the time was serious. Speculators would buy up old and unseaworthy ships as war was approaching, knowing that they could let them out later, at exorbitant costs, to a desperate Admiralty. Shipbuilders used low-grade timber and nails that rotted and rusted soon after the ship put to sea. Rope was shortened and, when coiled up, looked the correct length but the moment it was first put to use, the sleight of hand by the suppliers became apparent. Work was charged for many times over with disabled, if not actually non-existent, people on the pay roll. Fraudulent dockyard bosses became rich on the proceeds. The fact is that there was very little confidence in the Royal Navy; its outstanding reputation was yet to be made and Anson, a brave and resourceful sailor, was not confident in the political scene and loathed the shenanigans of wily civil servants and ministers. His main job was to ensure that operations were carried out without too much loss, disaster and courts martial.

Into this unstable world stepped John Byng. Born in 1704, he was the fifth surviving son of George and Margaret Byng. George was one of the most respected admirals in the navy. He had gained early political and career progression by enlisting the navy's support for William of Orange during the Glorious Revolution and thwarting the efforts of the Old Pretender in 1715 by cutting off Jacobite supplies from the Continent. In 1718, he was given the command of a large fleet in the Mediterranean to counter the Spanish and Austrian competition over their possessions in Italy. Off Cape Passaro, he decisively defeated the Spanish, preventing their attack on Sicily. Praise and honours were heaped upon him by a grateful government. He was made an Admiral of the Fleet in 1718, created Viscount Torrington and given the lucrative position of Treasurer of the Navy in 1721. On his accession, George II appointed him First Lord of the Admiralty.

Sons of illustrious fathers do not always live up to the hopes and expectations of their families but, in John's case, he appeared to do so. As a 14-year-old midshipman, he was present at Cape Passaro when the *Superb*, in which he was serving, captured the flagship of the Spanish commander-in-chief. Although not involved in significant action until the final chapter off Minorca in 1756, he rose steadily through the ranks of the navy. His first command, as captain, was of the *Gibraltar*, a twenty-gun frigate, in 1727. Various commands followed, but despite the War of the Austrian Succession starting in 1740, Byng was not involved in action, rather in relatively humdrum appointments in Newfoundland and the Channel. However, in August 1745, at the age of 41 he was made a rear admiral. While this was not as rapid an advancement as some others, he was, nevertheless, probably lucky to have reached this rank so soon. He then commanded a small squadron in home waters, preventing the French from helping Bonnie Prince Charlie.

In 1747, he was made second in command to Admiral Medley in the Mediterranean with a large fleet, preventing the French from attacking the Austrians, now British allies, in Italy. In August of that year, Medley died. Byng was promoted to Vice Admiral of the Blue and assumed command of the Mediterranean fleet. No doubt apprehensive about the French threat of invasion of the homeland, the government withdrew about a third of the fleet, putting Byng in the unenviable position of being able only to blockade Toulon properly or spread his ships, generally, along the French southern coast. He chose the latter, but with the conclusion of the war in 1748 Byng was recalled home having never actually been in action. Though never having commanded a ship, let alone a squadron, in battle, he had made no mistakes and the government, confronted with the difficulties of many who had, were happy to promote someone whom they clearly thought would be a safe pair of hands, and, after all, they told themselves, he did have experience of the Mediterranean.

But what of Byng the man? Society of the time expected men of Byng's background and standing to maintain a certain air of superiority and contempt for men who were perceived to be of lower status,

particularly civilians. Society would not have been disappointed. Byng, a
bachelor, now MP for Rochester with middle-aged widow Mrs Hickson
as his mistress, knew his place. He ran a house in Berkeley Square and
had built an imposing country seat, Wrotham Park, in Barnet. He was a
well-built man and a contemporary portrait shows him in a flamboyant
admiral's coat, with large cuffs and protruding lace, to full advantage.
He surveys his world with an air of pride and superiority. But does this
cloud the insecurity of the son of a great man, particularly in the same
profession? He was not known for his popularity and perhaps hid some
of this lack of confidence behind strict and austere behaviour – he was
known as a disciplinarian. He was fussy and precise over unimportant
and trivial details. Decision-making did not come to him easily and
although it is unfair to class this, in battle, as cowardice, it did not help
when the need was to encourage subordinates who looked to him for
guidance and leadership under stress.

In 1756, as the government realised the French threat of invasion
was becoming more and more hollow, its concentration returned to the
Mediterranean and the key strategic value of Minorca. Significant, and
worrying, intelligence was being received in London from the various
legations and consuls in the area that confirmed massing of French troops
and shipping in Toulon. Commodore George Edgecumbe, a high-quality
naval officer, was in command of the small Mediterranean squadron, con-
sisting of some eight ships. His force was far too small to be able to carry
out all the operations of blocking the French ports and projecting British
power at sea. The French threat was all too obvious. They could destroy
British trade and influence in the Mediterranean, combine with the powerful fleet in Brest and create a significant force in the Atlantic or send
heavy reinforcements to the Americas. Nevertheless, the French did not
have it all their own way; they experienced supply difficulties in making
ships ready for sea at Toulon and the French court was as riven with jealousies and back-biting as the British Government over what direction to
take. The two countries were still not at war. However, by February, with
the appointment of the redoubtable Marquis de la Galissonnière to command twelve ships of the line and the arrival of the Duke of Richelieu in
Toulon to command the army and stiffen resolve, the British could vacil-
late no longer and decided that Edgecumbe required reinforcing.

On 11 March 1756, Byng was promoted admiral and ordered to Portsmouth to fit out a squadron for service in the Mediterranean. He was not told how big it was to be or when it was to sail. This should not have been a problem. The Admiralty estimated that it required a fleet of forty battleships to defend England against invasion. At the time, there were some sixty-five in port or home waters, thus freeing twenty-five for a Mediterranean force. But there was still the nagging feeling that Britain was vulnerable to invasion, despite the increasing knowledge that it was virtually impossible. Of course, it suited the French to keep the pressure up. So Byng was allocated a mere ten ships of the line, with no frigates, store ships or hospital vessels – the Admiralty's theory being that, once he joined up with Edgecumbe, they would be just superior in numbers to the French.

Byng arrived in Portsmouth on 20 March and quickly discovered all was not well. His squadron was present with the exception of one ship, but he was 700 men short. The Admiralty made it quite clear he was not to make up numbers from the other ships' companies lying at Portsmouth and, moreover, he was to ensure one of the other ship's companies, not in his squadron, was to be made up before any of his. To compound this, he was astonished to hear that three ships of the line and two frigates, with crews he desperately needed, were to be sent off on a frolic of their own to deal with some French convoy in the Channel. It cannot have done his blood pressure any good to be told that he was also to take two drafts of soldiers with him; one lot were the absentees from the Minorca garrison and the other a small reinforcement for Gibraltar. On top of that, he was to distribute his Marines to the other ships and, in lieu, take on Lord Robert Bertie's 7th Regiment of Foot (now the Royal Fusiliers). The Fusiliers were not to replace the Marines (as close protection for the ships and boarding parties, etc.) but to be landed at Gibraltar. The governor of Gibraltar, Lieutenant General Fowke, was then to embark one of his Gibraltar battalions on board Byng's ships for Minorca. Order, counter-order and disorder followed. Anson protested that the Fusiliers must remain on board to carry out the Marines' tasks. The government then decided that Minorca would only need reinforcing with infantry if the French were actually invading, so the Fusiliers were to remain on board and Fowke was to add one of his battalions to the force only if Minorca was likely to be attacked. This shambles only added to Byng's anxieties.

The next day he received a letter from the Admiralty that he was to set sail 'with the utmost dispatch' and would receive sailing orders on the 24th. This was the result of a panic message from the British minister in Turin that the French fleet were on the point of leaving Toulon to invade Minorca. In the meantime, Byng's men were scouring the countryside for 'recruits' and the press gangs managed to collar the few who were either too drunk or disabled to escape. Nevertheless, Byng had made reasonable progress and, apart from lack of men, was ready to depart on receiving his orders to do so on 1 April. One can sympathise with Byng's heavy heart as he replied, 'With regard to the Instructions I have received, I shall use every endeavour and means in my power to frustrate the designs of the enemy, if they should make an attempt in the island of Minorca, knowing the great importance of that island to the Crown of Great Britain...and shall think myself the most fortunate if I am so happy to succeed in this undertaking.'

His shortage of men, even having scoured the hospitals, was still acute but over the next couple of days was largely made up with some pretty questionable individuals from other ships. The last ship of his squadron to join, the *Intrepid*, arrived but was in a state of disrepair, had not been warned for foreign service and was therefore short of provisions and ammunition. The remainder were better, but not much. All had been cleaned since December but two were leaky and others had been upgraded from old seventy-gun ships into more efficient sixty-fours, but were still not as good as the newly built sixty-fours. Others were below their gun rate. Out of a squadron of ten ships on a mission vital to the country, it was disgraceful that there should be so many deficiencies in ship capability, crew numbers and efficiency. None of this was the fault of the Admiral.

On 7 April, Byng was at last able to weigh anchor. His captains were a capable but undistinguished lot though even the most junior had nine years' seniority and the majority had previously been in the Mediterranean. He had served with only two of them before. There was no time or opportunity to work up the ships' motley crews or to train the squadron together in any tactics. They would have to rely on the

Articles of War and Fighting Instructions (a series of written tactical documents), send rowing boats over to the Admiral's ship to receive orders and use a complicated system of flag signals. In a world where 'being in the commander's mind' and initiative and intuition play such a great part, as became paramount in Nelson's time, Byng's little flotilla was hardly an inspiring one. But what had he actually been told to do? His orders dated 30 March 1756 were clear enough, quite properly leaving him enough flexibility, knowing he was fourteen days' fast sailing away from his base at Portsmouth.

On arrival at Gibraltar, he was to ascertain whether the French had passed through the Strait of Gibraltar and, if so, with how many ships. If some of them were transports, then it was likely they were bound for North America. He was then to take soldiers from his own ships, put them under command of Rear Admiral West (his second in command) and dispatch him to meet up with, and place under his command, those ships already either at Halifax, Nova Scotia or on their way there, to make a force superior to the French squadron. West was then to cruise off the coast of Louisbourg and the entrance to the Gulf of St Lawrence to seize the French ships.

If the French had not passed through the Strait, he was to proceed to Minorca without delay. If he had to detach West, he was still to set out for Minorca with the ships he had remaining with him.

If he found the French had attacked Minorca, he was to 'use all possible means in [his] power for its relief'. If the French had not attacked Minorca, he was to blockade Toulon to prevent them leaving the port. If any had managed to do so, he was to seize them in order to protect Minorca and Gibraltar. He was to protect British trade from Moroccan and Barbary raiders. He was to seize French privateers but take care not to extract them from Ottoman Empire ports in the Levant, nor to molest citizens of the Ottoman Empire. On arrival in the Mediterranean, he was to take under command the ships already there. Finally, if the French did evade his blockade of Toulon, and escape from the Mediterranean, he was to return to England and leave only enough ships behind to deal with the tasks he had been given.

This was fine as far as it went. Interestingly, Minorca did not appear to be the top priority; the escape of the French with reinforcements for

North America appeared to be uppermost in the minds of the government. But surely the first thing on anyone's mind would be the worst case: the French having invaded Minorca, overcoming the garrison with forces outstripping any that Byng had? What then? What actually was in their Lordships' minds when he was ordered to use all powers to relieve Minorca? An amphibious assault against Fort St Philip? With the Fusiliers already on board and a single, scratch, battalion made up from the four in Gibraltar? However, there were other possibilities. A British force, although outnumbered by the French, could land unopposed in another part of the island and then, if well led, harass the French from the interior. Meanwhile, British ships could blockade and intercept any French resupply from Toulon, thus starving out the large land component, which could not rely on local provisioning. They would, of course, have to take on the French Navy.

Byng's squadron had a rough passage to Gibraltar, only reaching it on 2 May 1756. Edgecumbe met him with the unwelcome news that the French had already landed in Minorca with between 13,000 and 15,000 men and thirteen men-of-war in support. However, Fort St Philip still held with a garrison of less than 2,500, bolstered by some of Edgecumbe's men whom he had left behind. Lieutenant General Fowke, the governor of Gibraltar, one of the more unsavoury characters to come out of this story, called a council together with the clear intention of doing absolutely nothing to help and retaining his four battalions on the Rock. He manipulated and unbalanced the recommendations, which he then made to Byng, with dishonesty and subterfuge, showing that Fort St Philip could not be reinforced and that to try to do so would merely be a waste of manpower. However, in order to cover himself, he finished by saying to Byng that, if he insisted, he would make a detachment available if he thought it necessary. As a senior army officer, instead of helping Byng with various options of how to deal with the Minorca situation, he was obstructive, deceitful and pathetic. Sadly, Byng, who clearly was extremely worried by the situation, did not have the character to see through this useless soldier. Nor did his second in command, West, a good man, who should have had the moral courage to intervene. Exacerbating the situation, and maybe one of the reasons why Fowke was so self-serving, was that the dockyards in Gibraltar were a run-down disgrace; buildings were decaying and the right provisions and stores, and experts for repairing ships, were not at hand. On 4 May, Byng wrote a stinging report to the Admiralty, which was quickly followed by one from Fowke, implicating Byng in the decision not to reinforce Fort St Philip. Byng's letter did not reach the Admiralty until 31 May. This not only was news those at home did not want to hear but it also gave everyone the uncomfortable feeling that the operation was doomed from the start.

On 8 May, without the reluctant Fowke's detachment but with the rest of Edgecumbe's ships under command, Byng set off with the whole of his squadron and, by 15 May, passed between Ibiza and Majorca, sailing south-east. Captain Hervey, a real hero and steadfastly loyal to Byng, was sent on ahead to deliver messages to General Blakeney at Fort St Philip if he could, and to carry out reconnaissance of the Minorcan coast and French shipping. All very sound, but Byng's letter to Blakeney was hardly encouraging. He told Blakeney that he had the Fusiliers on board whom he could land, subject to the General's advice, to defend Minorca. However, he warned that if he did so, because they had replaced the Marines, his squadron would then be ineffective.

Hervey managed to get close enough to Fort St Philip to see the English flag still flying and made his own signal to the fort. Byng was then becalmed some 3 miles from the fort but could hear the exchange of fire between the French and British. Infuriatingly, they had no wind to push them into the harbour from which they could take on the French land forces. At that moment the French fleet was seen to the south-east, making slow progress with the little wind that was unavailable to Byng, in the lee of land. Without hesitation, Byng signalled his squadron to give chase, and by seven o'clock in the evening the two sides were closing; however, neither wanted a night action, so Byng hove to near land in order to take advantage of the offshore breeze that would blow in the morning.

Back in the fort, apathy and indecision ruled. Hervey's ship was not seen until ten o'clock in the morning and by the time it had been decided what message should be sent to Byng, his ships were too far away for the rowing boat, with an officer to give a verbal report, to be able to reach him. The option, therefore, of taking advice from the besieged Blakeney, and landing a force to beat off the French, was lost forever.

As dawn rose on 20 May, the French were seen some 12 miles away to the south-east. Since Byng was between them and Fort St Philip, there was still an opportunity to liaise with the fort but he was loath to detach any ship from his force with battle looming. There now followed a duel of sailing expertise, each commander manoeuvring for position and the best possible wind advantage. The crews prepared for battle and the Fusiliers took up sniping positions. Soon after midday, the two fleets were abreast of each other, and with a check on his Fighting Instructions, Byng could be ready to attack. However, mindful of his 600-mile journey back to Gibraltar for any repairs needed, Byng was anxious to keep damage to the minimum. Battle was then joined with all the muddle and confusion brought about by lack of training, indifferent signalling methods and ships' captains not knowing exactly what they had to do. Movement by intuition and imagination was hampered by a slavish regard for conventional written instructions. Ships variously engaged each other at a range of 300 yards with cannon and small arms fire.

As in most battles, by land or sea, the fog of war descended. Smoke hung over the whole area and instant recognition of friend and foe became difficult, with ships advancing and withdrawing with the wind and what was left of their damaged sails and rigging. By five o'clock firing effectively ceased, and the French were seen moving away to the north-west, about 2 miles distant. Byng's force redeployed in case of French counterattack but the enemy soon disappeared into the night and Byng hove to. Pursuit of the French was not an option, given the damage to Byng's ships. For Galissonnière, attacking the British again was unnecessary; he had achieved his objective, which was to inflict so much damage on his opponents that they would be unable to relieve Minorca or blockade Toulon. So ended the Battle of Minorca, without a clear win for either side but a medium-term advantage to the French.

The following day, crews counted the cost. Two ships had got lost, but were later recovered, four were unfit for action and numerous repairs were required to most of the others. Had Galissonnière attacked then, he would have undoubtedly defeated the British. Additionally, Byng was worried about the quality of some of his captains who had not performed at all well in the battle. Byng then called for a council of war. Nowadays, this would be the time for a commander to give his views, listen to his subordinates and staff, and give out his orders. Sadly, this is not the way it happened then. The council was invited to suggest how their commander might carry out his instructions. However, it degenerated into a wide-ranging discussion, with everyone giving their views, portraying their own efforts in as good a light as possible, avoiding any blame for past inadequacies and seeking to do as little as possible in the next phase. Byng's council included the senior army officers. There were still a number of sensible and attainable options for the combined land and sea force to deal with the Minorca situation. Although the squadron was significantly depleted, it remained a worrying threat to the French resupply system for their forces in Minorca. The army officers should have been in a position to advise Byng how a land operation could be successfully conducted but they, weakly, went for the soft option and kept quiet. It seemed they had given up before they even started. It then became a self-serving discussion purely to justify the withdrawal to Gibraltar and leave Blakeney and his garrison to their fate. It was no good, however, Byng suggesting that it was a 'council' decision; it was his, as the senior commander, and he had to bear full responsibility for it. While it can hardly be construed as cowardice, it was, by any standards, a severe lack of judgement.

On 2 June, the bombshell exploded. A copy of Galissonnière's dispatch was obtained through allied informants, clearly revealing a French victory. This was enough to panic the government and, without waiting to hear from Byng, Admiral Hawke was dispatched to take command of the Mediterranean fleet and send Byng home. Byng's letters arrived on 23 June, covering his side of the affair. Politicians started to squirm with anxiety and self-protection. Byng's dispatch was edited, amended and suppressed to show everyone in a good light except him. On 27 June, Fort St Philip fell. The mob attacked Wrotham Park, Byng was burnt in effigy and the pamphleteers had a field day. On 26 July, Byng arrived at Spithead and was placed under arrest, disgracefully, by his brother-in-law Vice Admiral Henry Osborne. He was appallingly treated, being moved from pillar to post and effectively unable to organise his affairs, let alone a defence to what was clearly to be a court martial.

The useless Lieutenant General Fowke was court-martialled in August, properly found guilty and amazingly only suspended for a year. While this was not particularly severe, it boded ill for Byng. To put this into the perspective of the times, in the same documentation at the National Archives covering Fowke's court martial, three soldiers of the Coldstream and Third Guards were found guilty of desertion and sentenced to death. It was then ordered that only one would die and that they were to draw lots as to who it should be. In another case, an absentee of the Grenadier Guards was sentenced to 800 lashes with the cat o'nine tails. He was sent round four different regiments to be given 200 lashes by each one.

Pamphlets were published, both for and against Byng; these became the forerunners to our modern 'red top' newspapers. Satirists and the 'spin doctors' of the day, including even Dr Johnson ('for' Byng, but badly written) waded into print. It suited the government to allow the gutter press and the mob to do their job for them, rather than having the difficulty of having to defend themselves. This did not stop them, however, publishing scandalously inaccurate libel and a thoroughly unhelpful rebuttal to Byng's request for a number of witnesses. There was no drive for an early court martial, possibly because the government could see itself lurching towards a fall, and the trial of an admiral for failing his duty might (rightly) reflect badly on his superiors, bringing their demise to an earlier conclusion than they would have wanted. Nevertheless, delicate political negotiations took place, culminating in Newcastle's resignation, Pitt's assumption of the leadership and a revamped Admiralty, without Anson. Byng had two friends on the new Admiralty Board, his old second in command, West, and Temple, an avowed enemy of Newcastle. Unfortunately, Byng's old foe, Boscawen, remained.

On 14 December, the court martial was ordered with Byng to face a charge under the Twelfth Article of War:

Every person in the fleet who through cowardice, negligence or dis-affection, shall in time of action withdraw or keep back, or not come into the fight or engagement, or shall not do his utmost to take or destroy every ship, which it shall be his duty to engage, and to assist and relieve all and every of His Majesty's ships or those of his allies which it shall be his duty to assist and relieve; every such person so offending and being convicted thereof by the sentence of a court martial shall suffer death.

On the 28th, the court was sworn in with Vice Admiral Thomas Smith as president and three rear admirals and nine captains on the board. In those days, having no provision for a defending officer, Byng had to defend himself.

Prosecution witnesses were produced, including: West, whose standing as a member of the Admiralty Board was significant; General Blakeney, the elderly, promoted and ennobled erstwhile governor of Fort St Philip; senior army officers aboard ships and various captains, including Augustus Hervey, one of Byng's most steadfast friends. The evidence fluctuated from fully supporting Byng to being openly hostile, the latter coming mainly from those seeking to shine a better light on their own inadequacies. Some were revealed as liars, forgers, incompetents or just plain stupid. Byng himself called only two witnesses in his defence, to show that there had been no unnecessary delay at Gibraltar; it was impossible to land officers at the fort; he had demonstrated no cowardice or negligence in action; and, finally, it would have been impossible and unwise to follow up the French after the battle.

Byng's written defence was then laid before the court. This rested, in essence, on the inadequacy of his force to relieve Minorca once it had been successfully invaded. His orders had been to detach much of his strength, under West, to reinforce forces in the Americas, had the French passed through the Strait of Gibraltar. This meant a relatively small force for Fort St Philip in the absence of a French invasion of the island. He describes the battle and the superiority of the French. There was no evidence of any personal cowardice on his part. Had he pursued the withdrawing enemy fleet, there was a strong possibility that his own, now damaged, squadron would have been defeated. This would have exposed Gibraltar to attack. He had not lost Minorca; he was too weak to save it. Had those responsible sent double the force two months earlier, it would have been saved. Therein lay the blame.

There is an extraordinary sideline to this story. On 2 January 1757, Voltaire wrote a letter in English from his house in Switzerland to Byng. With it, he enclosed a letter from the Duke of Richelieu. The latter's letter was couched in glowingly supportive terms of Byng and could hardly have been more full of praise from one enemy to another. Had it been before the court martial, it would have, undoubtedly, had a substantially beneficial effect on Byng's defence. Owing to Post Office incompetence and highly suspicious interference by ministers and their functionaries, the letter did not reach Byng until 23 January, by which time all the evidence had been heard.

As the court considered its verdict, the cover-up was already being prepared by those who stood to lose much by their own incompetence, including Anson, Newcastle, Cumberland, Fox and even the King. A conviction was imperative. On 27 January, the court assembled to announce the verdict. They passed thirty-seven resolutions and, in accordance with Article Twelve, found the Admiral guilty and condemned him to death by firing squad, adding that 'they think it their duty most earnestly to recommend him as a proper object of mercy'. The resolutions were contradictory and thoroughly unsound. To have reached the conclusions they did, in the presence of a legally trained judge advocate, strains credulity. Article Twelve covers three criteria: cowardice, disaffection and negligence. Byng had been specifically cleared, in the resolutions, of the first two and the third was not mentioned. What, of course, they really meant was that they had found him guilty of an *error of judgement*. That may well have been so, but it was not a crime, let alone a crime carrying the death penalty. Commanders in all fields make errors of judgement from time to time. If they behave through idleness, stupidity or carelessness, it is not an error of judgement, it is negligence. There was no evidence to suggest Byng was idle, stupid or careless. He could not, therefore, be negligent, let alone so negligent as to amount to misconduct. The members of the court martial were clearly very uncomfortable with what they had done, yet felt their hands tied by the law. An urgent memorandum was therefore sent to the Admiralty, praying their 'lordships in the most earnest manner to recommend him [Byng] to His Majesty's clemency'.

The pro- and anti-Byng camps started to organise. The former was led by Byng's married sister, the redoubtable Sarah Osborne, reinforced by his old friend Captain Augustus Hervey. The hostile faction was, predictably, headed by Newcastle, Hardwicke and Anson, who could see the spotlight being turned on them to answer the very obvious question of why Minorca had not been properly and substantially reinforced earlier. The Admiralty Board saw an opening, and asked the King to appoint a panel of judges to consider the legality of the sentence. Little did they realise they had created a major problem for themselves, since the Law Lords had no difficulty with the *sentence*, which was laid down by law. What they were not asked was whether the *verdict* was legitimate, which clearly it was not.

It could be asked why the King did not merely exercise Royal Prerogative and mitigate sentence or even pardon Byng. However, it must be remembered that the monarch was in financial thrall to the City merchants who saw the loss of Minorca as a blow to their Mediterranean trade and needed a scapegoat to placate their shareholders. The King could not risk his funds drying up if he infuriated the City fathers.

Men of courage did risk their careers: Admiral Forbes of the Admiralty Board refused to sign the death warrant. A copy of his letter to the Admiralty is in the possession of one of Byng's descendants, Thane Byng, and clearly explains his concerns:

> It may be thought great presumption in me, to differ from so great authority as that of the twelve judges; but when a man is called upon to sign his name to an act, which is to give authority to the shedding of blood, he ought to be guided by his own conscience and not by the opinions of other men.
>
> In the case before us, it is not the merit of Admiral Byng, I consider; whether he deserves death or not, is a question not for me to decide; but whether his life can be taken away by the sentence pronounced upon him, by the court martial; and after having so clearly explained their motives for pronouncing such a sentence, is a point alone which has employed my serious consideration.
>
> The twelfth article of war, on which Admiral Byng's sentence is grounded, says, (according to my understanding of its meaning) 'That every person who in time of action, shall withdraw, keep back, or not come into fight, or who shall not do his utmost, &c. through motive of cowardice, negligence, or disaffection, shall suffer death.' The court martial does in express words, acquit Admiral Byng of cowardice and disaffection, and does not name the word

negligence. Admiral Byng does not, as I conceive, fall under the letter, or description of the twelfth article of war. It may be said that negligence is implied, though the word is not mentioned; otherwise the court martial would not have brought his offence under the twelfth article, having acquitted him of cowardice and disaffection. But it must be acknowledged, that the negligence implied, cannot be wilful negligence: for wilful negligence in Admiral Byng's situation, must have either proceeded from cowardice or disaffection, and he is expressly acquitted of both these crimes. Besides these crimes which are implied only, and not named, may indeed justify suspicion, and private opinion; but cannot satisfy the conscience in case of blood.

Admiral Byng's fate was referred to a court martial: his life and death were left to their opinions. The court martial condemned him to death, because as they expressly say, they were under the necessity of doing so, by reason of the letter of the law, the severity of which they complained of, because it admits of no mitigation. The court martial expressly says, that for the sake of their consciences, as well as in justice to the prisoner, they most earnestly recommend him to his majesty's mercy. It is evident then, that in the opinion and consciences of the judges, he was not deserving of death. The question then is, shall the opinions or necessities of the court martial determine Admiral Byng's fate? If it should be the latter, he will be executed contrary to the instructions and meaning of the judges; if the former, his life is not forfeited. His judges declare him not worthy of death; but, mistaking either the meaning of the law, or the nature of his offence, they bring him under an article of war, which according to their own description of his offence, he does not, I conceive, fall under; and they condemn him to death, because as they say, the law admits of no mitigation. Can a man's life be taken away by such a sentence? I would not willingly be misunderstood, and have it understood, I judge of Admiral Byng's deserts. This was the business of the court martial; and it is my duty to act according to my conscience; which after deliberate consideration, assisted by the best light a poor understanding can afford, remains still in doubt: and therefore I cannot consent to sign a warrant, whereby the sentence of the court martial may be carried into execution; for I cannot help thinking that however criminal Admiral Byng may be, his life is not forfeited by that sentence. I do not mean to find fault with other men's opinions; all I endeavour at, is, to give reasons for my own; and all I wish is, that I may not be misunderstood. I do not pretend to judge Admiral Byng's deserts, nor to give any opinion on the propriety of the act.

J. FORBES
Signed 6 February 1757, at the Admiralty

Byng's old second in command, West, resigned (the resignation was refused). Sadly, however, these were gestures that had little real impact. Byng, of course, was still a Member of Parliament so MPs enjoyed themselves by arguing the case across the floor to as little effect as some of the arguments in that chamber today. Even the rackety Sir Francis Dashwood, founder of the notorious Hellfire Club, spoke up for him. Pleas were made to the King again, by William Pitt, the Duke of Bedford and members of the Admiralty, but to no avail – Byng was merely granted a stay of execution for a fortnight until 14 March, while the case was re-examined by calling members of the court martial to the Bar of the House of Commons. This was akin to people appearing nowadays before a Commons Select Committee but certainly more intimidating, particularly for those who could see their career prospects evaporating if they gave the wrong answer. The fourteen days' breather speedily ran out.

At twelve o'clock on 14 March 1757 on the quarterdeck of the *Monarch*, a very composed and steady Admiral Byng knelt and let drop a white handkerchief as signal to the Marine firing squad to open fire, and instantly fell dead on their volley. Thus died a man unjustly blamed for the loss of Minorca to cover up the inadequacies of the King, the politicians Newcastle and Fox, and the Admiralty in the shape of Anson and other lesser men. After Byng's death, Voltaire published *Candide*. In it, the hero is puzzled by the execution of an English admiral and when he asks why, is told, '*Dans ce pays-ci il est bon de tuer de temps en temps un amiral pour encourager les autres.*'[1]

---

[1] 'In this country it is good to kill an admiral from time to time to encourage the others.'

The story does not quite end there. In All Saints Church Southill, in Bedfordshire, lie the vaults of the Byng family. On one lies the inscription:

To The Perpetual Disgrace
of PUBLICK JUSTICE
The Honble JOHN BYNG, Esqr.
Admiral of the Blue,
Fell a MARTYR to
POLITICAL PERSECUTION,
March 14th in the Year 1757 when
BRAVERY and LOYALTY
Were Insufficient Securities
For the
Life and Honour
of a
NAVAL OFFICER

On 14 March 2007, 250 years to the day that Byng was executed, his descendants gathered at the church to commemorate his death. Headed by the present Viscount Torrington and other members of the Byng and Osborne families, they laid a wreath and said prayers. The bell tolled fifty-two times for each year of his life. Encouraged no doubt by the government's blanket pardon, under Section 359 of the Armed Forces Act 2006, given to all those executed in the First World War, Viscount Torrington had previously written to the Secretary of State for Defence, Des Browne MP. He replied on 21 March as follows:

You have asked me to recommend a royal pardon for Admiral Byng as a way of redressing what is seen as 'the perpetual disgrace of public justice' arising from the proceedings. Having considered your letter, my view is that it would not be appropriate to exercise the royal prerogative in this case. I take this view not on the merits of the case but because it is a matter which has passed out of living memory and into history. In these circumstances, it has become a subject for historical scrutiny and not for government intervention.

I appreciate that this is a matter which means a great deal to descendants of the Admiral and that the two hundred and fiftieth anniversary of his death naturally focuses the thoughts of those who have a personal interest in the case. I hope, however, that you will appreciate my reason for declining your request.

Not satisfied with that, a petition signed by 600 people, representing the friends of All Saints Southill, the parishioners of Southill, Byng family members and the supporters of Admiral John Byng, was presented to the local MP, Alistair Burt, who laid it before Parliament on 19 March 2008 (Official Report Vol. 473, c. 1050). The petition:

Declares that the conduct of his trial and the verdict of his trial in December 1756 and January/February 1757, which resulted in his execution on 14th March 1757 was unfair and unjust. Further declares that he was made the scapegoat for the inadequacies of the Government and his Naval Superiors at the time, whom the Petitioners believe to have been responsible for the loss of Menorca to the French.

The Petitioners therefore request that the House of Commons urges the Ministry of Defence and the Ministry of Justice to review the trial and the verdict of that trial, resulting in Admiral John Byng being declared innocent posthumously; his Honour restored for him, his family and supporters.

The Secretary of State for Defence's response was:

The Admiral's case is well documented and I am aware of the considerable sympathy and admiration that many, not least his own contemporaries, have felt for him. Indeed, one cannot fail to admire his courage and generosity when faced with execution.

The petition alleges unfairness and lack of justice in the conduct of his trial. However, I should point out that the conduct of the Court Martial, its verdict and the sentence were the subject of comprehensive and extensive review at the time. Whilst fairness is a subjective concept, the matter of unjustness is not. A properly constituted Court Martial was held in accordance with the regulations in force at the time and resulted in a sentence that was fully in accordance with the then Articles of War. Although the thirteen senior naval officers who presided at the Court Martial were unanimous in their verdict, the Admiralty, Courts and Parliament exhausted all avenues available to them in seeking to absolve Admiral Byng of the charges against him. This included the final step in the appeal process, an application to the Monarch for clemency. This was refused.

This petition asks for the trial and verdict to be reviewed and for Admiral Byng to be declared innocent posthumously, thereby restoring his honour. Having considered this request several times previously, my view remains that it would not be appropriate to attempt to re-open this case. I take the view notwithstanding the merits or otherwise of the case but because it is a matter which has passed out of living memory and into history. In these circumstances, it has become a subject for historical scrutiny and not for Government intervention.

The last word must come from the family, who feel that for too long the name of Byng has been associated with cowardice in the face of the enemy. The fact is that, generally, members of the public are, understandably, ignorant of the true facts and are only vaguely aware of what happened. The Secretary of State is right to say that the matter has 'passed out of living memory and into history'. However, what is required now is an acknowledgement that, with a close examination of that history, an injustice has been done and can be put right. A comparable precedent, surely, is the nation's apology for its involvement in slavery; a matter certainly of history and not in living memory? What is written here, hopefully, equips the government and public to make up their minds and reach the conclusion that Byng must be *exonerated*. This has the effect of finding him not guilty of the charges; a *pardon* merely releases him from the punishment he received for the offences. Byng was a scapegoat for the inadequacies of others and must now be allowed to lie easily in his grave and his descendants remain satisfied that they have, at last, received the justice he deserves and which they have so determinedly sought over many years.

Our next scapegoat was also the victim of the inadequacy and skulduggery of the political and military machine. He, Captain Alfred Dreyfus, did not pay with his life, but with systematic persecution and a diabolically cruel exile and imprisonment.

FOUR

Captain Alfred Dreyfus

J'accuse

October 1894

Treason, though its perpetrators may have complicated characters, is carried out for relatively simple motives: ideas and ideals, money, blackmail, harassment or revenge. If the traitor can find a scapegoat, successfully blame him and cover his own crime so much the better. However, if then the scapegoat is, properly, found to be innocent and, to disguise their own errors and inadequacies, powerful authorities cover up the miscarriage of justice with byzantine complexity and intentional distortion of reality, then a descent into a surreal Kafka-esque world is inevitable. This is what happened to Captain Alfred Dreyfus of the French Artillery on 13 October 1894. A happily married man with not inconsiderable private income and a fervent love of his country and its military regime, he was about as far away from the stereotypical traitor as it is possible to imagine. But he was a Jew from German occupied territory.

———

The end of the nineteenth century, despite being later labelled la belle époque, was an extraordinarily difficult time for France. Abroad there was the paranoia of being surrounded by enemies. The creation in 1891 of the hostile Triple Alliance of Germany, Italy and Austria-Hungary drove France uneasily into the questionable arms of Russia. At home, the Third Republic, established after France's defeat in the Franco-Prussian War of 1871, struggled to deal with militant nationalism, anti-Semitism, separation of Church and State and the results of increasing industrialisation. The country itself was geographically divided, with the different regions often having little contact with each other, although this was rapidly becoming easier with the advent of railways and better roads.

There was a deep distrust of central government control from Paris. With the collapse of Napoleon III's attempts to have himself made emperor, the Republicans had been determined to turn France into a modern democracy. The influence of the Catholic Church was reduced by the secularisation of schools but the penalty was the antagonism of the many Catholics, a large majority of the population. Catholic clergy were, understandably, anti-Republican as they saw their influence waning and their flock, though nominally Catholic, beginning to drift. Jews and Protestants were in a minority but were seen as a possible threat to national identity, which traditionally based itself, although ambivalently, on a state religion.

Politics developed into a series of uneasy and shifting alliances. Parties lacked cohesion and stability and were vulnerable to the fashionable whim of the day. Scandal and disreputable behaviour rocked the government from time to time: the Wilson cash-for-honours in 1887, General Boulanger's bid for power in 1889 and the Panama bubble bursting in 1892 were all symptomatic. Kept women and high-class courtesans were accepted as part of the social milieu, alongside a tacit acceptance of bribery and corruption. General Boulanger shot himself on his mistress's grave and another highly placed politician died of a heart attack while having an amorous assignation with a lady in his office.

Industrialisation drew countrymen into the cities producing workforce tensions and disputes. Strikes were common and put down with force rather than negotiation, thus driving workers into the arms of the communists and socialists. Memories of the repression of rioters in 1848 and 1871 were still fresh in the minds of many. New rich of the bourgeoisie became increasingly separate from their roots and looked down on workers whom they regarded as socially beneath them. While articulate anarchist orators struck fear into the ruling class and the occasional assassination was exaggerated out of all proportion, workers, who, on the whole, preferred to remain outside political mayhem, were becoming increasingly conscious of their bargaining power. Nevertheless, an anxious State took great trouble over its security and intelligence apparatus, and developed detailed plans to mobilise the police and army in the event of civil disorder. Within the Second Bureau of the General Staff (Intelligence), the Section of Statistics was established. This bland name, of the sort loved by security services the world over, disguised a small counter-intelligence team organising and controlling agents. Headed by the enthusiastic Commandant Sandherr, it was staffed by a group of officers of varying quality.

Defeat at the hands of the Prussians, occupation of Alsace and Lorraine and the instability of politics fed the population's desire for revenge and stirred militant nationalism. What better organisation to put this into practice than the army. But the army was at a low ebb; beaten and humiliated; it needed to be restored to its former glory, and to become a modern fighting machine capable of taking on its old enemy. Major initiatives were taken by the war ministry including obligatory service. New training systems and exercises were begun, out-of-date regulations were rewritten, weapons updated and the Staff College (École Supérieure de Guerre) created. A powerful defensive network on the northern and eastern borders was established. A new interest in the profession of arms arose and the officer corps achieved a prestige envied by its civilian counterpart. An increasing number of officers were recruited from the ranks of the aristocracy and Catholic families. The bourgeoisie, who saw a commission as a stepping stone to social respectability, were eager to enlist. Nevertheless, patronage and nepotism still reigned in a hidebound posting and promotion selection system. The army, however, represented stability and the values of the old order. Its loyalty was not in doubt and it saw itself outside the grubby world of self-serving politicians. Therefore, to a certain extent, it was anti-Republican and opposed the new democracy. Additionally, it tended to become isolated from society and poorly integrated with the nation, living in military cantonments under its own conventions. It was used to conducting its affairs in accordance with its own rules and would not tolerate interference from outside. Sometimes those rules would inevitably come into conflict with natural justice.

Anti-Jewish feeling had effectively evaporated during the nineteenth century in France and indeed, much Jewish money funded the reconstruction after the Franco-Prussian War. However, with the devastating collapse of the Union Générale bank in 1882, when many people lost enormous sums of money and were ruined, the 'Syndicate' – the imaginary Jewish financial consortium – was blamed. At the same time, the

Jewish population of Paris increased to some 40,000. This was as a result of an influx from the Jewish communities in Alsace after the occupation (people such as the Dreyfus family) and those fleeing the pogroms of Central Europe. While previously the old Jewish families, many of whom were very wealthy and highly respected, were tolerated, the poor refugees from the East, speaking no French and bringing with them weird customs, were not. In the wake of increasing industrialisation, the hard-working, money-making Jew was resented by those who thought Paris would deliver fortunes without making much effort.

The army was not immune to this influence. The worst example of anti-Semitic literature was *La Libre Parole*, a newspaper run by Édouard Drumont. This paper contained all the usual invective but in April 1892 it began a series of articles on Jewish officers in the army. Since Napoleon's time, French Jewish officers had fought with distinction and exceeded the proportion per head of the civilian population. Drumont cynically portrayed this as an example of clandestine manoeuvring by Jews to ingratiate themselves with their country. Some officers resigned as a consequence, but others took up the challenge and fought duels. In one, a Jewish officer was killed and a significantly large crowd attended his funeral. This led the Minister of War to make a strong statement condemning any racist division in the army. But within the ranks there were many who were endemically opposed to Jews and easily influenced by Drumont and his cronies.

Alfred Dreyfus was born in Mulhouse, Alsace, on 9 October 1859 to a family of wealthy Jews. After the Franco-Prussian War ended with the Treaty of Frankfurt in 1871, most of Alsace and a third of Lorraine was annexed by the Germans. Inhabitants of Alsace could opt for French citizenship but, if taken up, had to leave the province within a stipulated time. This the Dreyfus family did, and they settled in Basel, hoping to return in due course. A sensitive and shy child, Alfred found school difficult and tended to withdraw into himself. It was therefore a surprise to his family when he decided to become an officer in the French Army. Feelings of resentment, and nationalism, against the occupier of his homeland are easy to understand, but he was also attracted to the well-regimented pattern of life exemplified by the institutionalised organisation of the army of the time. As in his own family life, he saw the army providing a safe, predictable model where things ran on established lines, people knew where they stood in strict hierarchical layers and behaviour followed a well-understood code. He realised that, as a Jew, there would be difficulties to overcome but, in 1878, there were a number of successful Jewish officers in the army and the vicious propaganda against them had not yet begun. Dreyfus found the precision and discipline very much to his taste and, in 1882, was commissioned into the Artillery. Described as intelligent, zealous and conscientious, nevertheless his brother officers found him shy, lonely and haughty. Those living on their pay resented this product of the new rich bourgeoisie and were, to a certain extent, suspicious of a German-speaking Alsatian. One can see how a clever, hard-working individual, who found exams easy, might not have fitted comfortably with his more rumbustious, idle, fun-loving fellow officers.

In 1890, he married and was admitted to the French Staff College, the École Supérieure de Guerre. For many officers this was a significant hurdle; for a Jew, it was an outstanding achievement. Working extremely hard, he passed out ninth out of eighty-one with excellent reports and a recommendation to serve on the General Staff. Nevertheless, there were uncomfortable currents running. Anti-Semitism was on the rise and there were those who clearly had anxieties about Jews in sensitive positions. However, as a potential high achiever, Dreyfus was posted to the General Staff as a trainee, to be passed round the different departments to learn the ropes for two years. With no financial worries, a very happy family life, now with two children, life looked good. On the Staff, Dreyfus was becoming, though, an uncomfortable colleague; he asked lengthy and portentous questions, propounded his ideas at inappropriate moments and airily gave his views to the distaste and embarrassment of his superiors. He believed in advancement on merit and despised the sycophancy of some of his fellows who saw career progression mainly dependent on the cultivation of influential senior officers. He was easy to dislike, particularly by those who were jealous of his money, found him conceited and arrogant and were not, in any case, well disposed towards Jews. Despite all that, with his profound belief in his country and the hope for the eventual recovery of his homeland, his dedicated loyalty to the army and his balanced and contented home life, he did not under any circumstances fit the treachery criteria.

At the other end of the spectrum was Marie-Charles-Ferdinand Walsin Esterhazy. Born in 1847 he was descended, through a bastard line, from the aristocratic Hungarian Esterhazys and, with his parents dead by the time he was 19, inherited a not inconsiderable sum of money and the ownership of a chateau west of Paris. He was a sickly child and used this as an excuse to meander through his early schooling, never obtaining a baccalaureate and, at 20, failing the entry exam for Saint-Cyr, the French officer cadet academy. He spent the next two years idling his way round the fleshpots and expensive courtesans of Paris and, not surprisingly, it was not long before his money ran out and he fell into the hands of moneylenders and creditors.

An unattractive character of Walter Mitty delusions, he fancied himself as an officer and somehow managed to obtain a commission in the Papal Legion in 1869. From there he transferred to the French Foreign Legion in North Africa but was swiftly recalled in 1870 to take part in the disastrous Franco-Prussian War. Although, along with many others, he was demoted to second lieutenant in the aftermath of the war, it was not long before he managed to obtain a regular commission as a captain. Posted to Paris, for the next ten years he passed himself off as a count and cultivated the gullible, unintelligent, idle and wealthy near-aristocracy and layabouts. Boastful and deceitful, he regaled anyone silly enough to listen with his tales of personal bravado and military escapades, though contemporary images have him looking more like a sleazy salesman than a dashing war hero (see plate IV).

Not without a certain ability to write, he found a niche on a periodical commenting on French defence affairs with pretensions to be an expert on military science. As a result of the contacts he made, he was posted as a translator to the Second Bureau of the General Staff (Intelligence) in 1877. Later attaching himself, in 1881, to the French expedition to Tunisia, he managed to fabricate a document reporting his outstanding performance at a battle at which he had not even been present. Mentioned in dispatches, he returned to Paris to receive the adulation of his admirers and, hopefully, membership of the Légion d'Honneur. This was not to be and his financial affairs descended into an even worse state. He fended off bankruptcy with various low-level, dishonourable and near-criminal ruses and even managed to borrow money from a compliant mistress. There was now only one way out of his predicament: to sell his soul and his country for money.

The German military attaché in Paris was the urbane and charming Colonel Maximilien von Schwarzkoppen, a military diplomat highly suited to a milieu of febrile and paranoid intelligence work, coupled with the louche moral attitudes of the 1890s. Probably bisexual, he managed to carry on liaisons simultaneously with other men's wives and the Italian military attaché, Major Alessandro Panizzardi. Drafts of letters, and ones he received, would be carelessly torn up and thrown into Schwarzkoppen's wastepaper basket from where they would be retrieved by Madame Bastian, a cleaner at the embassy, who was in the pay of French intelligence, operating under the codename 'Auguste'. She also pilfered letters left in pigeonholes in the concierge's office. Her handler was the rough-hewn and zealous Commandant Henry of the Section of Statistics.

On 20 July 1894, Esterhazy called at the German Embassy under the pretext of obtaining a visa to visit Alsace but, in fact, to offer his services as a spy, explaining that he was driven to it by penury. Schwarzkoppen was not particularly impressed but was instructed by Berlin to maintain the link. Later Esterhazy appeared again with a document of little intelligence value and asked to be given a fixed monthly salary. Schwarzkoppen refused, saying that his contacts were only paid for the specific items they produced. Having said that, Schwarzkoppen was, nevertheless, very interested in what Esterhazy might reveal. In fact, Esterhazy did then produce a not insignificant plan of artillery mobilisation that Schwarzkoppen was keen to see. So, despite his bombastic and extravagant talk, Esterhazy – in Schwarzkoppen's eyes a low-level and unreliable agent – was able to lay his hands on some items of value.

That September, General Auguste Mercier, minister of war, was told to his horror that a bordereau, or memorandum, of importance had fallen into the hands of the Section of Statistics via their source in the German Embassy. The bordereau had either come from Schwarzkoppen's wastepaper basket or the concierge's pigeonholes. Much later, Schwarzkoppen protested – to cover his own extraordinary laxity and negligence – that it could not have come from his wastepaper basket but must have been filched from the concierge's office. The probability, however, is that it was the former because it arrived torn into pieces. The bordereau clearly emanated from a French officer in the pay of the Germans. It went as follows:

> Having no indication that you wish to see me, I am nevertheless forwarding to you, Sir, several interesting items of information
>
> 1. A note on the hydraulic break of the 120 and the manner in which that part has performed;
> 2. A note on covering troops (several modifications will be effected by the new plan);
> 3. A note on a modification of Artillery formations;
> 4. A note pertaining to Madagascar;
> 5. The Sketch for a Firing Manual for the country artillery (March 14, 1894);
>
> This last document is extremely difficult to procure and I am able to have it at my disposal for only a few days. The Ministry of War has distributed a fixed number of copies to the regiments, and the regiments are responsible for them. Every officer holding a copy is to return it after manoeuvres. If you would then take from it what interests you and keep it at my disposal thereafter, I will take it. Unless you want me to have it copied in extenso and send you the copy.
>
> I am off to manoeuvres.

Mercier was appalled but could see that if he had the traitor unmasked, it would not do his own position any harm. He immediately issued orders to General Raoul de Boisdeffre, Chief of the Army General Staff, and his deputy, General Charles Gonse, to find the culprit. From the contents and turn of phrase, an immediate assumption was that the traitor could only be an officer from the Ministry of War, most likely within the General Staff and one familiar with artillery matters. Sandherr, chief of the Section of Statistics, scoured his files to match handwriting, without success. Next, it was surmised that it had to be someone who had been affiliated to all four of the bureaux so was one of the 'learners' who were doing their attachments. There were three or four artillery officers who had served apprenticeships, one of whom, it was recalled, was Dreyfus, who had not been reported on particularly well when serving in the Fourth Bureau. A specimen of Dreyfus's handwriting was obtained, which bore a resemblance to that in the bordereau. A snag was that the bordereau wrote of being 'off to manoeuvres' whereas Dreyfus had not been on any, nor, actually, had any of the other General Staff learners. But the investigators were not to be deflected. With the inexorable momentum of a boulder rolling downhill, the officers involved convinced themselves that Dreyfus was their man. All they now needed was a proof of handwriting accompanied, if possible, by a confession.

Although Mercier had made up his mind, he thought it expedient to give himself some cover by reporting the matter to the president of the Republic and the prime minister. Cabinet colleagues were nervous of a diplomatic incident with the Germans, who were liable to initiate legal action on the flimsiest of evidence. However, Mercier harangued them with the importance of the defence of the country and how vital it was to deal with treason. In practice, he had already set his plan in motion by briefing Commandant du Paty de Clam, an officer with a bizarre reputation and behaviour to match, to carry it out.

On Monday, 15 October 1894, Dreyfus appeared at the Ministry of War, instructed to do so by a summons relating vaguely to an inspection matter, but to come in plain clothes. He was met by Commandants Georges Picquart and du Paty de Clam. To his astonishment, Dreyfus was asked by du Paty to write a note for him to General de Boisdeffre as he had hurt his hand. Du Paty then began to dictate the text of the stolen bordereau while Dreyfus wrote. Seeing what he had written, du Paty stopped halfway through and placed his hand on Dreyfus's shoulder with the words, 'In the name of the law I arrest you. You are accused of the crime of high treason.' Flabbergasted by this extraordinary experience, Dreyfus vehemently refuted the charge. Du Paty then quoted an extract from Article 76 of the Penal Code while showing Dreyfus a revolver in a drawer. It was clearly intended that Dreyfus should be offered the 'gentleman's way out' but he was not, quite understandably, going to give his detractors that satisfaction and firmly maintained his innocence. Du Paty briefly asked him some questions without showing him any documentation, before handing him over to Commandant Henry to be conveyed, in secret, to the Cherche-Midi prison.

Commandant Forzinetti, governor of the prison, was a man of common sense and, indeed, compassion. He had been told to accept Dreyfus into the prison but keep the matter secret without letting his superiors know. He was very concerned about Dreyfus's extremely distressed behaviour and condition, prompting him to think that Dreyfus was a possible suicide risk. He thoroughly disapproved of du Paty's impromtu visits to interrogate Dreyfus, which were designed to catch him asleep and off guard, and to intimidate him. In desperation, Forzinetti had Dreyfus seen by a doctor and reported the matter to his superior, General Saussier, the military governor. Saussier, a jovial bachelor with an extreme fondness for women, was also, effectively, commander of the field army and had as much power as Mercier, whom he could not stand. He was astonished and considered the ministry had made a grave error. He fully supported Forzinetti and told him to report on Dreyfus's behaviour and du Paty's absurdities.

Du Paty continued to press for a confession and instituted an investigation into Dreyfus's past which, to his delight, revealed evidence of previous liaisons with ladies not noted for the strength of their knicker elastic. Dreyfus protested that these were all before he married and were things of the past. These peccadilloes, if proved, were not actually going to get the accusers very far and something much more substantial in the way of evidence was required. A notorious anti-Jew, Bertillon, in the Justice Department, concocted an extraordinary theory that Dreyfus had forged the bordereau himself. Therefore, if the writing did not look like his, it was because he had disguised it. Either way, the accusers were going to win. However, with even more handwriting experts who differed in their conclusions, du Paty was not fully convinced they would win in a court of law.

At that moment the press came to the rescue. On 29 October, a leak to *La Libre Parole* revealed the 'extremely important arrest ... of an individual ... accused of espionage'. It did not name Dreyfus, but by the 31st his name was out. The press then had a field day, and the anti-Dreyfus and Jews-infiltrating-the-army scenario became a campaign headed by *La Libre Parole* and Drumont, backed up by many others and not just confined to the more salacious journals. Extraordinary blood-curdling vituperation was laid against anyone a Jew and anything Jewish. It was of the nature to be seen again in 1930s Germany. No proof or evidence, it seemed, was required to support unbelievable libel before it was published. All France's wrongs and difficulties were laid at Jews' doors and every single one was in the pay of the enemy. Not only were Jews slated but the government, particularly Mercier, was castigated for allowing Jews into the army in the first place and then delaying the announcement of Dreyfus's arrest in the hope the scandal would die down. The fragile government could not now back out. Nervously, the German Government, supported by the Italians and Austrians, denied any connection with Dreyfus. Whether the public believed that or not was another matter. Despite his misgivings and disgust at what was happening, Saussier, as military governor of Paris, had to issue an order to open an investigation. The examining magistrate, d'Ormescheville, produced a report of breathtaking inaccuracy, which finished:

> Along with his extensive knowledge, Captain Dreyfus possesses a remarkable memory; he speaks several languages, including German, which he knows thoroughly, and Italian, of which he claims to have only a vague notion. He is moreover, of a rather supple – even obsequious – character, quite suited for relations of espionage with foreign agents. He was thus the perfect choice for the miserable and shameful mission that he inspired or accepted and to which – quite luckily for France, perhaps – the discovery of his intrigues has put an end.

On 4 December, as a result of this investigation, Dreyfus was remanded to be tried by court martial. His elder brother, Mathieu, one of a small number who come out of this story with great credit, managed only at this stage to brief a lawyer, Demange, to see the papers. Despite all the accusers' efforts, the only 'evidence' against Dreyfus remained the bordereau and its ambivalent authenticity. Demange was no fool; could the accusers start to worry about an acquittal? A number, by now, had a lot to lose. Sandherr and Henry of the Section of Statistics, together with du Paty, got their heads together and reviewed the vast amount of material obtained by 'Auguste' from the German Embassy. Some of the more amorously exotic exchanges between the attachés, Schwarzkoppen and Panizzardi ('My dear Bugger, Farewell, my little dog') needed little embellishment, but there were others that required a certain amount of date changing and embroidering of fact. The accusers had now become conspirators. They knew too much about each other and what they had done. Things had gone too far. Any weakness and they would fall. They had to cling together and convict Dreyfus. The dossier was certainly going to be 'sexed up'.

The trial began, in the prison, on 19 December 1894. The prosecution demanded it be heard in camera. Demange was not surprised; for days the press had been divided over the issue and so his summary, which he was determined to read to the court, played to those who wanted the trial to be open to the public. He was unsuccessful; the president of the court refused his plea and decided the trial was to be held in closed session. There then followed the most extraordinary travesty. Witnesses for the prosecution – du Paty, of course, behaving like some prima donna; Henry, pointing to Dreyfus as 'the traitor' based on absolutely no evidence; the bizarre handwriting witness who maintained Dreyfus had forged his own handwriting – gave their evidence. Demange, quite properly, put his case that the bordereau could not have been written by Dreyfus and there was no evidence to support it. He went on to say that there was no motive; the defendant was a loyal son of France. Critics would later say that Demange, being a criminal lawyer, would have been more used to driving doubt into the minds of a jury rather than dealing with the more narrow-minded and unimpressionable officers on the board. Nevertheless, his defence was impeccable. A series of character witnesses attested to Dreyfus's probity and patriotism.

The seven-man court then retired. While they were deliberating, du Paty brought a sealed envelope from the Minister of War, Mercier, to the president of the court with strict instructions that it be opened and the contents read solely by the board. Mercier had acted alone. He told none of his colleagues, the president of the Republic or the prime minister. The document was then read in private by the members of the court martial board. It contained more supposed evidence from the Section of Statistics to prove Dreyfus was the traitor. Once read, the documents were returned to du Paty. The defence was totally unaware of this extraordinary violation of justice. The court reopened and a unanimous verdict of guilty was handed down with a sentence of deportation for life and military degradation. Demange, Mathieu and the Dreyfus supporters were appalled. Dreyfus himself, taken back to his cell, was beside himself with despair and grief. Mercier ate a very good dinner that night.

The only grounds for appeal were if there had been some irregularity in the court martial procedures. There were none, at least none known by the defence, so any appeal application was immediately ruled out by the court. The press was jubilant, even the broadsheets. It was not a good time to be a Jew in France.

Before his exile, Dreyfus was to be subjected to the most appalling indignity: the degradation. For a country like France, which prided itself on being the arbiter of style, fashion, sophistication and gentlemanly behaviour, this was something out of the Middle Ages. On 5 January, units of the Paris garrison were drawn up in a square in the École Militaire in Place de Fontenoy. The public were not admitted but there was room available for the press and various VIPs. The streets and buildings outside were thronged with people. Dreyfus was marched out, under escort, into the freezing cold of the square. All that was missing was Madame Defarge and the *tricoteuses*. The commanding officer raised himself from the saddle of his horse and brandishing his sword aloft, shouted, 'Alfred Dreyfus, you are no longer worthy of bearing arms. In the name of the people of France, we dishonour you.' Then a large sergeant major stepped forward. Seizing Dreyfus's already loosened shoulder straps and trouser stripes, he tore them from the uniform. His badges of rank were thrown on the ground. Taking Dreyfus's sword, he broke it over his knee – it had previously had a notch filed into the blade to make this possible. Somehow preserving his equanimity, Dreyfus was paraded round the square in front of the troops before being bundled into a prison van for the journey to La Santé Prison.

He was subsequently taken to Île de Ré from where, on 22 February 1895, he was transported by ship to the hellhole of Devil's Island, 27 miles from Cayenne in French Guiana, from which he was not to return for over four years. Out of sight, out of mind – or so the conspirators thought.

For the Dreyfus family there was a complete void; they felt powerless to do anything. They could not contact Alfred and the authorities had washed their hands of the affair. The Germans denied any part in the scandal and, in January 1895, Mercier resigned as minister of war but not before delivering the Dreyfus documentation, including the 'secret' letters to the court martial board, to Sandherr, the chief of intelligence. However, on 21 February, at a meeting of the Dreyfus family doctor with the new president of France, Félix Faure, it was revealed that Dreyfus had been convicted on the basis of documents to which the defence had not been privy. This devastating news was allowed to be disclosed to the family but not made public. Nevertheless, it was becoming generally known, as the members of the court martial found it very difficult to keep it to themselves. Extraordinary though it seems, this violation of judicial practice was less important than the fact that Dreyfus was seen as a traitor and deserved all he got. Public apathy won and Mathieu Dreyfus despaired of ever obtaining justice for his brother.

In spite of this, things were about to change. Sandherr, by now a very sick man, was succeeded by Commandant Georges Picquart. Picquart was an officer of outstanding reputation and an unusually high moral sense. Coincidentally, he had been an instructor of Dreyfus's at the École de Guerre. He had also been present at the notorious handwriting 'interview' between Dreyfus and du Paty. He had monitored the trial on behalf of the Chief of the General Staff, de Boisdeffre, and had been present at the 'degradation'. On his handover from Sandherr, he was told of the secret documents at the trial and, if he needed them, Commandant Henry had them in his files.

Picquart, however, was no particular supporter of Dreyfus, and had no doubt of his guilt. He set about sorting out his office and instituting some new rules and procedures. Some of the shiftier agents were dismissed, Henry was to bring intelligence material directly to him without having sifted it first himself, and the German and Italian attachés were brought under increasing surveillance. Then, in March 1896, a torn-up document, known as a *petit bleu* from the thin blue express paper it was written on, came into the hands of the Section of Statistics from its source in the German Embassy. It had not been seen by Henry. It was explosive – not only was it a draft note from von Schwarzkoppen, though not in his handwriting, to an agent, but also the name and address was on the reverse. It was Esterhazy's. On the same day, a further torn-up draft was delivered. Written in amateurish code, it clearly expressed von Schwarzkoppen's dissatisfaction with Esterhazy's performance; his actions were too compromising and costly for what was being produced. He was being warned.

It immediately struck Picquart that there was another traitor at large. He asked Henry about his relationship with Esterhazy, as they had worked together some years before. Henry replied that they had lost contact but knowing what was in the secret file and its forgeries, it cannot have been long before Henry must have realised that with Esterhazy's exposure, the light would soon be focused on him. He probably appreciated even before Picquart that the bordereau was written by Esterhazy. Curiously, Picquart failed to let his superiors – de Boisdeffre, his deputy, Gonse, and the Minister of War – know of this significant material. Nevertheless, he started an investigation into Esterhazy but results were disappointing and, by the end of July, he informed the chiefs of his suspicions. They were not enthusiastic about starting another Dreyfus Affair but reluctantly sanctioned Picquart to continue his investigations. Esterhazy, in the meantime, having no idea he was under suspicion, plagued the authorities with demands to be given congenial appointments. Two of Esterhazy's letters fell into Picquart's hands and, with increasing disquiet, he compared the handwriting with a photocopy of the original bordereau. There was absolutely no doubt – Esterhazy was the writer of the bordereau, not Dreyfus.

Picquart called for the secret dossier in Henry's safe, expecting some revelation proving Dreyfus's guilt in some other way than the bordereau. To his astonishment he found no such thing; the documents were insignificant. He was now convinced and, on 1 September 1896, produced a full report for de Boisdeffre. Embarrassed that he had delayed reporting the arrival of the *petit bleu*, he altered the date of its receipt. Both de Boisdeffre and Gonse ordered Picquart to keep the matter of Dreyfus separate from Esterhazy. Picquart could not understand it; as far as he was concerned, Dreyfus had been wrongly convicted and here was the proof. The military were starting to close ranks. They preferred a judicial error, orchestrated by Mercier, to be covered up rather than free an innocent man. Picquart was appalled and determined to set a trap for Esterhazy. When he explained it to the chiefs, they refused to allow it in that it was 'unworthy' to deal with a senior officer in this way, forgetting that they had done exactly that to Dreyfus.

The Dreyfus family now returned to the fray and, on 18 September, Dreyfus's wife, Lucie, sent a petition, drafted by their lawyer, Demange, to the Chamber of Deputies. In it she explained that she was aware of a newspaper's exposé of the 'secret' dossier asserting her husband's guilt, which had not been disclosed to the defence. The expected denial from the Ministry of War was not forthcoming and she therefore concluded that her husband was innocent. She demanded justice. Unfortunately, this was all lost in the euphoria of the Russian czar's state visit; national pride and aspirations were far more important than the life of a prisoner on Devil's Island.

Picquart was also starting to annoy his chiefs with his obsession, which was becoming uncomfortable not only for them but also for the old hands in the Section of Statistics. Could he be posted somewhere remote like Indo-China perhaps? Instead, on 14 November, he was given forty-eight hours to hand over his appointment and leave for the French eastern frontier to carry out some intelligence tasks. Gonse took over the files and saw that the case needed a discovery of some overwhelming evidence against Dreyfus. Henry set to work to create such evidence. Was this to ingratiate himself with his masters, misplaced loyalty, to enhance his own prospects or to protect his old colleague, Esterhazy?

On 10 November 1896, lightning struck; Le Matin published a facsimile of the bordereau. Picquart was at once suspected of leaking it and was summarily dismissed by a panicking Minister of War. Von Schwarzkoppen immediately recognised the writing and realised that Dreyfus had been wrongly convicted. But what could he do? He could hardly reveal Esterhazy as his agent. Doubts were now beginning to appear in the minds of even the most hardened anti-Dreyfusards, as they

had come to be known. Henry set about his 'investigation' with customary zeal, creating further fictional documents. In December, Picquart
was posted to North Africa to 'take charge of the intelligence service in
Algeria and Tunisia'. Like Dreyfus, he was placed safely out of the way,
but not before he had written a full account of the case and put it in a
sealed envelope in June 1897, with his will, to be opened only on his
death. He also briefed his old lawyer friend, Leblois, but swore him to
secrecy. The latter then heard of Auguste Scheurer-Kestner's belief in
Dreyfus's innocence; Scheurer-Kestner, as vice president of the Senate,
was a powerful and influential individual and Leblois could not resist
telling him the whole story but insisted that he would not make use of
the material without agreement.

Meanwhile, the conspirators, now headed by Gonse, were digging
themselves in deep. They were suspicious of Picquart's connection with
Scheurer-Kestner, even from afar, and they were aware of the latter's
meeting with Leblois. They decided that Esterhazy should be warned.
He was irrational, mentally unhinged and could not be trusted to behave
well under pressure. The faithful du Paty was summoned and drafted an
anonymous letter to Esterhazy, warning him of exposure by the Dreyfus
family. The letter was written, on 17 October 1897, by Henry's wife who
was now firmly in on the plot. On receiving it, Esterhazy lost his nerve
and rushed to von Schwarzkoppen who sent him packing with scant
sympathy. Esterhazy could now only rely on his 'protectors', du Paty
and Henry, who were busy forging further documents for the dossier.
They now identified Picquart as the main threat. After all, he was the one
man who knew the whole plot and who was involved, but his scrupulous
loyalty kept him aloof.

Scheurer-Kestner and Mathieu Dreyfus were trying their best, the
former approaching his old friends in government but with little success. Esterhazy, having recovered some of his previous confidence, wrote
increasingly insubordinate and ludicrous letters justifying himself to the
president, the prime minister and minister for war. The plotters dreamt
up fictitious telegrams to Picquart, couched in pseudo code to suggest
that he was involved in stolen documents in the Dreyfus case. These
telegrams were 'intercepted' by intelligence before he received them.
Picquart was questioned by his superior officer and there was clearly

no case to answer but, it had to be said, that he had been in Paris at the material time.

Spurred by an ever-more vindictive press, Mathieu could contain himself no longer and made public a letter he had written earlier to the Minister of War, denouncing Esterhazy as the author of the bordereau. Picquart joined him by complaining to the minister that he had been slandered by Esterhazy. An investigation was initiated and General de Pellieux, governor of the Seine military district, was entrusted with carrying it out. This was a setback for the conspirators in that it might cast light into some of their murky doings. In order to protect Esterhazy, du Paty and Henry had gone far beyond their original misdeed. Esterhazy appeared oblivious of the sword hanging over him and gave increasingly lurid stories to the press, which lapped them up. De Pellieux was strongly 'guided' by the Chief of the General Staff, de Boisdeffre and his number two, Gonse, with the result that, astonishingly, Esterhazy was cleared but Picquart was firmly under suspicion.

De Pellieux was told to reopen his investigation and Picquart was recalled to France to answer the accusations. Clearly, Esterhazy was again going to be cleared. However, into this pantomime appeared a spurned mistress of Esterhazy's, Madame de Boulancy. He had borrowed money from her, which was never repaid, and swindled her into the bargain. She was out for revenge. She handed over some highly indiscreet letters of Esterhazy's in which he had railed against France and expressed his hatred of the French Army. On 28 November, *Le Figaro* published the worst of these. 'Forgeries' cried the other newspapers and, even if true, weren't we all guilty of youthful indiscretions and saying things in the heat of the moment? Although Mathieu was blamed for orchestrating all this, the Dreyfus family saw it as an opportunity, because surely now de Pellieux would have to summon handwriting experts? The conspirators would not want this, coupled with a risk that other crudely forged documents might be brought into the open. De Boisdeffre then personally vouched for the authenticity of two of the documents, knowing them to be forgeries, to prevent de Pellieux examining them. De Pellieux refused to call handwriting experts on the basis that they had all been involved in the Dreyfus case, and was content merely to question Esterhazy about the identity of the remaining documentation.

A straight dismissal of any charge against Esterhazy, however, might provoke serious disquiet. Even the press, while delighted to publish his rubbish, had seen through him. Perhaps it would be better to try him by court martial and acquit him? A sort of 'show trial' like those much favoured later by Stalin but, in this case, to exonerate a guilty man rather than the other way round, might be the solution. This would have the added advantage of reinforcing Dreyfus's guilt. After careful briefing, Esterhazy wrote to de Pellieux demanding that his honour should be restored by being tried by court martial. His request was met with the alacrity of an efficiently planned operation and the customary manipulation took place to whitewash Esterhazy while making severe innuendoes against Picquart. It took the court three minutes to consider a unanimous verdict of acquittal. Esterhazy became, overnight, the hero he had always dreamed of being. The following day Picquart was arrested and Scheurer-Kestner relieved of his appointment of the vice presidency of the Senate. The conspirators had won and the Dreyfus Affair was over. But was it?

Émile Zola was one of the most widely read, although not altogether uncontroversial, authors of the time. The Dreyfus Affair reinforced his deep-seated abhorrence of the anti-Semitic movement and reflected the themes of his novels: the persecuted innocent victim of bourgeois hypocrisy and political machination (*La Conquête de Plassans, La Débâcle* and *Lourdes*). From a meeting with a number of the Dreyfusards in November 1897, he became fully committed to correcting the wrong. A series of Zola's commentaries appeared in newspapers; these were not always to the liking of the conservative nationalists but were tolerated because of his popular standing. Esterhazy's acquittal proved the final straw – had France lost its senses? On 13 January 1898, *L'Aurore* published probably one of the most famous letters ever to a newspaper, entitled 'J'accuse'; in it, Zola addressed the president of France to exhort him to correct this miscarriage of justice. The letter was some 4,500 words long, named names and was vitriolic in its accusation against the 'agents of harm to society'.

Support was immediate from intellectuals, writers (Proust), artists (Monet), socialists and lawyers and, indeed, many ordinary people to whom Zola was a literary hero. In the meantime, Picquart had been discharged from the army and his pension stopped. His lawyer was suspended from the Paris Bar. Character assassination was developed against Zola and the murky hand of the forger Henry was all too apparent. Fearing that he could not receive a fair hearing, Zola's lawyers persuaded him to leave France, and on 19 July he arrived in England.

Earlier, the new minister for war, Cavaignac, having had access to the secret dossier, reaffirmed, publicly, Dreyfus's guilt. The conspirators then suffered a severe blow. Christian, Esterhazy's cousin and the carrier of messages between Esterhazy and du Paty, fed up with being swindled and robbed, declared that the telegrams to Picquart in Tunisia had been forged by Henry. Esterhazy was locked up, ironically in the same prison as Picquart, but subsequently freed. Cavaignac – a man of stubborn rectitude – determined to clear his own mind as to the validity of the documents in the dossier, which he believed to be legitimate, ordered a hard-working and indefatigable staff officer, Captain Cuignet, to revise and sort the documentation. In doing so, to his astonishment Cuignet realised that two letters had been 'cut and pasted' and the paper was different. On 30 August, Cavaignac confronted Henry in the presence of de Boisdeffre and Gonse. Henry eventually broke and blamed his actions on orders from above – the usual escape route for anyone obeying an illegal order. Cavaignac was unimpressed and Henry was imprisoned. De Boisdeffre resigned and Gonse lost his job. Late the following day, Henry cut his throat and on 1 September, Esterhazy left France for England. The Dreyfusards were back in action.

On 3 September, Lucie Dreyfus, Alfred's wife, forwarded a formal submission to the Court of Cassation (roughly equivalent to the High Court in the United Kingdom or the Supreme Court in the United States) for the revision of her husband's conviction. An inevitable series of delays then took place with the lawyers and politicians of both sides jockeying for position. Matters were brought to a head by the death of President Faure in the arms of his mistress, and the election of his successor, Émile Loubet. Loubet, a bluff, simple soul of peasant origin, was, allegedly, pro-Dreyfus. Whether that was so or not, on 29 May 1899, the Court of Cassation annulled the verdict of the court martial of 22 December 1894 and remanded the case to the military authorities in Rennes for a retrial. Dreyfus was to be brought home from an exile of unbelievable hardship of four years, two months and five days. Picquart was pardoned, released and restored to his rightful position in the army. On 1 July, Dreyfus was once again in the arms of his beloved and supporting family.

The retrial lasted from 7 August to 9 September. The army now saw itself bitterly defending its position and the senior people within it at the time of the original conviction and subsequent cover-up. Witnesses were rehearsed in their lies, hearsay evidence was allowed and irrelevances paraded. Men of dubious integrity went unchallenged. One of Dreyfus's lawyers was subject to an attempted assassination. On 9 September, the court handed down a guilty verdict by a majority of five to two, with a sentence of ten years' detention of which five had deemed to have been served. Dreyfus would not, though, have to return to Devil's Island.

Waldeck-Rousseau, the prime minister, was nervous. How was this sentence to be carried out? Was Dreyfus to be sent to prison? If so, where and what would be the conditions? The world's press were howling with astonishment and anger. There was talk of imposing sanctions against France and boycotting the World's Fair in Paris; there were demonstrations outside French embassies in New York, London, Milan and Antwerp. Waldeck-Rousseau was less concerned about that than a return to peace among his own population, justice seen to be done and a final end to the affair. How was this to happen?

On 1 January 1900, Waldeck-Rousseau declared an amnesty in the Dreyfus case. This was not actually what some Dreyfusards had in mind but, effectively, declared that there was to be no further litigation in the case and no further criminal trials. Rightly, Waldeck-Rousseau wanted to take France forward and put the affair behind everyone. It was not until 12 July 1906 that the Rennes verdict was annulled and Dreyfus cleared of all charges.

It is too simple to say that Dreyfus was victimised because he was a Jew. That was part of it but the problem went much deeper than that. However, because he *was* a Jew, it made it easier for his accusers, given the country-wide, not solely within the army, virulent anti-Semitic feeling, to make him the scapegoat for all the ills of the country and the army. Once he had been wrongly convicted and his accusers realised they had the wrong man, the spiral of deceit and cover-up makes Watergate and the 'sexing up' of the Iraq dossier look comparatively tame. Primarily, Dreyfus was the casualty of the army's inadequacy and lack of self-confidence after the Franco-Prussian War.

The army itself was nervous of Alsace-Lorraine officers and paranoid about infiltration by agents and double-agents. Men such as Mercier, de Boisdeffre and Gonse, let alone wasters like Esterhazy and the unbalanced du Paty, backed up by the loyal but incompetent forger, Henry, created a cesspool that cast its stink over future generations of French Army officers for whom the Dreyfus Affair was something to remember with deep shame. They were only slightly balanced by men of integrity like Scheurer-Kestner, Picquart and Cuignet.

The fragile and ever-changing political atmosphere reflected the anxieties of the Church, the old guard aristocracy, fervent Republicans and the Nationalists. The press had much to answer for, and their hounding of Dreyfus as a representative of all that they hated about the Jews was only marginally stemmed by writers such as Zola and Lazare, and lawyers like Demange. Dreyfus amazingly survived the horrors of Devil's Island and never ceased to honour his country when he could have been forgiven for rejecting it after the unbelievable harm it had done him and his family.

A victim of hounding in a different way and by a different kind of society, the so-called Lost Cause, is General 'Pete' Longstreet, the man who lost Gettysburg.

FIVE

Lieutenant General James 'Pete' Longstreet

The 'Old War Horse' of Gettysburg

July 1863

Of all the battles ever fought by Americans throughout the world, Gettysburg still remains the one most deeply embedded in the national psyche. It epitomised the anguish of the Civil War: North versus South, family against family, slavery versus abolition. Yet, it was more than that. It was, at the time, and remained, the biggest and costliest battle of the war, with over 45,000 killed, wounded and missing. Although it was not the final engagement, it marked the beginning of the end. The Northerners now realised that victory was within their grasp and the Southerners knew that they would have to come to terms as their ability to fight on diminished.

Even more importantly, for the South, their hero General Robert E. Lee had failed. How could this happen? There must be a reason for it. It was impossible, in Confederate eyes, for this man to have been out-manoeuvred and out-fought by General Meade. He must have been let down. How and by whom?

Jeb Stuart, the charismatic cavalry reconnaissance commander, had ridden off and left Lee blind to enemy layout and strengths. General Richard S. Ewell's nerve collapsed and he failed to take the vital ground of Cemetery Hill, preferring to remain in Gettysburg town. Nevertheless, the fingers of disappointed ex-Confederates, promoters of the 'Lost Cause', pointed at Longstreet, one of Lee's corps commanders; the man who had argued with his leader, was allegedly late on the second day and was then responsible for not supporting Pickett's breakthrough.

Lee always accepted personal responsibility for the loss of Gettysburg,

but after his death, on 12 October 1870, the full weight of Southern bit-
terness and acrimony turned on Longstreet. He no longer had Lee to
protect him and those, such as Jubal Early, who had little to be proud
of in their own Civil War performance, saw him as the scapegoat for all
their post-war misery. Longstreet lost the battle, therefore Longstreet
lost the war. For many years, his detractors had it all their own way
and Longstreet did not help himself in some of his activities, so it was
not until relatively recently that he was cleared when the truth of why
Gettysburg was lost and the Lee mythology became much clearer.

In the early nineteenth century the United States was a collection of
states, rather than a united nation. Government functions of education,
transport, health and public order were carried out at state or local level,
with little more than a nod to Washington. A few national institutions
such as churches and political parties provided some sort of coherence
but, on the whole, states went their own way and guarded their right to
do so. Gradually, however, changes in technology and in the economy
were bringing different areas of the country into much closer contact.
Transport improved with newly built canals and roads. Importantly, railways were constructed to provide passenger and freight infrastructure.
Improvements in printing led to cheap newspapers, and the development
of the telegraph system carried relatively up-to-date information across
the vast distances.

To the non-American, the Civil War was only about slavery; the
South needed, for economic reasons, to retain its slaves and to the North,
the very idea was abhorrent. Indeed, Abraham Lincoln said the 'war was
in some way about slavery'. But it went deeper than that. Americans were
people of principle; the Declaration of Independence, the Constitution
and the Bill of Rights were relied on to guide them through trouble. These
principles, though, had different meanings to the North and South. The
might of the republic and its overall power clashed with the unalienable
right of the individual and the independence of his state.

The art of compromise, another great quality of Americans, was lost
in the clamour of eloquent rhetoric for war. The Confederacy saw it their
right to secede from the Union and, in 1861, appointed not only their

own president but also a Secretary of State for War. People who had been at one against the common colonial enemy, Britain, now divided against themselves with the same popular passion. Their differences became more important than unity and the values that had cemented them since 1781. To the Union, secession was defiance of its rule of law and a rebellion against its authority. To the Confederacy it was simply a matter of defending its territory and repelling invasion, even if that meant strategic forays into Northern areas of influence.

Many Southerners had no connection with slavery, owned no slaves or were not reliant on income produced by slave labour. In a population of some 5 million, only 48,000 owned more than twenty slaves. Yet this did not stop the small-holding subsistence farmers or those who owned nothing fighting for what they considered to be their right. While a vast majority of Southern whites were not slave owners, arguably everyone living in the south was connected to slavery in some form or fashion. Slavery gave a distinctive tone to the whole pattern of Southern life. Although large plantation owners were few, they were wealthy and powerful, and often in politics. Far from opposing slavery, small farmers saw that, with hard work, they could pull themselves upwards to the planter class. Deep down lay the view that blacks were an inferior race who could live in a civilised society only if disciplined through slavery. Southerners developed an elaborate pro-slavery argument, defending the institution on biblical, economic and sociological grounds.

The ultimate outcome of wars is often decided by each side's access to materiel and resources. While the South, on the face of it, was wealthy, its actual prosperity depended on the capital value of slaves and income from labour-intensive cotton, sugar and tobacco plantations. If the slaves went, so did the plantations. The North, on the other hand, had iron, steel and coal, and manufactured goods, with transport infrastructure underpinning enormous potential. In the long run, there would be no economic contest.

The catalyst for war was the election, in December 1860, of Abraham Lincoln as president on an anti-slavery ticket. This provoked the secession of South Carolina, swiftly followed by Mississippi, Florida, Alabama, Georgia, Louisiana and Texas. Lincoln was not an abolitionist but insisted that slavery should not be extended into areas of the United

States that had not yet formally become states. The South believed that slavery would not survive unless it did. Not only was this an economic issue but also one of political balance in Congress, where new slave-owning states or non-owning ones would be represented. The struggle had been particularly brought into focus by the Mexican War (1846–7). Peace gave the non-slave states the opportunity to incorporate the newly gained Texan territory into the 'free' states. Importantly, California, previously Mexican, was invaded by gold-rush prospectors who were mainly Northern free-staters. On top of this, the Fugitive Slave Act of 1850 allowed slave owners to pursue runaway slaves into the free states to the outrage of the Northerners. This further pushed the two sides apart and room for compromise steadily evaporated.

In early 1861, the seceding states met in Montgomery, Alabama, drafted a constitution calling themselves the Confederate States of America and elected a president, Jefferson Davis. Despite efforts on the part of moderates on both sides, war was now inevitable and on 13 April 1861, the Union base, Fort Sumpter, surrendered to a Confederate force after a bloodless exchange of fire. The American Civil War, also known as the War Between the States, the War of the Rebellion or the War of Northern Aggression, began. It was to last until 1865 and cost a higher percentage of lives lost per head of population than any war the United States has been involved in since.

James Longstreet's background was not unlike a number of Confederate generals'. Essentially, he reflected the times in which he lived. He was born on his father's cotton plantation in North Augusta, South Carolina on 8 January 1821 but always considered himself from Augusta, Georgia. Unsurprisingly, he became an excellent horseman and shot, and enjoyed the country life. He was physically strong, self-reliant and made friends easily. At the same time he could be moody and taciturn and his manners had a rough edge. He could never be taken for an aristocrat like his later commander, Robert E. Lee.

His father died in 1833 and he then lived in Augusta at his uncle's house. His uncle, Augustus, was a pillar of local society and had a benign influence on Longstreet. In 1838 he entered West Point military academy.

His class contained a number of men who later became household names in the Civil War. A sociable young man, Longstreet was affectionately known as 'Old Pete' among his fellow cadets, and he made a number of friends with whom he kept in contact throughout his adult life: one of these was Ulysses S. Grant, who later married a cousin of Longstreet's. He graduated from West Point in 1842, coming fifty-fourth in a class of fifty-six, sixteen of whom would go on to be Civil War generals.

Officer training at West Point was fairly basic and aimed to turn out company commander-level officers, suitable for the Frontier Wars, without any grand design on generalship. What Longstreet learned and experienced over the years after West Point was far more important to his later military life. In the Mexican War, he served as a company commander and adjutant (executive officer) of an infantry battalion. This was an important education in what motivated soldiers, how to get the best out of them and what leadership really meant. It also provided an essential grounding in the benefits of efficient administration. He was involved in a number of tough battles, and in one he was severely wounded. After the war, he served in the dull commissary of the Department of Texas but it did give him the experience of administering 1,500 soldiers, and their accompanying horses, over vast and inhospitable terrain. Further experience as the commander of Fort Bliss gave him the responsibility of, albeit small, independent command.

Although he never commanded large numbers of men before becoming a brigadier, he was on a par with others of the same age and experience. There is no evidence that his tactical opinions owed any influence to great military thinkers; his ideas seemed, sensibly, to derive from first-hand experience in battle. On the whole, he was more used to being in the attack than defence and while this, for the most part, was successful against the Mexicans, he realised how strong a well-prepared defensive position could be, even with fewer men than the attacker. There had been a couple of uncomfortably close-run things at Churubusco and El Molino del Rey.

Longstreet continued his career in the US Army for the next ten years, serving in Texas, Kansas and New Mexico, steadily moving up the ranks to become a major in 1858. Meanwhile, the political climate between the states deteriorated. When Alabama seceded from the Union in January 1861, Longstreet, like many other officers brought up in the South, turned loyally to his home state, Georgia. He resigned his commission in the US Army in May and joined the forces of the Confederacy as a lieutenant colonel. He arrived at the Confederate capital, Richmond, Virginia, in June and was appointed brigadier general. Sent to Manassas Junction, Virginia, he took command of a brigade of Virginia infantry.

The battle at Manassas, which became known as Bull Run, was the first major conflict between North and South. Longstreet's brigade fought on 18 July 1861 and, three days later, were in reserve during the actual battle at Bull Run. Although a Confederate victory, the battle demonstrated the bloody character of the war to come. During that winter, while both sides regrouped, Longstreet was promoted to major general. In early May 1862, he was involved in the skirmishes at Yorktown and Williamsburg. Then at the Battle of Seven Pines, on 31 May, Longstreet led the Confederate attack. This was not a success as he committed his troops piecemeal instead of concentrating them. However, when General Robert E. Lee was appointed commander of the Army of Northern Virginia, Longstreet quickly proved his ability, winning Lee's confidence at the Seven Days campaign near Richmond in late June. In mid August 1862, Lee engaged Union forces at the Battle of Second Manassas. A Union victory under Major General John Pope seemed highly likely but, on 29 August, Longstreet arrived with five divisions to assault a 2-mile-long section of the Union flank. One of the worst battles of the war, Second Manassas resulted in 25,000 casualties and proved a victory for the South.

Then, on 17 September 1862, came Antietam, the bloodiest battle of the Civil War. There were more casualties than at the landings on Omaha Beach in June 1944 or Iwo Jima in February 1945. The carnage still causes a chill in American hearts. The battle gave President Lincoln the excuse to issue the Emancipation Proclamation on 22 September, which stipulated that all slaves in Confederate territory were to be forever free. From now on the North held the moral high ground against slavery and any European support for the South withered away.

His performance at Antietam earned Longstreet the affectionate nickname 'Old War Horse' from General Lee, who promoted him to lieutenant general on 11 October and gave him command of the First

Corps of Virginia. At the same time Thomas 'Stonewall' Jackson took command of the Second Corps. Longstreet's qualities were thoroughness and a methodical nature; he preferred the steadiness of defence rather than the riskier and more dashing attack. Lee trusted and listened to him, but did not always agree with him.

General Robert E. Lee was, and still is, an American icon, particularly of the South. By any standards, now as then, Lee was a great man, not only through his many accomplishments but in the way he lived and behaved. While, like many great men, he had his share of flaws, it is not difficult to understand how the myths built up around him and how challenging it was for his adherents to accept any failings on his part. He was what every man who aspired to be a Southern gentleman hoped to become.

Some men, sons of high-achieving fathers, find it difficult to live up to their fathers' reputations; others, sons of wasters and profligates, struggle throughout their lives to overcome the disadvantage of their birth and often succeed. Lee was one of the latter. Born on 19 January 1807, he was the son of 'Light Horse' Harry. He never really knew his father, who was seldom at home and left permanently when Robert was 6, dying when he was 11. Harry Lee was a bluffer, spendthrift, reckless speculator and jailed bankrupt. The only lessons Robert could learn from his father were how things should not be done.

Lee graduated from West Point military academy to become an engineer, fighting in the Mexican War. Later he transferred to the cavalry to gain a command. While he was a man of courage, he preferred non-confrontation and hoped problems would go away if they were ignored. His nephew, Fitzhugh Lee, who fought under J. E. B. (Jeb) Stuart as a cavalry officer, wrote in 1894, 'He had a reluctance to oppose the wishes of others, or to order them to do anything that would be disagreeable and to which they would not consent.' This was to affect his later life in how he behaved with his superiors and subordinates. He was somewhat aloof, avoiding crowds and people who were not close friends. He was highly self-disciplined and controlled, was difficult to know well and even his family were never that close to him. He thrived on duty to his fellow human beings, to the detriment, possibly, of his own happiness. Looking out from the paintings and photographs of the time, Lee is the epitome of the Southern gentleman, immaculate in his grey Confederate

uniform, conveying self-confidence and assurance. But there was something missing – perhaps the frustration of a man imprisoned by his own
strictures prevented him living a freer life of his own and expressing a
more outgoing nature? How much did this affect his relationships with
his commanders and, in particular, his 'Old War Horse', Pete Longstreet?

Following defeat at Chancellorsville in May 1863, Union troops – the
Army of the Potomac – under their inept and vacillating commander,
General Joseph Hooker, withdrew north over the Rappahannock River.
Lee saw this as an opportunity to drive north, through Pennsylvania,
with a number of objectives. The first was to force the Northern army
from its relatively secure positions north of the Rappahannock into open
ground more favourable to his form of manoeuvre warfare, at which he
was so expert. He would then threaten Philadelphia, Baltimore and New
York, in addition to Washington. At the same time, this would relieve
pressure on his rear areas in Virginia. Lee was convinced that he needed
a significant and final victory over the Northern army to negotiate peace
from a position of strength. As time went on, the disparity between the
Union ability to reinforce and replenish against the Confederate dwind-
ling reserves of men and materiel would become more acute.

On 3 June, Lee left Fredericksburg, using the Shenandoah Valley as
cover, then switched northwards towards Winchester, Harpers Ferry
and Harrisburg. He now had Jeb Stuart commanding the cavalry, First
Corps under James Longstreet, Second under Richard Ewell and Third
under Ambrose Hill, totalling about 75,000 men. Identifying Lee's
axis of advance, Union cavalry surprised Jeb Stuart's cavalry at Brandy
Station on 9 June. In this, the largest cavalry action of the Civil War,
the Northerners got the better of the Confederates, although sustaining
marginally higher casualties. Nevertheless, Lee pushed on, throwing the
Northern command into further paroxysms of dismay and indecision.
Lincoln had had enough of the useless Hooker, who had now completely
lost his nerve, and replaced him with George Meade, a man of a different
stamp: experienced, robust and well respected by his troops. Meade now
thought through the problem properly. Lee was the invader and therefore had to attack; withdrawal would be an admission of defeat. Lee's

forces were spread out and Meade's relatively concentrated; if Meade concentrated even further, on ground of his own choosing, Lee would be forced to attack him.

This was exactly what Lee wanted to avoid but he was now forced to concentrate his troops in an area between Chambersburg and Gettysburg. Southern reconnaissance parties reported Gettysburg and the surrounding area occupied by Union troops. Lee had lost touch with Stuart, on whom he relied for intelligence on the enemy strength and positions, so was, to a certain extent, acting blind. (Stuart was not to reappear until midday on 2 July having not been heard from since 25 June.) Nevertheless, on 1 July, Lee and Longstreet rode towards Gettysburg from where the sound of artillery and small arms could already be heard. The ground of Gettysburg has been described as an inverted hook (see map opposite). Lying in a semicircle south of the town are Cemetery and Culp's Hills, about 80 and 100 feet respectively, with another slightly south again. Stretching from there, for 5 to 6 miles southwards, is the shank of the hook, the high ground of Cemetery Ridge with, at its southern point, Little Round Top and Big Round Top Hills.

It was not Lee's intention to allow his troops to engage in small individual skirmishes, but rather to concentrate and bring significant force to bear at a particular point. However, as in most battles, the unexpected happened. Some of Hill's corps engaging Union troops on the ridges west of Gettysburg were joined by Ewell's from the north. This resulted in a stroke of good fortune for Lee in that he had now caught the Northerners between Hill and Ewell. The result was to expel the enemy from Gettysburg in confusion. A number made for the high ground of Cemetery Hill. If they could be pursued while still in disarray, Lee's troops would be in possession of this vital ground. Accordingly, Lee sent a staff officer to Ewell's headquarters to tell him, 'that it was necessary to press "those people" in order to secure possession of the heights and that, if possible, he wished to see him do this'. He went on: 'if he found it practicable, but to avoid a general engagement until the arrival of the other divisions of the army'. By modern standards this sounds more like a wish than an order. Perhaps it was the way in which Lee liked to 'direct' his commanders rather than giving them clear, unequivocal orders. In Ewell's defence, he was new to corps level command and was not used to

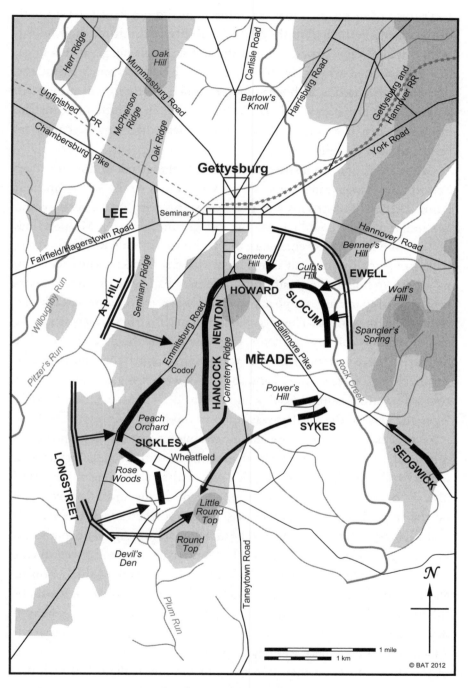

Battle of Gettysburg, 2 July 1863

Lee's form of direction. He was confused; he did not know the strength of the enemy and whether they had the ability to reinforce their hilltop positions and was worried that Lee did not want to engage, at this stage, in a full-blooded assault. In the event, it left Ewell too much latitude to do what he wanted, which was not very much. His staff was infuriated; an important chance was missed. Years later Ewell admitted his mistake but, in essence, it was Lee's for not giving clear, direct and unequivocal orders to take the hills.

That afternoon Longstreet told Lee that things could not suit them better; the Confederates could now swing round to the south, and left flank, of the Union troops and put themselves between the enemy and Washington. They could choose suitable ground, threaten Meade's lines of communication and challenge the Unionists to attack. It was really what Longstreet wanted all along. He was averse to taking the enemy on, frontally, up hill and in positions where they had, at least, some opportunity to prepare fire support plans and work out counter-attack and reinforcement options. There is an old military maxim that has stood the test of innumerable engagements: the odds favour the defender 3:1. Lee disagreed; there was the enemy, he was going to attack them and finish it. But Lee's men were scattered and too many were using the few available routes forward, leading to delay and confusion. Jeb Stuart, Lee's trusted 'eyes and ears' of the cavalry, was still on a mission of his own elsewhere.

As the day wore on, more and more Union troops took up positions on the high ground, Cemetery Ridge, running south from Cemetery Hill to the two Round Top Hills. A quick reconnaissance by one of Lee's staff officers brought gloomy news of enemy positions and likely strength on the ridge. Lee decided, therefore, that no further attack was feasible that evening. With hindsight, had he attacked immediately, he might still have caught the enemy in disarray. Lee tentatively directed Ewell to take Culp's Hill, Longstreet to take the left (southern) flank of the Unionists and Hill to 'threaten' the centre. The signal for Ewell to attack would be the sound of Longstreet's guns. This operation was to take place the next day, 2 July, subject to further reconnaissance. The inference was that the attack should take place as early as possible. Although Lee had no idea of the strength of the enemy in front of him, he realised full well that time was short and he would have to strike before Meade could bring up even more troops and artillery. Again, Longstreet was dubious but Lee refused to accept his suggestion for a southern flanking movement. No exact timings for the attack were issued. These and further coordinating instructions were to be left to the following day when the exact enemy positions could be identified.

Before first light, Longstreet met up with Lee and his staff. Lee, suffering from dysentery, was jittery, unusual for a man who was normally so cool, and sent out reconnaissance parties to establish what ground was actually held by the enemy. Longstreet still tried to persuade Lee to outflank the enemy to the south but Lee was determined to take the enemy on as soon as possible. He refused Longstreet's appeal to wait until Pickett's Division had arrived. Lee confirmed his orders to Ewell on a visit to his headquarters but, again, failed to issue timings except that 'report circulated that the attack of Longstreet would be delivered at 4 o'clock'. Clearly, this was a late start time for a major battle but Longstreet's men had to take a 6-mile covered approach route, which would take much of the day.

Lee did not give Longstreet the order to start until 11 a.m. and Lee could have had no misunderstanding of how long it would take to get the men into action. Nevertheless, the time taken for Longstreet's men to complete their approach march irritated and frustrated Lee. Was Longstreet, like Achilles, 'sulking in his tent'? There is evidence that he did not conduct himself with his customary dash and zeal but by four o'clock, Longstreet was ready.

At the last moment, two of his divisional commanders realised that the enemy positions did not end at the southern tip of Cemetery Ridge but ran out south and west towards the Emmitsburg Road until they reached a peach orchard and a wheat field, then arched back south-westwards to an area known as Devil's Den close to the Round Top Hills. Meade's people were clearly in very much more substantial positions than the Southerners had anticipated. Earlier Confederate intelligence was now clearly, and dangerously, out of date, if not faulty from the very beginning. Highly embarrassed, Longstreet had little option but to continue his plans unchanged. Lee was not on the spot to make immediate decisions and, in reality, did not influence much on that day.

Realising that Round Top was still only partly occupied, Hood,

Longstreet's right-hand divisional commander, requested a southern flanking movement but it was refused. After some hard fighting,
by nightfall Longstreet's men had achieved partial success; they occupied the entire Devil's Den area, including the wheat field and orchard.
Crucially, however, the Unionists still held the line of Cemetery Ridge
and the Round Tops. Success would have been greater had Hill's corps
been more effective and Ewell's attacked earlier than 6.30 p.m. The
whole enterprise lacked coordination and management. Lee failed
to order Hill to support Longstreet or sharpen up Ewell's assault.
Had Longstreet busied himself more and reacted quicker, rather than
allowing himself to be upset by Lee, his attack could have undoubtedly
gone in earlier, but not hours earlier. There was never any question of a
'sunrise attack'.

Buoyed by this limited success, Lee ordered Ewell and Longstreet to
attack again the following day. The Confederates still had their aggression
and offensive spirit. To be fair, Lee really had little option; to withdraw
would be tantamount to giving in and accepting the war was effectively
lost; to attack had all the possibilities of winning. Meade was worried
too. He called his commanders together to put the options to them. Stay
and fight? If stay, wait to be attacked or launch an attack from where
they were? Or withdraw to another position? The decision was made to
stay and fight.

Early the following day, Lee had no intention of waiting for yet more
delay, so rode round to Longstreet to ensure he got going. Longstreet
still maintained that a flanking move was on the cards. Given the losses
the Confederates had sustained and lack of gun ammunition, there was
now considerably less merit in this. Additionally, Lee was concerned
that, if his army did so, it would be unable to live off the land in a station-
ary position waiting to be attacked. In essence, his men could be starved
out. Longstreet then said that he needed reinforcing for an operation of
this magnitude since he had had to leave two of his divisions (Hood's and
McLaws's) in their present positions to withstand any enemy counter-
attack. Lee accepted this and gave Longstreet two of Hill's Divisions,
which were much closer to the objective, in addition to Pickett's Division,
which had just arrived.

Longstreet was now ordered to attack not the left flank of the Union force but into the centre of Cemetery Ridge. Longstreet expressed some very understandable doubts. Lee, however, insisted that the attack take place as ordered. Discretion by subordinate commanders, so much Lee's earlier modus operandi, was no longer allowed. Having put his point of view and been refused, like any good subordinate, Longstreet got on with it. By midday, Ewell had unsuccessfully tried to take Cemetery and Culp's Hills. While, again, this lacked any coordination with Longstreet, it did have the effect of forcing Meade to keep troops on his right flank occupying those two features.

The Confederate fire plan started at 1 p.m. but half an hour later Pickett's troops were formed up and ready but gun ammunition was starting to run low. Fire from enemy guns on Cemetery Ridge then slackened and Pickett's men started to appear from the woods out into the open at about 2 p.m., an advance of some 1,400 yards. They stood little chance under the withering fire of the Unionists, who had had time to recce their defensive positions and bring down very effective fire. There were isolated breakthroughs but many fell, some turned and ran and others gave themselves up as prisoners. Lee, now in the gun line, saw what was happening and ordered the distraught Pickett to withdraw the remnants of his division behind the hill on which the guns were positioned and to be prepared to withstand the inevitable counter-attack from Meade. Lee realised the battle was over, if not the war, and now he must prepare for a retreat, not just a tactical withdrawal.

Had Lee intended Pickett to receive more support than he had? Where were the two divisions of Hill's corps that he had put under Longstreet's command? Longstreet maintained they were needed to protect the Confederate right flank. Had they reinforced Pickett's charge, the battle might have been won. But had they done so and been destroyed with Pickett's men, the war would have been certainly lost that afternoon. Was this Lee's decision or Longstreet's?

Lee gambled on Gettysburg bringing the war to a point of mutual exhaustion when peace could properly be conducted. It failed and it was Lee's fault, which he always admitted. Blame can be laid on some of his subordinates but it was his style of suggestion rather than definitive orders, and too light a rein on his generals, which let him down.

This devastating defeat forced the South into a defensive war and encouraged the Union to push south into north-west Georgia. Gettysburg has been described as the 'High Tide of the Confederacy'. From now on the only way for the tide to go was out. Nevertheless, there remained some bloody and prolonged fighting, including bitter trench warfare. Unionist General William Sherman carved a path of devastation through Atlanta into Savannah that became known as 'Sherman's march to the Sea'.

Longstreet and his men remained in eastern Tennessee and joined Lee in Virginia in late April 1864. In May, Longstreet, under Lee, fought off Grant near Chancellorsville, part of a prolonged battle that became known as the Wilderness Campaign. Wounded by a bullet that passed through his throat and into his shoulder, Longstreet was forced to retire until October. Meanwhile, stalemate battles at North Anna and Cold Harbor continued to drain Confederate strength.

When Longstreet rejoined his command, Lee was defending the Confederate capital of Richmond against Grant at nearby Petersburg; the battle deteriorated into trench warfare until Union troops finally breached Richmond's fortifications on 3 April 1865. The Army of Northern Virginia was now in full retreat. On Sunday, 9 April 1865, Longstreet accompanied Lee to Appomattox, West Virginia. There, in the town's small courthouse, the war between the states was formally brought to a close. It is, however, a common misconception that the war finally ended here. In fact, General Joe Johnston surrendered the Army of Tennessee, as well as the districts of the Carolinas and Georgia, at Bennett Place, near the modern city of Durham, North Carolina, on 26 April – a much larger surrender, indeed the largest of the war.

To understand why Longstreet was so vilified after Lee's death in 1870, one has to realise the context in which it happened. The South had lost the war and was now plunged into misery and economic uncertainty. Slavery, on which much prosperity depended, had ended; families had lost significant numbers of able-bodied men; farms, houses and plantations had been laid waste and bankruptcy stared many in the face. Carpetbaggers from the North abounded. The war needed to be presented in the best possible terms – thus the myth of the Lost Cause was developed.

Instigated by white Southerners, a number of them former Confederate generals, the Lost Cause created and romanticised the 'Old South' and the Confederate war effort, often distorting history. It was one in which nostalgia for the Confederate past was coloured by a collective amnesia of the disgrace of slavery. It provided a comforting cloak over the dishonour of defeat and relied on a number of assertions: secession caused the war, not slavery: slaves were loyal to their masters and were unsuited and unprepared for freedom; the Confederacy was defeated militarily only because of the Union's overwhelming advantages in men and resources; all Confederate soldiers were heroes, the chief among whom was General Robert E. Lee; Southern women put up with their suffering and the loss of the men folk with stamina and saintly stoicism. It was, of course, much more complicated than that.

Proponents of the Lost Cause alleged that the Confederates were not defeated on the battlefield; rather, they were overwhelmed by massive Union resources and manpower. Robert E. Lee virtually said so in his famous farewell address to the Army of Northern Virginia at Appomattox courthouse on 10 April 1865, when he declared that the army had been 'compelled to yield to overwhelming numbers and resources'. While this was true to a certain extent, it gives little credit to the Union Army and its more successful generals. It also understates the Confederacy's not insignificant wartime industrial capacity and its ability to field and supply its army. The Confederacy was actually self-sufficient in military hardware by 1863.

Confederate soldiers were idealised and it was not considered dishonourable to be defeated by overwhelming numbers. The heroic 'Johnny Reb' became immortalised in poetry and song. Of course, most Confederate soldiers fought with enormous courage under appalling conditions but, it has to be said, desertion was particularly high on both sides. A total of between 10 and 15 per cent of Confederate soldiers were absent without leave at any one time. In June 1862, Longstreet estimated that of the 32,000 Virginian soldiers under his command, 7,000 were absentees. More soldiers were executed for criminal offences, both North and South, than in all other wars combined in which American forces served.

For many years the mythology surrounding Lee gave him godlike status in the eyes of diehard Confederates. Together with Stonewall Jackson, killed at Chancellorsville in 1863, they were the icons of the Lost Cause adherents. The *Southern Historical Society Papers* (SHSP) with major contributors such as Generals Jubal Early and Pendleton were instrumental in maintaining the legend. The Pulitzer prize-winning biography of Lee written by Douglas Freeman in 1935 reinforced this view. If Lee was God then Freeman's book was the Bible.

Freeman identified a number of reasons for the Gettysburg disaster. The first was Stuart's lack of contact with the enemy, which denied Lee good intelligence on enemy strength and movements. Second was Ewell's failure to take Cemetery Hill on 1 July; Ewell was used to Stonewall Jackson's very direct control but not Lee's more discretionary direction. Third, the Confederate frontage on 2 July was far too extended (more than 5 miles), making coordination and communication difficult let alone the consequent inability to concentrate maximum force at a given point. Then there was Longstreet's delay in attacking on 2 July. Freeman describes Longstreet as sulking and stubborn after Lee's refusal to take his advice. He maintains that it was Lee's misfortune to have to employ a man whose inclination was to go on the defence, in the attack. However, he does not spare Lee; he writes that 'Lee's temperament was such that he could not bring himself either to shake Longstreet out of his bad humor by a sharp order, or to take direction of the field when Longstreet delayed'. Finally, he asserts that the most fundamental reason for the failure was the lack of coordination in the attack due to the recent reorganisation of the army after Stonewall Jackson's death. Its command structure was inexperienced and unpractised.

It was not until shortly before Freeman's death that he realised, in the light of further evidence, or lack of it in the first place, how much he had wronged Longstreet. At a speech in May 1953 at the Chicago and Richmond Civil War Round Tables dinner, he said Lee regarded Longstreet as the ablest and most successful of his five Confederate generals but, by then, it was too late to revise his outstanding four-volume book.

Gettysburg of course was an unmitigated disaster for Lee and the Army of Northern Virginia. Not only did General Meade repel the Confederate invasion, but he also removed the last vestige of operational initiative from Lee. Within weeks of the battle, the conflict returned to Virginia. Lee's catastrophic losses, particularly among his experienced commanders, put the army on the defensive for the remainder of the war. For an army famed for its mobility and its striking power, the Army of Northern Virginia never recovered its command or its offensive capability. While the Confederate Army would survive and remain a powerful threat, Gettysburg was the beginning of the end.

Why did the South lose this vital battle? For Jubal Early and the Lost Cause there had to be a reason. It could not possibly have been any mistake by Lee. Neither could it have been the soldiers' fault; they fought as bravely as they had ever done. Artillery and commissariat could not be criticised. Command and leadership was without question. However, what about the 'sunrise attack' on the second day of the battle – the attack by Longstreet's corps that failed to materialise until four o'clock in the afternoon? If it had gone in at first light as ordered by Lee, the Confederate Army would have overwhelmed the Union, Gettysburg would have been won and peace could have been negotiated on acceptable terms. The loss of Gettysburg was clearly, then, Longstreet's fault, leading to the loss of the war and the collapse of the South.

The Lost Cause supporters simply could not accept the reality that the Pennsylvania campaign marked two major blunders by Lee. First, he failed to listen properly to the alternatives put to him by his staff and commanders, particularly Longstreet. Then he underestimated the strength of the enemy based on faulty intelligence and inadequate reconnaissance. This led to what Lee termed 'the expression of discontent in the public journals at the result of the expedition'. As a consequence of that criticism, Lee tendered his resignation on 8 August 1863, but Jefferson Davis refused it. The fact is that, for the first time ever, Lee was simply outsmarted by his opponent and his command and control over his army and its leaders was inadequate.

The anti-Longstreet cabal, led by Generals Early and Pendleton, and the editor of the SHSP, the Reverend J. William Jones, a one-time padre in the Confederate Army and friend of the Lee family, always claimed it was Longstreet who started the controversy over the reasons for the defeat at Gettysburg. Soon after the battle, Longstreet had written to his uncle. The letter was, of course, personal.

Camp, Culpeper Courthouse,
July 24, 1863.

My Dear Uncle: Your letters of the 13th and 14th were received on
yesterday. As to our late battle, I cannot say much. I have no right
to say anything, in fact, but will venture a little for you alone. If it
goes to aunt and cousins, it must be under promise that it will go no
further. The battle was not made as I would have made it. My idea
was to throw ourselves between the enemy and Washington, select a
strong position and force the enemy to attack us. So far as is given to
man the ability to judge, we may say with confidence that we should
have destroyed the Federal army, marched into Washington, and
dictated our terms, or, at least, held Washington and marched over as
much of Pennsylvania as we cared to, had we drawn the enemy into
attack upon our carefully chosen position in his rear. General Lee
chose the plans adopted; and he is the person appointed to choose
and to order. I consider it a part of my duty to express my views
to the Commanding-General. If he approves and adopts them, it is
well; if he does not, it is my duty to adopt his views, and to execute
his orders as faithfully as if they were my own. I cannot help but
think that great results would have been obtained had my views been
thought better of; yet I am much inclined to accept the present condition as for the best. I hope and trust that it is so. Your programme
would all be well enough, had it been practicable; and was duly
thought of, too. I fancy that no good ideas upon that campaign will
be mentioned at any time that did not receive their share of consideration by General Lee. The few things that he might have overlooked
himself were, I believe, suggested by myself. As we failed, I must
take my share of the responsibility. In fact, I would prefer that all the
blame should rest upon me. As General Lee is our commander, he
should have the support and influence we can give him. If the blame
(if there is any) can be shifted from him to me, I shall help him and
our cause by taking it. I desire, therefore, that all the responsibility
that can be put upon me shall go there and shall remain there. The
truth will be known in time, and I leave that to show how much of
the responsibility of Gettysburg rests on my shoulders.

Most affectionately yours,

J. Longstreet.

To A. B. Longstreet, LL. D., Columbus, Ga.

It would be difficult to find anything wrong with that letter. There was nothing underhand in it; Longstreet explains that he put forward his views, which were rejected, and then he got on with his job. He accepts that some of the blame for the defeat is also his. Jones claims that the letter was made public shortly after Lee's death in 1870 by which time criticism of Longstreet was already being voiced. If it was, it was the first time Longstreet had made any response to the rumour and innuendo.

Who then were Longstreet's enemies – the cabal? Apart from the good Reverend, there was General Jubal Early. He was one of Ewell's divisional commanders and involved in the failure to press home the attack on the Union right on Cemetery Hill on day one of the Gettysburg battle. It was he who had given the order to burn Chambersburg in 1864 and been sacked by Lee after his defeat by Sheridan on 20 October 1864 at Cedar Creek. Although Lee remained his idol it might be felt that, in denigrating Longstreet, he had some of his own inadequacy to conceal. He had been an earlier critic of secession and only changed to supporting the South at the last moment; a number of people remembered this. Skulking in self-exile in Mexico and Canada after the war, he only returned to America in 1869.

General William Pendleton was Lee's commander of artillery. He was the officer instructed by Lee to carry out a reconnaissance of the main enemy positions after first light on 2 July to confirm the Confederate intelligence and establish the exact objective for the attack on the Union frontage. In the *Official Record of the War of the Rebellion*, Pendleton is quoted, 'Soon after sunrise, I surveyed the enemy's position toward some estimate of the ground and the best mode of attack. So far as judgement could be formed from such a view, assault on the enemy's left by our extreme right might succeed, should the mountain there be of no insuperable obstacle. To attack on that side, if practicable, I understood to be the purpose of the commanding general.' It is curious therefore that he could have expected Longstreet's attack to have been going in at exactly the same time. He also had some baggage. In September 1862,

Lee had given Pendleton command of the rear protection force after the Battle of Shepherdstown, ordering him to hold the river crossings until the morning. Despite a commanding position from which to defend the fords, Pendleton lost complete control of the situation. Panicking, he woke Lee after midnight and reported his position lost and all his guns taken. This turned out to be a highly exaggerated account, as he lost only four guns, but had prematurely withdrawn his infantry. The newspapers cruelly reported this incident for the remainder of the war, and unflattering rumours and jokes were spread by soldiers throughout the army.

The first real attack on Longstreet occurred on 19 January 1872 in a 17,000-word address at Washington and Lee University by Early on the anniversary of Lee's birth. It was flowery and pompous, completely, possibly deliberately, missing the main point. This was, of course, that while Lee wanted to attack at first light, *he could not do so because Longstreet's men were not in position.* A first light attack was a standard classic operation; night fighting seldom took place in any large numbers purely because of command and control problems, so an attack at dawn when, hopefully, the enemy were still half asleep and the whole of the rest of the day was clear for combat, was the best option. The difference between the desire and what was possible is obvious. Longstreet's corps was simply not in a position to attack at dawn (4.30 a.m.). Despite Lee's aspiration, he was an experienced enough commander to know the problem; hence no evidence whatsoever of any orders, as such, for a dawn attack. Early's conviction that the dawn attack would have resulted in a 'brilliant and decisive victory' can be firmly placed in the 'what if' bin of military history. It was merely wishful thinking.

The following year, it was Pendleton's turn to pursue the attack in much the same vein. He was particularly vicious, alleging that Longstreet failed to attack at dawn on the morning of 2 July as ordered by Lee. He also questioned Longstreet's conduct throughout the battle and his loyalty to Lee. Phrases such as, 'culpable disobedience' and 'treachery' larded his talk. Thomas J. Goree and other Longstreet supporters felt that Pendleton was taking advantage of Longstreet's unpopularity to make these assertions. Goree added that it was 'preposterous and absurd, and must be to every soldier of the Army of Virginia, the idea of such an old granny as Pendleton presuming to give a lecture or knowing anything about the battle of Gettysburg. Although nominally Chief of Artillery, yet he was in the actual capacity of Ordnance Officer, and, as I believe, miles in the rear. I know that I did not see him on the field during the battle.'

Another ally was one of Longstreet's divisional commanders, Lafayette McLaws, slightly surprising since Longstreet had removed him from command in 1864. McLaws, however, could not allow Pendleton's falsities to go uncorrected. He sent Longstreet an account of the battle in which he wrote that there were no orders for a dawn attack. He maintained that had there been, it would have meant sending exhausted troops over un-recced ground against enemy positions of unknown strength. Further, he said that any delay by Longstreet's men was purely because Lee had insisted Longstreet take the concealed approach.

Longstreet did not respond immediately but in the spring of 1875 wrote to a number of officers on Lee's staff to verify whether Lee had issued orders for a dawn attack on 2 July. Colonel Walter H. Taylor replied on 28 April, 'I can only say that I never before heard of the "sunrise attack" you were to have made as charged by General Pendleton'. On 7 May, Colonel Charles Marshall wrote, 'I have no personal recollection of the order to which you refer. It certainly was not conveyed by me, nor is there anything in General Lee's official report to show the attack on the 2nd was expected by him to begin earlier, except that he notices there was no proper concert of action on that day.' Colonel Charles Venable says, 'I did not know of any order for an attack on the enemy at sunrise on the 2nd, nor can I believe any such order was issued by General Lee.' Finally, General Armistead Long, Lee's military secretary at the time, wrote, 'I do not recollect of hearing an order to attack at sunrise, or at any other designated hour, pending the operations at Gettysburg during the first three days of July 1863.'

Unfortunately, Longstreet could not leave it there and on 3 November 1877, the *Philadelphia Weekly Times* published a very full account of the campaign and Battle of Gettysburg, 'The Mistakes of Gettysburg', in which he criticised Lee, asserting that he made a series of errors that Longstreet pointed out to him at the time. There was an unpleasant tone of arrogance and unnecessary exaggeration. He also alleged Lee had altered his original official report, in which he assumed all the blame for the defeat at Gettysburg, by writing afterwards 'a detailed and somewhat critical account of the battle' from which Longstreet's critics had acquired their ammunition. In other words, he accused Lee of altering his original report in order to damage him. This so infuriated those who admired Longstreet, including some of Lee's staff officers who had supported him earlier on, that it effectively alienated them. With some clever manipulation and selective quotation of various replies, Early was able to put loaded questions to a number of people, which resulted in increasing condemnation of Longstreet. What came to be known as the 'Gettysburg Series' in the SHSP gave the impression that Longstreet was guilty of being responsible for the loss of Gettysburg only after exhaustive examination of the facts and evidence.

However, he did have some supporters. His old friend and companion, T. J. Goree, wrote to him:

> With my heart full of gratitude, I often think of you and of many acts of kindness shown me, and the innumerable marks of esteem and confidence bestowed upon me by you during the four long and trying years that we were together. Although we may differ in our political opinions, yet I have always given you credit for honesty and sincerity of purpose, and it has made no difference in my kindly feelings towards you personally, and I trust that it never will.

Interestingly, the survivors of Pickett's Division fully supported him against Early. Speaking to the *Buffalo Evening News*, during the 75th Anniversary Reunion at Gettysburg, a former officer in Pickett's Division remarked,

> Longstreet opposed Pickett's Charge, and the failure shows he was right ... All these damnable lies about Longstreet make me want to shoulder a musket and fight another war. They originated in politics and have been told by men not fit to untie his shoestrings. We soldiers on the firing line knew there was no greater fighter in the whole Confederate army than Longstreet. I am proud that I fought under him here. I know that Longstreet did not fail Lee at Gettysburg or anywhere else. I'll defend him as long as I live.

The same year Longstreet published his memoirs *From Manassas to Appomattox*. It put his point of view but he was no writer or master of spin to match his enemies. He gave praise where it was due and revenged himself on a few of his enemies such as Fitzhugh Lee, who had published a biography of his uncle the year before, in which he castigated Longstreet. The book came over as the vain recollections of an ageing and stubborn general who had lost his objectivity. While the Lost Cause had its adherents, there was always going to be a villain and it was Longstreet.

Despite health problems and his continuing fight with the cabal, Longstreet's later life was relatively happy. His beloved wife, Louise, died aged 62, in January 1890. In September 1897, aged 76, he married Helen Dortch. Aged 34 – born in the year of the Battle of Gettysburg – she had never been directly involved in the war; nevertheless, she defended her husband's reputation tirelessly after his death from pneumonia on 2 January 1904 until she herself died in 1962. Helen continued to speak out in defence of her husband, publishing *Lee and Longstreet at High Tide: Gettysburg in the Light of the Official Record*.

Longstreet outlived Pendleton, who died in 1883, and Early in 1894. The 70-year-old Reverend Jones kept going, however, and published yet more slander in 1906, claiming that Lee 'did not hesitate to say in the intimacy of private friendship that he had lost the battle of Gettysburg mainly because of Longstreet's disobedience of orders'. For many years the legacy of the Lost Cause lived on and, with it, the denigration of Longstreet. Even notable historians such as Douglas Freeman, as late as 1935, relied overmuch on the dubious contents of the SHSP. It was not until the 1950s and 1960s that Longstreet's rehabilitation really took off with Glenn Tucker's *High Tide at Gettysburg* and *Lee and Longstreet at Gettysburg*.

At the same time, Lee's iconic status started to be revised and the myth-makers of the Lost Cause shown for what they were. Alongside this, it was inevitable that Longstreet's actions at Gettysburg could be put into perspective against Lee's. William G. Piston's *Lee's Tarnished Lieutenant* remains a powerful standard work and shows conclusively how the Lee image had been manipulated by Jones and Early. This was reinforced in 1993 by Jeffry Wert's *General James Longstreet*.

Longstreet was an outstanding leader of men and a thoroughly experienced commander who had not only physical courage but also the moral courage to face up to his superior when he felt things were wrong. Like many great men, he had his flaws but they were outweighed by his qualities. The embittered losers of the Civil War needed a god – Lee – and someone whom they could blame for their misfortunes – Longstreet. He became the ideal scapegoat.

While no general but a mere lance corporal, the next victim suffered military injustice in its most abhorrent form. Just as much the scapegoat as Longstreet, Robert Jesse Short was executed to cover for the failings in command, administration and leadership of the notorious reinforcement camp of Étaples in 1917.

SIX

Lance Corporal Robert Jesse Short

Mutiny at Étaples

October 1917

The gravestone in plot VIII I 43 in the Commonwealth War Graves Commission Cemetery in Boulogne East bears the following inscription:

26/626 LANCE CPL
JESSE ROBERT SHORT
TYNESIDE IRISH N.F.
4TH OCTOBER 1917
DUTY CALLED
AND HE WENT FORWARD
EVER REMEMBERED BY
HIS WIFE & CHILDREN

Sadly, he did not go forward when duty called in quite the sense that the epitaph suggests. He was executed by firing squad, having been convicted of mutiny by court martial.

———

In the second half of August 1914, the German armies swept nearly all before them. Driving through neutral Belgium, they forced the French and the very small British Expeditionary Force (BEF) almost to Paris. There they were stopped by the Allied counter-attack at the Battle of the Marne. The German offensive had suffered from inadequate resolution at the highest level, poor command and control over the various armies and unsatisfactory reconnaissance. They had diverted two army corps to

the Eastern Front to help deal with the Russian threat, and other forma-
tions had to be used to besiege Antwerp. It had been touch and go, but
they had been held. Failing again to break through at the First Battle of
Ypres in late October, the Germans concentrated on the Eastern Front
and settled down to a largely static line of defence in the West, with fortified trench lines stretching from Nieuwpoort on the Channel to the
Swiss border. There was no way round these defences and the Allies were
then committed to the terrible cost in manpower of trying to batter their
way through for the next three years in order to recover the ground the
Germans were occupying. Here were the well-known set-piece attacks
of Neuve Chapelle, Loos, the Somme, Arras, the Third Battle of Ypres
and Cambrai. Meanwhile, the French were engaged in major battles in
the area of Vimy Ridge, elsewhere in Artois, on the Aisne, in Champagne
and at Verdun. Much fighting was done at the lower level, however –
patrols and raids, sometimes at company strength (100) but, more often,
by a dozen men. Well-sited machine guns decimated attackers but the
greatest casualties were caused by artillery and mortars. Under appalling
conditions, leadership, and the maintenance of morale, became absolutely essential.

In order to understand what later came to be called the 'Bull Ring'
mutiny at Étaples in September 1917, it is important to put into context
what men faced on the Western Front at the time. Then, as now, the
life of an infantryman has often been described as 90 per cent boredom
interspersed with 10 per cent sheer terror. There is a general view that
this was a permanent existence in a water-filled trench, exposed to endless artillery fire with sallies 'over the top' from which one was unlikely
to return. The reality was somewhat different. Troops would be rotated
between front-line positions and areas to the rear. Typically, a division
would have two of its brigades in the forward trenches and one out, with
each brigade having two battalions of its four in the line. Often, a battalion had only two companies forward and the other two in direct support
and in reserve further back ready to deploy. So, a man could expect to
spend about ten days a month actually in the front-line trenches. Clearly,
this varied depending on the tactical situation and there would be surges
from time to time. However, each division would come out of the line, as
a complete formation, to rest, have leave and carry out refresher training.

This rotation was vital to morale and played an essential part in allowing the soldier to have one of the things he needed most: to know 'what he was on'. However ghastly the front line was, there was always an 'out of battle' time to look forward to – hot food, a warm bath of sorts and clean clothes. As we shall see, this was not so in the French Army.

Medical arrangements were good and, barring casualties from shot and shell, after the first winter the sick rate was less than in the army in peacetime, a sure indication of good morale. Of course, there were particular ailments allied to the conditions, such as trench foot. This was caused by long exposure to waterlogged trenches and lack of circulation in legs and feet. It caused great discomfort and there was little the doctors could do about it. Food was adequate, healthy, balanced and seldom fell below 4,000 calories per day. As the war went on the German Army could not match that when subjected to blockade from the Royal Navy and while the French exceeded it, the quality of food was so poor, it was one of the contributory factors to their mutinies.

Drummed into British officers from their earliest training was the order 'weapon, soldier, self' and, for instance, woe betide any junior platoon commander who went to the officers' mess before inspecting his men's rifles and feet after a route march or operation. Once out of the line, the men's welfare was just as much the officers' responsibility as it had been in the trenches.

Up to January 1916, the British Army was manned by volunteers and thereafter mainly by conscription. Some 5.5 million passed through the system – about a quarter of the adult male population – half of whom were volunteers. In the later stages, some of the regimental identity was diluted by men being rebadged and drafted to regiments other than their own as operational needs dictated. Nevertheless, reinforcements were speedily assimilated and drafts were quick to 'muck in' with their new companions. Good leadership, as ever, hastened the process. In the early years of the war, regiments recruited locally and if, for instance, you lived in Somerset, then, naturally, you joined the Somerset Light Infantry. Some regiments were raised specifically as a result of the drive for volunteers in 1914. Robert Short, for example, enlisted in the 26th Northumberland Fusiliers (3rd Tyneside Irish) on 2 December 1914. This was a typical battalion of Kitchener's New Army. Kitchener, Secretary of State for War at the outbreak of hostilities, recruited an army of a million volunteers with the aim of beating the enemy through attrition. Short's battalion, locally raised by the mayor of Newcastle, was full of enthusiasts. Sadly, though, this process, while keeping chums together had a devastating effect on communities when battalions suffered mass casualties. Later rules were made to prevent brothers serving in the same battalion to avoid hardship to a single family, though, of course, this could be upsetting for brothers who, naturally, wanted to serve together. (In the Scots Guards this unofficial rule applied to officers until the late 1960s.)

Men like Robert Short, who was a miner by trade, often came from rough and poor backgrounds and army life, with its three meals a day, your own bed and a gang of companions, could be attractive. It was a relief from mind-numbing, back-breaking manual labour with little hope, or opportunity, of self-advancement. Life in a Glasgow tenement slum, a single cold water tap, no bath, a lavatory shared with the other tenants and the whole family in one bed was something from which men were glad to escape. The regiment became the family, and the security, which many lacked in the civilian world. Discipline may have been harsh but, toe the line, and you were protected and looked after. There was also the hope of promotion. The regiment was a well-ordered and clearly directed organisation, which reflected the values of the Edwardian institutional world. Men fought well among their friends.

———

So how did Robert Short fit into the vast tapestry of the army before and after 1914? Born in Bedwelty, Wales on 13 August 1886 to a coal miner father, he is variously called Jesse Robert, Robert Jesse, or just Jesse or Robert. For sake of ease, we shall call him Robert Short. On 13 January 1905, he enlisted in the Welsh Regiment at Aberdare to serve for nine years with the Colours and two in the Reserve. He joined the 1st Battalion at Gravesend on 26 January (coincidentally where the author joined his, fifty-six years later). On 19 April, he went absent without leave and was taken into custody four days later. He was summarily dealt with by his commanding officer, given twenty-one days' hard labour and returned to duty on 18 May. He was discharged on 18 December that year as being incorrigible and worthless, although there is no record of what prompted this. Not to be put off, he then enlisted in the South Wales Borderers on 6 October 1906 as Private Jesse Morris. However, his past caught up with him and he was tried by District Court Martial, found guilty of having previously been discharged with disgrace, desertion and losing equipment by neglect, and sentenced to fifty-six days' hard labour and discharge with ignominy.

By 1911, he had moved to Gateshead and, on 25 September, married Dinah Low, giving his occupation as coal miner/putter. On 2 December 1914, he again enlisted, this time in the 26th Battalion, Northumberland Fusiliers (3rd Tyneside Irish). He concealed his past with the simple ruse of lying about his age. The Battalion arrived in France in January 1916 as part of the 103rd Brigade in the 34th Division at the same time as the 24th Battalion. The 24th Battalion then amalgamated with the 27th on 10 August 1917. By September 1917, it is highly likely he would have at least fought in the Battle of the Somme in July 1916. On 1 July 1916, the first day of the battle, the division, which consisted of Short's brigade, a brigade of Tyneside Scottish and a brigade of two Scots and two English battalions, suffered a stunning 6,380 casualties – well over half its attacking infantry. The 24th Battalion, Northumberland Fusiliers had 620 casualties and the 27th had 539.

It seems at about this time Short was sent to Étaples as being unfit for some reason but, in due course, he must have been cleared for service, as his posting order to 8th Northumberland Fusiliers is in his record. He was, though, shot before he was transferred. The medal roll of the Northumberland Fusiliers of 31 March 1920 shows Short to have been an acting corporal in the 24th, 24th/27th and the 8th Battalions. On the roll is a manuscript entry to the effect that he was not, unsurprisingly, awarded the Victory or British War Medals, but 'sentenced to be shot by FGCM. Shot 4-10-17. Forfeited for mutinous conduct 12-9-17'.

Was he a good soldier who fell foul of peacetime restrictions? If he wasn't up to it why did he re-enlist, not once but twice? He lost no time when the call came in 1914. If he was such a 'waster' why did he volunteer, certainly with the risk of his previous record surfacing? He could easily have gone on being a miner until conscripted, and even then might have been in a 'reserved' occupation, mining being so important to the war effort. Perhaps he didn't like mining? Maybe, now being a married man with two children, he had thrown over his rackety past and become a small pillar of society. After all, he was good enough for someone to think he rated promotion to corporal, even in acting rank. Later, his records show him to have been graded 'Exemplary'. Typically, in the army, then as now, there were soldiers who were very good on operations and in battle. That is what they enjoyed, not the life in barracks under the steely eye of the sergeant major, drilling, parading, swabbing and cleaning kit. Additionally, the availability of drink in and around barracks, which could not be obtained in the field, could tempt the frustrated and bored soldier to behave badly. Was Corporal Short one of those?

By mid 1917, the British had established a number of large resupply bases in northern France to maintain its huge army. Étaples, near Boulogne, was the BEF's principal depot, specifically providing reinforcement manpower. It was a vast network of camps, dumps and hospitals among the sand dunes on the outskirts of the town (see map of Étaples opposite). It was the biggest BEF base in France with sometimes up to 50,000 men in transit and training. It provided a hospital staging post for those wounded being evacuated to England and a mortuary for the dead, buried at what has now become the Commonwealth War Graves Commission Cemetery north of the present town on the old cemetery site. It can hardly have been a morale raiser for a brand-new recruit, about to go up the line, to witness trainloads of wounded, some dying, being brought into the base. Within it were a series of Infantry Base Depots (IBDs). Linked to the complex, on the flat, sandy area was a training ground known as the 'Bull Ring'. This was an infantry training area to lick new drafts from England into shape before sending them up the line to their battalions.

The base also updated and retrained men returning from leave and sick leave or having recovered from wounds before being sent to the front. This is not an abnormal procedure and is practised today where there has to be an administrative process for equipping men joining or returning to their units in the field. Their regiments could have moved since they left them and there was a requirement to ensure men knew the latest detail on, for instance, deployments, security measures and

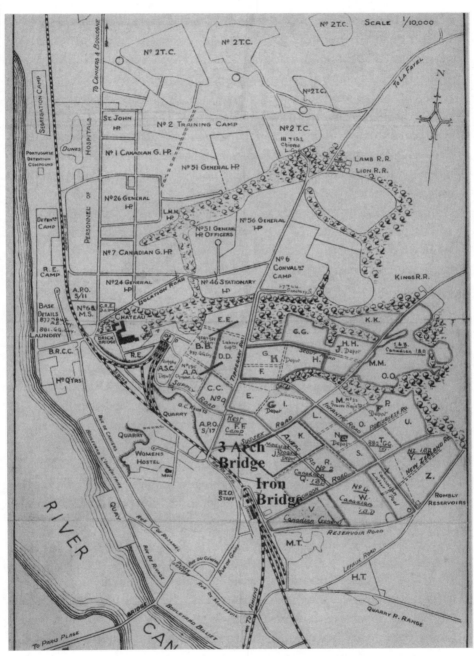

Contemporary map of Étaples training camp, 31 March 1918

any new developments. At Étaples, however, NCO instructors had become unnecessarily obsessed with spit and polish, ritual and over-institutionalised training. This included retraining highly experienced veterans of the trenches who, not unnaturally, resented being mucked about by men who had probably seen very much less action than they had. The instructing staff were universally disliked and, as they wore yellow armbands, were known as 'canaries'. They were seen as people who had a 'cushy' job away from danger and the action. Men who might have fought at the Somme or had been released from hospital, resented being made to parade at 6 a.m. or take part in tedious and harsh training on a cold beach.

Conditions in the camps were poor. Food was dull, unimaginative and there was not much of it. It was served in squalor and the mess tents stank of stale food and crowded humanity. There were no recreational facilities, apart from a cinema, and the canteens were few and over-subscribed. Some were of the YMCA variety; others were manned by upper-class ladies like Lady Angela Forbes. The marginal fleshpots of Étaples, such as they were, were across the railway line and strictly out of bounds. Even more enticing, across the river Canche, was Le Touquet Paris Plage, the well-known Edwardian high society watering hole.

Martinet military police NCOs oversaw discipline. Officers on the staff of the base were not those who had distinguished themselves in battle, and probably never would. A battalion commander, ordered to produce an officer to join the staff at Étaples was hardly likely to nominate his best and, indeed, it was probably an opportunity to get rid of his worst. Men were not in any kind of regimental grouping, nor led by their own officers or NCOs. There was therefore no essential 'duty of care', which provided such a necessary cohesion to the maintenance of morale.

The base was badly run and had all the ingredients for trouble. Housed with the British were Australians and New Zealanders. The Australians had an outstanding reputation in battle but their discipline behind the lines was infamous. It should not be forgotten, though, that all Australians were volunteers and not conscripted. (Any death sentence imposed by court martial had to be confirmed by the Australian governor general. None ever was, so no Australian in the war was executed.) Somewhere like Étaples was a place that no self-respecting Digger was prepared to put up with and he would have had willing supporters among his British mates.

On Sundays no training took place in the afternoon after church parade. With little to do and nowhere to go, the devil made work for idle hands and Sunday, 9 September 1917 was no exception. About noon a corporal from 27 IBD warned the military police that the New Zealanders intended raiding the police hut as a result of a New Zealand corporal being arrested earlier. These sorts of threats by the Australians and New Zealanders were fairly common, so no notice was taken. Nothing actually came of it; however, at about 3 p.m. the guard ('picquet') on the railway bridge into Étaples (Three Arch Bridge) arrested a New Zealand gunner called Healy. He claimed to have committed no offence but was, nevertheless, roughed up by the police. (It is possible that he was returning from a little bit of illegal leave.)

Gunner Healy's arrest was witnessed by others and, by four o'clock, a crowd of bored onlookers, augmented by those leaving the afternoon performance at the cinema, gathered to jeer at the police. At about 5.30 another New Zealander demanded the release of the supposed prisoner and so was taken to the guardroom to see for himself that the man (Healy) was not under arrest and was not there. The crowd, unaware of this and sensing mischief, started to throw stones and looked as though they were going to rush the police hut. One of the camp police, Private Reeve, drew his revolver and fired two or three shots over the heads of the crowd. The shooting enraged the crowd, which now numbered between 3,000 and 4,000 in the area of the police hut and Three Arch Bridge. The police had disappeared.

At 6.15, Captain Guinness, the camp adjutant, saw the crowd and was told of the police shooting. He immediately reported to Colonel Nason, Officer Commanding (OC) Reinforcements, who ordered a picquet of one officer and fifty other ranks from the New Zealand Depot. This picquet turned out with rifles and bayonets, but no ammunition. Colonel Nason then went to the police hut and, seeing the seriousness of the situation, ordered two further picquets, each of a hundred other ranks with officers from 19 and 25 IBDs. A further picquet of one officer and fifteen other ranks was also detailed from 18 IBD. At the Officers' Club, Colonel Nason ordered all officers to rejoin their depots immediately, and each depot was ordered to send three officers to Three Arch Bridge to persuade the crowd to return. There were now about a thousand men wandering around Étaples town having a generally good time.

At about 7.30 p.m. a group tried to break into the Sevigne cafe, where two policemen were hiding. Several officers held back the crowd, and the town was clear by 9 p.m. (Much later, lurid fictionalised accounts were written of officers being thrown into the river, but this did not happen.) This was, effectively, disobedience and insubordination by a large number of men who had nothing better to do; the real threat to officers or property was minimal. The core of the problem was the resentment felt against the military police. That night the soldiers returned peacefully to their camps by about 10 p.m. without further incident.

By Monday morning, matters seemed to have returned to normal. Lieutenant General Asser, General Officer Commanding (GOC) Lines of Communication, arrived to be briefed. Steps were taken to prevent further outbreaks and as the military police were clearly unable to cope with the situation, Major Henderson, OC 25 IBD, was ordered to take charge of the town and command any guards and picquets. A Board of Inquiry sat to collect evidence concerning the events of the previous day. (The findings of this Inquiry sadly no longer exist.) Orders were given that all officers were to be present in their depots from 5.30 to 10 p.m. This, however, failed to prevent disturbances by men who had tasted the freedom that had been so severely denied them in the base camp.

At 4 p.m. bodies of men broke through the picquets into the town and held noisy 'meetings'. During the afternoon and evening, several cars were damaged. A picquet of two officers and a hundred other ranks from the Lewis Gun School, Le Touquet, was sent to Paris Plage but disturbance there was minimal. At 6.30 p.m. a mob of 200–300 marching along the river road towards the detention camp were met and addressed by the base commandant, Brigadier General Thompson, and were led by him, assisted by Major White, Major Dugdale and Captain Strachan, back to camp. On the Canche bridge, a crowd of 1,000, which was milling around, was also addressed by the Commandant and began to disperse, clearly not intending to make any further trouble. About 8 p.m. another small party of about a hundred attempted to get at the Field Punishment Enclosure, where they thought military policemen were hiding. They dispersed quietly when told to by the Commandant. At 9 p.m. Major Cruickshank, the New Siding Rail Transport Officer, saw a crowd of a hundred opposite the town station. Apparently, they thought there were police in the station and tried to enter. They were almost immediately persuaded to return to camp. Throughout, there was no animosity towards the officers; it was evidently the military police the crowds were after.

By Tuesday, 11 September, however, Brigadier General Thompson was beginning to become extremely nervous. Brigadier General Horwood, Chief Provost Marshal of the Armies, visited Étaples during the morning. He was strongly urged to report to the adjutant general that troops from outside were urgently needed, and he promised to do what he could. A call for cavalry, after a muddle over the telephone, was refused but it was agreed to send up to 700–800 men of the Honourable Artillery Company (HAC) stationed nearby in Montreuil.

At about 4 p.m. a crowd again broke through the picquets on Three Arch Bridge and went into Étaples. Others pushed aside the picquet on the river Canche bridge and went towards Paris Plage. None of the picquets made any determined effort to prevent this happening. Whether they felt powerless to do so, or were in sympathy with the crowds, is not clear. The mob of about a hundred near Paris Plage was brought back to camp by Major Cruickshank. En route they were joined by other men and reached camp some 300 strong, where they dispersed quietly.

However, at about 9.15 p.m., Captain E. F. Wilkinson, 1/8th West Yorkshire Regiment, who was in charge of a mixed picquet composed of West Yorks, Manchesters and Canadians on the bridge over the river Canche, was approached by a group of about 70–80 men. They were carrying noticeboards taken from the camps and were waving sticks with red and coloured handkerchiefs attached to them. The crowd broke through the picquet, which did nothing to stop them, and then pushed the four officers to one side. Wilkinson ordered the officers to fall their men in by regiments. He then shouted at the picquet. While he was doing this, Corporal Short came back from the crowd that had just broken through and told the men they were not to listen to Captain Wilkinson. He said, 'What you want to do to that bugger is to put a stone round his neck and throw him into the river.' Wilkinson ordered him to move along.

He refused to do so but Wilkinson was powerless to arrest him with his unreliable picquet. Short then moved on to speak to the Canadians further away and Wilkinson was able to grip his men. He detailed an NCO and four men to arrest Short if he came back and started shouting. A little while later, Short returned and was promptly arrested.

On Wednesday, everyone was confined to camp but at about 3 p.m. troops again broke bounds, with picquets still failing to make determined efforts to stop them. One thousand men marched to Paris Plage and then returned to camp without causing any damage – 366 of the HAC (not the 700–800 originally promised) did not arrive until that night. Lieutenant Colonel Cooper, commanding 1st HAC, took over command of Étaples guards and picquets from Major Henderson. Nevertheless, it was felt that 400 of them would not be enough, so the 19th Hussars of the 9th Cavalry Brigade and four machine guns were stood to at an hour's notice. That day Corporal Short's court martial took place.

On 12 September, General Haig recorded in his diary that 'the Adjutant General reported some disturbances which had occurred at Étaples due to some men of new drafts with revolutionary ideas who had produced red flags and refused to obey orders. The ringleaders have been arrested, and the others sent to the front.' On Thursday, 13 September, General Asser again visited Étaples and made some changes. Captain Longridge, 16th Lancers, took over duties of assistant provost marshal (APM) from Captain Strachan, the officer responsible for the military police, and Major Dugdale, APM Lines of Communication, took over command of all guards and picquets. Ten military policemen were removed and 120 others drafted in from three different areas. The 1st Royal Welsh Fusiliers (22nd Infantry Brigade) and 22nd Manchesters (91st Infantry Brigade) were to be sent to Étaples at once. The cavalry and machine guns were stood down.

Some 200 men broke out of camp that evening, but most of them were back in camp again by 9 p.m. Two of the ringleaders were injured by entrenching tool handles while trying, unsuccessfully, to force the picquet now provided by the HAC. From roll calls taken at tattoo that day, only twenty-three men were absent. Asser reported to Haig, who wrote in his diary for 23 September, 'that drafts there [at Étaples] got out of hand due to having 50,000 new drafts there without sufficient officers to control them. Some men with Republican ideas got among them, raised red flags and made a disturbance. I decided to carry out the training in future at Corps Schools, of which we have 17 for 20 Corps. This will keep drafts away from the dockers at the Bases. These are said to be very republican!'

In the Commandant's report for September, no mention of the mutiny is made, but training at Nos. 1 and 2 Training Camps was to a great extent closed down, with infantry reinforcements going straight up to the front to complete their training, with the exception of the New Zealand Division. The Commander-in-Chief probably reached the right answer but not quite for the right reason: red flags were handkerchiefs, there were no Republicans and no one was near any dockers.

To understand why the officers in the British Army were so paranoid about mutiny in 1917, we must look at what happened to the French. There were deep-seated reasons for the French mutinies of 1917 but what finally drove the *poilus* to despair and revolt was the failure of General Nivelle's offensive in April. The attack went in on the 16th with the customary courage of French soldiers. German wire entanglements were not cut as they should have been, slowing the infantry down, and the artillery fire went far ahead of them and was ineffective against well dug-in enemy positions. The French were taken in the flank by machine guns from positions untouched by shellfire. Swift German counter-attacks were launched against disorganised and floundering attackers. By nightfall the assault had ground to a halt. Heavy casualties overwhelmed the forward medical services, which had anticipated a swift success with light wounded. By the formal end of this debacle on 9 May, the French had lost 100,000 casualties.

On 20 May, the mutiny, which had been simmering since the beginning of the month, began. For thirteen days during the failure of the Nivelle offensive and the muddle, indecision and order/counter-order, French soldiers were ordered to and fro in meaningless, exhausting and tedious marches in rain, sleet, high winds and biting cold. There was little rest and no cover from gunfire or the elements. Food was poor, badly cooked and in short supply. Washing, laundry and sanitation facilities were wholly insufficient. Agitators, stirrers and grousers had a field day and, fuelled by quantities of cheap wine, many refused to return to the Front. Officers and NCOs eventually gained control and managed to get them going. Nevertheless, they could not restore discipline or dare to single out ringleaders for punishment.

Mutiny – real mutiny, not just disobedience – when soldiers refuse orders and challenge their officers, is the greatest fear of a commander. It is almost worse than defeat in battle. Once discipline and obedience dissolves, authority has no means to hold people together. The confidence between officers and men that maintains the cohesion and trust so essential to fighting together is irredeemably lost. Between 20 May and mid June, no fewer than fifty-five French divisions were affected by disturbances to a greater or lesser extent. Many of them had taken part in the disastrous attacks of 4 and 16 April. Half the army were therefore mutinous. If the Germans knew this, what then? Would troops fight for their country or abandon their units and spread the revolution, like the Russians? (Operations had started, of course, in March at the same time as the Russian Revolution.) Troops in the line tended to be more reliable so far but would they be affected? The French managed to retain security and imposed effective censorship. Even Haig was not aware of the true situation until 2 June. Nevertheless, rumours and chat inevitably spread at soldier level and it would have been naive to think that France's allies had no inkling of what was going on.

On 12 September 1917, Corporal Short was court-martialled, the day after the disturbance in which he was involved and, subsequently, arrested. He was charged with

> Endeavouring to persuade persons in His Majesty's Regular Forces to join in a mutiny, in that he at Étaples, on 11th September 1917, endeavoured to persuade a Picquet not to listen to their officers but to lay down their arms and go with him and referring to the Officer in Command of the Picquet said to the Picquet, 'you ought to get a rope, tie it round his neck with a stone and throw him into the river,' or words to that effect.

Under the Rules of Procedure governing how a court martial should be conducted, Short should have been given twenty-four hours' notice of the court martial being held. This was not done, according to Brigadier General Thompson, the base commandant, 'owing to the urgent necessity of bringing the accused to trial, having regard to the present disturbance'. A Summary of Evidence against him was read to him in the presence of the witnesses making the statements. He was not offered, nor, as far as can be seen, did he request, the services of a defending officer.

The proceedings were swift and merely involved five prosecution witnesses. Short declined to cross-examine any of them and merely made a brief statement: 'I wish to state that I had a drop too much to drink and did not know what I was doing or saying. I have been in the Army for eight years and in France twenty-two months. I am a married man with two children and am very sorry for what I have done.'

The court returned a guilty verdict and condemned him to 'Suffer death by being shot'. This was confirmed by Field Marshal Haig on 30 September 1917.

On the face of it, there was nothing particularly wrong with the proceedings of the court martial apart from the extreme haste. Undoubtedly, for a charge of this seriousness, he should have had a defending officer or afterwards, at least, had an officer to advise him on the merits, or otherwise, of an appeal. Short appeared resigned to his fate. He had faced disciplinary proceedings before and he probably thought he was lucky that his previous record was not before the court. Additionally, he lied about his length of service in the army. Not that any of these matters would have made any difference to the verdict and sentence. The 'system' had made up its mind and Short was to be held responsible for the disturbances. An early court martial would prevent further mayhem and divert any blame that might be directed onto those actually responsible for the state of affairs leading to the mutinies. Senior officers, in the knowledge of what had happened to the French, could hope that by executing Short so swiftly, any copycat mutiny in the British Army would be nipped in the bud. Haig could rest easy that the republicans had been kept at bay.

There is a temptation to judge what happened by the standards of today. This would be an error, as the Vice Judge Adjutant General James Stuart-Smith put it on 1 August 1984: 'History abounds in trials and sentences capable of being seen through later generations as harsh and patently unjust. The view traditionally taken has always been that they must be accepted as part of history and that it is not the business of one generation to sit in judgment on the legal process of its forebears, what ever compassion they may feel.' However, there is nothing against taking a view today by the standards of the time.

Short's verdict and sentence were perfectly proper. In respect of mutiny, Section 7 of the Army Act 1881, reapproved by Parliament in 1913 and in the 1914 *Manual of Military Law*, states that 'Every person subject to military law who … causes or conspires with other persons to cause any mutiny or sedition in his Majesty's Armed Forces' or who 'joins in, or, being present, does not use his utmost endeavours to suppress any mutiny … shall on conviction by Court Martial be liable to suffer death or such less punishment as in the Act'. Mutiny is defined in Part One of the *Manual of Military Law* as 'collective insubordination, or a combination of two or more persons to resist or induce others to resist lawful military authority'. Was Short correctly charged? Probably, although a clever defending officer might have persuaded the court that Short was certainly guilty of insubordination and disobedience, but not mutiny. There might have been some merit there in an appeal. Or, indeed, an appeal against the severity of the sentence (others were also convicted of mutiny but received hard labour custodial sentences, not execution).

This really brings us to conclude whether what was going on at Étaples was actually mutiny or, effectively, mass insubordination against the whole ethos of, and conditions at, the camp and the treatment at the hands of the military police and the 'canaries'. Despite Haig's understanding, from the information available to him there was no political overtone, no socialist encouragement and no involvement with 'dockers'. The 'red flags' were handkerchiefs, officers were, on the whole, respected and no one sang 'the Internationale'. There was no class tension or anti-war spirit. A few cars were vandalised but property was respected and the camp was not burnt to the ground. The fleshpots of Étaples and Le Touquet Paris Plage were not ransacked for their liquor and women. Even the police hut, surprisingly, remained intact. This was not a revolution inspired by ringleaders and conspirators. When rounded up by their

officers, men meekly returned to camp. There was no evidence whatsoever at his court martial that Short had planned a mutiny, nor had anyone
else. None of this reflects what had happened in the French Army and
what the British military hierarchy was so frightened of. There was no
mutiny, as such, at Étaples.

Short suffered for the inadequacy of the system and those responsible for it. Étaples was a vast, ungovernable set-up. The military
police and 'canaries' were inadequately controlled and supervised by
low-quality officers who panicked when troops refused to cooper-
ate. Did the Commandant really think he was going to turn a cavalry
regiment and machine-gun detachment onto the 'mutineers'? Colonel
(acting Brigadier General) A. G. Thompson was commissioned in the
Royal Engineers, and before the war was the commandant of the Royal
Military Academy, Woolwich. It is said that during a visit to Woolwich,
General French criticised Thompson's lax attitude and emphasis on the
social life of the cadets to the detriment of their military training. If true,
this certainly could have harmed his future, and command of Étaples
can hardly have been seen as a career move. He apparently had a dour
and taciturn personality, and was seen to be negligent and uncaring. He
clearly lacked the administrative and leadership skills to handle a place
the size and complexity of Étaples. He would have been anxious not to
receive further criticism from above, so how much better to blame the
troubles on socialist agitators and revolutionaries, and demonstrate his
zeal and efficiency? Backed by the inadequate Captain E. F. Strachan,
the APM in charge of the military police, Short was an easy and convenient scapegoat.

Why didn't the British Army mutiny? We have seen why the French
did. What was the difference? In addition to the disturbances at Étaples,
there were two other mutinies in the BEF on the Western Front: 12th
Battalion, South Wales Borderers in January 1916, and a mortar detachment of 38th (Welsh) Division in 1917. Additionally, there was collective
refusal to obey orders at Blargies Military Prison Camp near Rouen in
1916 and the mutiny of 1st Battalion, Australian Expeditionary Force,
which protested that it was being used too often as the leading assault

unit of the BEF. Apart from Short, two other soldiers were executed for mutiny in 1916 for separate incidents at Blargies Prison: a New Zealander, Private Braithwaite, and Gunner Lewis of the Royal Field Artillery. When it is considered what soldiers had to endure throughout the war, this is infinitesimal.

British soldiers, on the whole, obeyed their officers through habit, discipline and respect. Officers were expected to lead from the front and then look after their men when they were out of the line. Good leadership was the key to maintaining morale. Unlike the French, who put their divisions into the line and left them there until they were exhausted, the British adhered to a strict regime of rotation, so men always knew, bar accidents, how long they had to put up with the worst. Welfare, medical and leave arrangements were far better than the French. British workers who enlisted in the army were used to tedium, hardship and subordination. They had, nevertheless, their own values, with a resilience and optimism backed by an enduring sense of humour. Their closest mates became their substitute family. On leave they could return to a peaceful country not ravaged by an enemy.

For Robert Short, though, the story does not end there. In recent years there has been a drive, now successful, to have those shot for cowardice and desertion, pardoned. The arguments both for and against have been compelling. Then in 2006, the Government passed the Armed Forces Act. It is a formal annual requirement, but that year it contained a section entitled: '359 Pardons for servicemen executed for disciplinary offences: recognition as victims of First World War'.

This mass pardon applied to 309 soldiers. However, what it actually meant was that the sentence had been commuted. The conviction was not quashed nor was the sentence changed. Neither did the pardon imply any criticism of procedures and processes or of the decisions and actions of the commanders at the time. Lying on Robert Short's court martial file, signed by the Secretary of State for Defence, Des Browne MP, is his formal pardon (see plate XIII). However, it did seem odd that Short's pardon was included with those who had been shot for desertion or cowardice. His name was not put forward by the 'Shot at Dawn' campaigners, so why did he feature? A letter from the Ministry of Defence of 30 November 2009 explains:

> Unfortunately, about 60% of military service records from WW1 were destroyed in the Blitz and those that survived are generally sparse. This lack of documentary evidence made it exceptionally difficult to examine individual cases in any detail. It is for this reason that Ministers felt that the fairest and most acceptable approach was a pardon for all those in the group, which recognised that death was not the fate they deserved but was believed, at the time, to be necessary for the prosecution of the war. Consequently the Pardon was granted collectively and not on an individual basis. The Pardon covers the whole group of those executed during WW1 under the Army Act 1881 and the Indian Army Act 1911. Offences included desertion, cowardice, striking a superior officer, asleep at or leaving a post, disobedience showing wilful defiance of authority, casting away arms, and mutiny. Mutiny was included in the list of offences because the differences between cowardice, desertion and striking an officer on the one hand and mutiny on the other do not seem clear cut. Each of the three single Services accepted that view. The offences of murder, treachery, treason and pillage were excluded.

Robert Short was no longer the scapegoat.

We now move to the other end of the scale – a holder of the VC and the commander of a division, Jackie Smyth was the luckless casualty of inadequate preparation, system failures and orders given to him by superiors totally out of touch with reality.

SEVEN

Major General Jackie Smyth VC MC

Disaster of the Sittang Bridge

February 1942

For many years, the disaster of the Sittang Bridge in Burma (now Myanmar) in 1942 was held up at the Staff College, Camberley, as an example of how not to conduct a bridge demolition. When the bridge was blown, some two-thirds of the 17th Indian Division was stranded on the enemy side of the Sittang River. The divisional commander who ordered its destruction was acting Major General Jackie Smyth VC MC. He was sacked and reduced to his substantive rank of colonel. He was not only relieved of command but also removed from the army; he never held another military post for the rest of the war. In fact, the demolition of the bridge turned out to be merely a minor irritation to the Japanese, barely affecting their headlong drive to Rangoon (now Yangon) and the conquest of Burma.

Was Smyth totally responsible for this debacle? What prompted him to take what was seen as precipitate action? Were there others involved? Was it convenient to make him, as he himself considered, the scapegoat for the loss of Burma? Or was he, as many of those directly affected by the demolition thought, merely incompetent? Was his judgement affected by a serious medical condition?

Burma is a mass of dense jungles, with rivers carving steep gorges through precipitous mountains and ridges, but it also has wide open plains and rivers sometimes with a breadth of a couple of miles, which are often crossed by ferries rather than the few bridges. Of these rivers, the Irrawaddy and the Salween are the largest (see map on page 136). The former is the main artery, navigable for 800 miles, being joined 50 miles west of Mandalay by the Chindwin. The Salween is only navigable at its mouth, with the towns of Martaban (now Mottama) and Moulmein (now Mawlamyine) either side of the 3-mile-wide estuary. Eighty miles west of Martaban, the Sittang River flows north to south, presenting a significant obstacle during the monsoon season.

In 1942, crossing the Sittang required ferries, with the exception of a single-track railway bridge carrying the Rangoon–Martaban line. The bridge was about 500–600 yards long, with eleven spans of 150 feet each. The river below the bridge widened out to about 1,000 yards and had a strong current. Roads were mere cart tracks and most were impassable to wheeled traffic, the main movement being conducted on the rivers. The exception was the Burma Road running from Rangoon to the Chinese border at Wanting, one of the surviving lifelines supplying Nationalist China and a constant source of concern to the Japanese. Drenched in the monsoon from May to October and parched for much of the rest of the year, the country is inhabited by a people with widely differing, independently minded tribal regions and cultures – the Shans, Nagas, Karens and Burmans, for example.

Burma was one of the more unpleasant places in the world in which to fight. Disease, climate and terrain made it arguably the worst. Foot rot, dysentery, ulcers, gangrene, malaria and other tropical infections unknown to doctors were rife. A mosquito found every area of unprotected skin and leeches every orifice – the latter were only successfully dealt with by a lighted cigarette end. Clothing disintegrated and boots fell apart through sweat and in the damp heat or monsoon downpours. Weapons rusted instantly and supplies of drinking water, food and ammunition depended not on a quartermaster's direction of a sophisticated European or North African echelon but a haphazard system of mule trains struggling through rivers, mud and over barely passable tracks. Maps were few and unreliable. Jungle training, in 1942, had been virtually non-existent and the closeness of the bamboo and pitch-black night instilled fear even in the stoutest hearts. Radio equipment was basic below divisional level and hardly worth its weight, with batteries, so the staff tended to rely on an erratic telephone system.

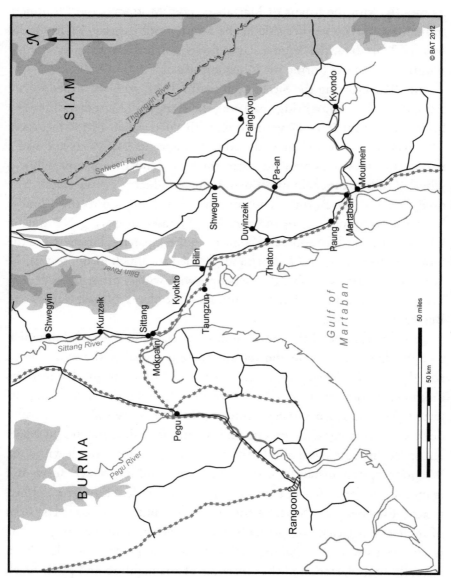

Burma area of operations, February 1942

The Japanese soldier, with his veneration of ancestors and total loyalty to the Emperor, was vastly different to his European, Indian or Burmese enemies. Regulations forbade soldiers to be taken prisoner and his highest duty was to be killed in battle, which would automatically allow him to join his gods. Suicide was the accepted way out if captured or overrun, as even then suicide was aggressive – the soldier lay on a primed grenade so when his body was moved the grenade exploded, killing him and his enemy. Discipline was brutal, but bearing in mind many of the recruits came from a harsh peasant existence where life was vicious and cheap, it had negligible effect. Although the Japanese Army lacked the quantity and sophistication of its opponents' technical hardware, its soldiers' ability to live off the land on a diet of rice and to be able to put up with extraordinary privations made them a formidable foe. Contrary to Western belief, the Japanese were not initially well-trained jungle fighters; however, they had considerable combat experience and were well trained in the basics. They were not reliant on roads and were experts at by-passing opposition and using the unexpected approach, outflanking their enemy. They achieved astonishing (to Western eyes) distances with aggressive speed. Perhaps their major asset, however, was that the Japanese were totally underestimated by almost everyone on the British side from General Sir Archibald Wavell, Commander-in-Chief (C-in-C), downwards. Major General H. L. 'Taffy' Davies who served on Field Marshal Slim's staff, and subsequently commanded a division, said,

> At this time there was no real appreciation of the formidable character of the foe we were facing. General Wavell himself regarded the Japanese as a second-class enemy. This illusion persisted even after we had lost Malaya and Burma and after the experience of the Americans in the Philippines and elsewhere. In fact the Japanese Imperial Army, with its savage, hardy and completely fanatical infantry element, constituted as formidable an enemy as have ever been faced by any British Army. In addition Japanese armies had been specially trained in ideal training areas, for the type of campaign on which they were setting out.

Slim himself, in his memoir *Defeat into Victory*, admitted:

The strength of the Japanese Army lay, not in its higher leadership but in the spirit of the individual Japanese soldier. He fought and marched till he died. If 500 Japanese were ordered to hold a position, we had to kill 495 *before it was ours* – and then the last five killed themselves. It was a combination of obedience and ferocity that made the Japanese Army, whatever its condition, so formidable, and which would make any army formidable. All armies talk of fighting to the last round and the last man. The Japanese alone did it.

Second Lieutenant John Randle, commanding a company of the 10th Baluch Regiment wrote, 'The Japs fought with great ferocity and courage. We were arrogant about the Japs, we regarded them as coolies. We thought of them as third rate. My goodness me, we soon changed our tune.'

Although Burma was secondary to Japan's main aim of taking all Dutch East Indies, together with Malaya and the Philippines, in order to maintain its oil, tin and rubber supplies using Singapore as its main naval base, it would be useful to seize Rangoon to cut off supplies to the Chinese on the Burma Road. On 15 January 1942, the Japanese crossed the Thai border into Burma and on the 17th, bombed Moulmein. Then, on the night of 30 January, elements of the Japanese 55th Division attacked Moulmein in force, with the 33rd Division circling round to the north. What had the British to face them?

The strategic defence of Burma was a shambles; its administration came under C-in-C India but operationally it answered to C-in-C Far East in Singapore. Complacent, unloved and swept under the carpet was an inevitable conclusion reached by anyone who bothered to think about it. Churchill saw North Africa as the priority and rejected any thought of Singapore being attacked or any need, therefore, to provide extra assets to the region, let alone specifically to Burma. In July 1941, General Sir Archibald Wavell, removed from command of the Middle East where he had failed to grapple successfully with the inadequacies of the British Army, was appointed C-in-C India. Vainly, he tried to be allowed to assume operational command of Burma where he quickly realised how unprepared the staff, units and command and control were to defend it.

He anticipated any Japanese attack would come from Indo-China onto the Burma Road and then into India, but the main preoccupation was with Singapore, although, even as late as 8 November 1941, he wrote, 'I should think the Jap has a very poor chance of successfully attacking Malaya and I don't think, myself, that there is much prospect of his trying.'

The Japanese bombed Pearl Harbor on 7 December 1941 and attacked Hong Kong the following day, simultaneously landing in the Philippines. With that, Churchill conceded and placed Burma under Wavell's command, who replaced the army commander there with Lieutenant General Hutton. However, even more changes in the command structure were afoot. On Christmas Day, Hong Kong fell and Wavell was made Supreme Allied Commander of a new coalition in the South-West Pacific of American, British, Dutch and Australian forces (ABDA) with his headquarters in Java (formally on 15 January). Defence of Burma was on his mind but, with no reinforcements available and all his many other problems, there was not much he could do about it. He did, however, make Jackie Smyth a major general and give him command of the 17th Indian Division with the aim of stopping the Japanese as far to the east in Burma as possible. The threat to Singapore was becoming critical and on Sunday, 15 February, it finally surrendered to the Japanese. The ABDA set-up was now ineffective and Burma returned to the command of C-in-C India, as Wavell had always wanted it to.

In the Burma command, inadequate intelligence meant that the British relied entirely on guesswork as to the expected thrusts of the Japanese. The best guess was that they would come from the north, but that was soon shown to be woefully wrong. Contemptuous of the Japanese Air Force, the British planes were aged and barely maintained, and, in practice, outnumbered by the enemy. The army consisted of only two British battalions – the 1st Battalion Gloucestershire Regiment, which was significantly under strength, and the 2nd Battalion King's Own Yorkshire Light Infantry. There were four battalions of Burma Rifles, reinforced by six battalions of the Burma Military Police, which converted to infantry columns in 1941. They included Punjabis, Sikhs and Gurkhas. Artillery and engineers were minimal. There was not only a lack of basic military equipment and arms and ammunition, but also, importantly, a complete absence of essential training, some of which was still based on operations

on the North-West Frontier, let alone specific instruction for jungle warfare. The Burma Army was militarily bankrupt.

———

The main characters in this tragedy were General Sir Archibald Wavell,
Lieutenant General Thomas Hutton and Major General Jackie Smyth.
The brooding presence of Winston Churchill, far away in London,
totally out of touch and issuing a flood of peremptory signals, perme-
ated the atmosphere.

General Sir Archibald Wavell was a man who inspired respect and,
for those close to him, affection. He was self-effacing and taciturn and
this kept him apart, to a certain extent, from the soldiery who did not
take to him in the same way as they did to Generals Slim and Messervy
('Uncle Bill' and 'Frank'). His silences were legendary, yet rather than
displaying a lack of comprehension as to what was being discussed,
they communicated a feeling of confidence when he made it plain he
had missed nothing. Many of his contemporaries found him difficult,
Churchill being the prime example, but others, such as Generals Brooke,
Dill and Montgomery, much admired him. His critics accused him of
being overcautious and lacking in decision-making, vacillating and evasive. Yet, given the immense problems he had to face in high command,
the evidence for this is thin. Perhaps his greatest gifts, certainly to those
closest to him in times of immense stress and danger, were his imperturb-
ability and self-control; quietly, he despised open shows of emotion. He
never flapped and only occasionally lost his temper. He was a modest
man who lacked showmanship and appeared mildly surprised at each
promotion and higher appointment.

On 22 June 1941, when Churchill removed him from command of
the Middle East – 'a new eye and a new hand were required' – Wavell
did not disagree; he was tired and dispirited by his failures in Greece
and Crete and the near loss of Egypt. He needed a long rest and time
to recuperate. However, against advice, he was appointed to command
India without even a chance to come home briefly to sort out his private
life. It seemed that he was being relieved of one of the most important
commands to be put out to quieter pastures, to sit, as Churchill put it
'under a pagoda tree'. The appointment surprised many as Wavell had no

experience of Asia and Indian troops. He knew little of the Japanese and despised them as being third-rate. He failed to take the Japanese threat seriously, although, to be fair, the intelligence assessments were abysmal. With the short-lived ABDA coalition, Wavell's spread of responsibility was so vast that it was almost impossible for him to keep properly in touch with the myriad problems that arose. The consequence was the inevitable issuing of orders that arrived too late or instructions that bore little relation to what was happening on the ground at the sharp end. His complete failure to realise the speed, power and aggression of the Japanese military machine and his condescending attitude to their race was his undoing.

Lieutenant General Thomas Hutton took over command of the army in Burma on 27 December 1941. In the First World War, he had distinguished himself as a Royal Artillery battery commander, winning two Military Crosses. Since then he had become a consummate staff officer but had little contact with soldiers, with the exception of the time he commanded a military district at Quetta. Latterly he had served both Auchinleck and Wavell as their chief of staff in India. On the face of it, it seemed an odd appointment for Wavell to make. Good chiefs of staff do not necessarily make good commanders in the field, although that is not always so. Wavell was so appalled by the state of preparation for war in Burma that, as he thought he had time for the administration, organisation and training to take place, it seemed that a man of Hutton's background and experience was best suited to that task. On 18 January 1942, Wavell wrote to Hutton, 'I fancy the Japanese have got their hands too full at the moment to attempt an attack on Burma, but it may come later dependent on what happens at Singapore and in the Philippines.' Much later, when everything had gone wrong, Wavell replaced Hutton with General Harold Alexander, a commander of a completely different ilk.

Hutton was a quiet, decent, unimpressive, non-extrovert character – unkindly described by James Lunt as looking 'more like a head gardener than a general'. The days had gone when generals commanded from the fastnesses of their rear areas and soldiers needed to see their chiefs, particularly when things were going wrong, to exude confidence and show they cared. Hutton simply did not have time, or the ability to make time, to get among his troops in the way that Slim did. Through no fault of his own, he did not know his commanders, such as Smyth, well enough for them to establish a mutual trust and bond. Consequently, interaction was subject to personalities and where they were very different, the inevitable clash occurred. In relation to Wavell, it would have taken an enormous amount of moral courage to resist the (often out-of-touch and irascible) orders coming from Java. Hutton was resolutely loyal to his boss and, no doubt, in considerable awe of such a renowned figure. Leo Amery, then Secretary of State for India and Burma, did send a telegram, on 18 February 1942, to Wavell saying, 'Have heard doubts cast on Hutton's quality as a fighting leader. Have you any misgivings as to his being the right man? Your telegrams so far have been entirely appreciative.'

Hutton himself did appreciate the vital importance of Rangoon once Singapore had ceased to become the key naval base, even before it surrendered. However, he was forced into the forward defence of Burma by Wavell and, of course, by those such as Churchill and the Viceroy of India who were even more out of touch with the realities.

Major General John (always known as 'Jackie') Smyth assumed command of the 17th Indian Division on 4 December 1941. James Lunt described him as 'a bright, perky and friendly little man, with a wonderful ability to put young officers like me at ease. There was no side to him; he was neither grimly taciturn like Wavell, nor curiously unimpressive, like Hutton. He was alert, relaxed and willing to listen, even to a 25-year-old junior staff captain like me ... we thought he was tremendous.' However, not everyone would agree. A long time after the war, when Hutton had become very sensitive to Smyth's defence over his actions on the Sittang, a friend wrote to Hutton:

I would not worry about J. Smyth. It is quite clear by now that he has a bee about that affair and is determined to bring it into every book he writes, regardless of the subject ... The truth is that almost up to the 2nd W W he was the blue-eyed boy of the Indian Army. Only to the few was it known that he had become a flaneur, useless professionally, and he's made a lot of influential enemies who were just waiting for him to trip. His reputation as the I.A. [Indian Army] teacher at Camberley was NIL. Since he firmly believed he was marvellous he never got over the shock of being sacked and it has remained with him like a stomach ulcer ever since. ... J.S. has long become a bore and only he doesn't know it.

Smyth had a Victoria Cross and a Military Cross. There are few people, particularly soldiers, who are not, to a greater or lesser extent, in awe of a holder of the VC. The Military Secretary's department, responsible for honours and awards in the army, has a rough grading of gallantry awards based on the chance of the recipient losing his life in the action. For example, the winner of the Military Medal, sadly no longer awarded, would stand a 60 per cent possibility of death. For a VC, it was 100 per cent – it is not surprising that so many are posthumous.

On 13 April 1941, as a substantive full colonel, Smyth left for India. On arrival, he was given command of a brigade in Quetta. Then the blow struck. He was diagnosed with an anal fissure with the added problem of a bout of malaria. This required hospital treatment, which was not entirely successful, leaving him with a half-healed, recurring problem. On 18 October, he was appointed to command the 18th Indian Division in the rank of acting major general. He realised that in his state of health he could not possibly command in the field, but as the 18th Division had yet to be formed and would then need to be trained for at least six months, he felt confident that by the time it was ready for active service he would be fit himself. He persuaded the senior medical officer of this who, consequently, raised no adverse medical report.

On 4 December, Smyth was ordered to assume command of the 17th Indian Division, which was warned for immediate overseas posting. Glossing over his continuing medical problems, he accepted the appointment with alacrity. It is difficult to imagine him turning it down, citing a pain in his bottom. The division had been speedily trained in mechanised warfare for operations in the Middle East but needed considerably more experience before the soldiers would be fit to take on a first-class enemy. Two of his brigades were promptly sent to Singapore. He was sent to Burma, with his one remaining brigade – the 46th Indian Brigade – to follow.

Smyth, rightly, saw himself as a fighting soldier with experience bar none. Sadly, though, the real problem was his health. No matter how physically strong and mentally robust, a commander, at whatever level, must not have some gnawing pain which, however much he tries to ignore it or play it down, will inevitably affect his judgement. His pain was such that, at times, he had to be given strychnine injections to relieve it. This was not the condition in which to tackle the problems and hardship he was about to face.

Hutton's directive from Wavell, which he merely handed on to Smyth, was 'gain time and kill Japs'. In this he was egged on by the governor, Dorman-Smith, who was anxious that any yielding of territory would have a catastrophic effect on Burmese morale. The delay imposed on the Japanese was to allow time to reinforce and prepare Rangoon for the inevitable attack. Rangoon was the key to the Burma Road resupply system and the only effective port into Burma. The Japanese, therefore, were simply to be kept as far away from it as possible. Thus the idea of a forward defence was embedded in Hutton's mind by Wavell with little real consideration as to how this was to be done apart from unrealistic thoughts of strong defensive positions from which bold counter-strikes could be mounted. In an appreciation on 10 January 1942, Hutton, however, wrote, 'Even with the foreseeable reinforcements, that is up to the period mid–end March, our operational resources are so limited as to preclude anything except a defensive attitude possibly combined with very local offensives.'

Even without any worthwhile intelligence on the strengths of the Japanese forces facing them (two divisions in fact), the balance of forces to accomplish this weighed heavily against the pathetically half-trained, under-equipped and under-strength British.

Wavell's grasp of the situation, or rather lack of it, is illustrated by this entry in his official dispatch:

I suddenly received in Java a series of telegrams describing Rangoon in immediate danger and the situation as critical. I did not understand how the threat could be urgent since I knew that General Hutton had been prepared for the possible loss of Mergui and Tavoy [well east of the Salween River], and it did not seem likely that a Japanese force large enough to imperil Rangoon could have appeared without any warning. Telegrams from Burma were arriving with great delay so that I was usually behind a situation that changed rapidly. ... I did not consider the situation immediately serious, provided that reinforcement of Burma with land and air forces proceeded without delay, and that some naval force was provided to prevent a landing near Rangoon from the Tenasserim coast.

Nevertheless, Smyth's 17th Division was ordered to hold Moulmein in January 1942; without it, Japanese bombers had the run of airfields to the east, well within reach of Rangoon. In the absence of a full, well-trained division, supported by a regiment of artillery, Smyth knew Moulmein was indefensible. It was in a bad tactical position, on the far side of the river, with no question of any mutual support from Martaban on the other (western) side of the wide estuary. Additionally, his divisional frontage, extending north up the Salween River to Pa-an and Papun, was thinly defended and susceptible to being taken out in small isolated groups and penetrated from the flanks – tactics at which the Japanese were to show themselves uncomfortably adept. Battalions were sometimes as much as 40 miles apart. Due to the abysmal lack of intelligence, the British had simply no idea of which way the Japanese were likely to come, thus had to spread their meagre forces to cover every conceivable approach.

Smyth's division was a muddle of units. Two of its three brigades had been sent to Malaya, leaving the weak 46th Brigade (commanded by Roger Ekin), which had been categorised as 'unfit for any form of operations without further training'. It had been earmarked for Iraq, where further training was to take place, and had, of course, no experience of the jungle. Smyth was reinforced by the 2nd Burma Brigade (commanded by Bourke, then Ekin), the 16th Indian Brigade ('Jonah' Jones) and the 48th Gurkha Brigade (Noel Hugh-Jones), the latter two having to wait in Rangoon for their transport before they could be sent forward.

There was a serious lack of signals assets and engineers, in addition to the scarcity of gunners. The division even lacked anti-malarial drugs. Mechanised, the units were inevitably tied to the roads and lacked the mules, and expertise, to use the jungle tracks and paths. The division never had time to train as a cohesive force and the commanders did not know each other. There was no reason why the troops should have any mutual trust. The locally raised Burma Rifles battalions were simply not up to determined Japanese assaults. Smyth and his commanders realised this and suggested they be used in a guerrilla role, operating well forward and on the flanks to give early warning of enemy thrust lines. This was vetoed out of hand by Hutton who thought it might betray a lack of confidence in the Burmese.

From the very start Smyth insisted that the only possible defence of Rangoon was from a position on the west bank of the Sittang River. He anticipated he not only would have time to prepare a substantial defensive position on ground of his own choosing but also, by the time of the expected Japanese assault, hoped to have been reinforced by the tanks of the 7th Armoured Brigade, which was expected in Rangoon on 21 February having been diverted en route to Java by Wavell on 6 February. The ground west of the Sittang consisted of dried paddy fields and was therefore much more open than the jungle and, despite the small banks (bunds) between fields, was to the tank commanders liking, giving them decent arcs of fire and room to manoeuvre.

The Japanese Army, on the other hand, consisted of the 33rd and 55th Divisions, the former of 16,000 and the latter of 14,000 men. While they had not fought in the jungle before, they were a battle-hardened and experienced force, having fought together in China and French Indo-China (Vietnam). Sadly for the British, they were probably the most ruthless and efficient forces in the world at the time.

On 23 January 1942, Hutton overruled Smyth's plan and told him to hold Moulmein at all costs. On the night of 30 January, 8,000 Japanese attacked and overwhelmed the 2nd Burma Brigade, defending Moulmein on the eastern bank of the Salween. The Japanese made light work of these troops and the brigade commander, Ekin, signalled that he could not hold his positions in daylight. He was given permission to withdraw at will, and the scramble for the ferries to get back over the Salween to Martaban ensued. The brigade lost over 600 men and morale, particularly of the Burma Rifles, was severely dented. The collapse had begun.

In a subsequent report, Hutton accepted that the defence of Moulmein required two brigades, and reinforcements, even if available, would find it impossible to get into the perimeter holding the town. Although the

ABOVE **I.** Captain Jahleel Brenton Carey pictured in the *Illustrated London News*, 16 August 1879

LEFT **II.** Louis Napoléon Bonaparte, Prince Imperial of France

BELOW **III.** Statue of the Prince Imperial, Royal Military Academy Sandhurst

ABOVE **IV.** USS *Indianapolis*, 1945

RIGHT **V.** Captain Charles McVay III, 1945

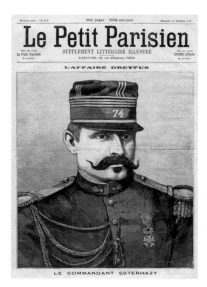

ABOVE **VI.** Ferdinand Walsin Esterhazy, featured on the front page of French newspaper *Le Petit Parisien*, 12 December 1897

RIGHT **VII.** Captain Alfred Dreyfus

ABOVE **VIII.** Admiral John Byng

LEFT **IX.** Wrotham Park, Barnet: the country seat of Admiral Byng

ABOVE **X.** Lieutenant General James 'Pete' Longstreet

RIGHT **XI.** General Robert E. Lee, 1863

ABOVE **XII.** Corporal Short's headstone, Commonwealth War Graves Commission, Boulogne

RIGHT **XIII.** The 2006 pardon of Corporal Jesse Robert Short

This document records that

Cpl Jesse Robert Short of the
24th Battalion, Northumberland Fusiliers

who was executed for mutiny on
4 October 1917 is pardoned under Section
359 of the Armed Forces Act 2006.

The pardon stands as recognition that he was
one of many victims of the First World War
and that execution was not a fate he deserved.

Secretary of State for Defence

LEFT **XIV.** Major General
Jackie Smyth VC MC

ABOVE **XV.** Lieutenant General
Sir Charles Warren

LEFT **XVI.** General Sir
Redvers Buller VC

ABOVE **XVII.** Officers of 28th Commonwealth Brigade, 1951

Left to right
- Lt Col John MacDonald, CO 1 KOSB
- Lt Col Frank Hassett, CO 3 RAR
- Brigadier George Taylor
- Unknown visitor
- Lt Col John Moodie, CO 16 Fd Regt RNZA
- Lt Col John Barlow, CO 1 KSLI

RIGHT **XVIII.** Brigadier George Taylor DSO and Bar

LEFT **XIX.** An officer from the 4th Regiment of Foot, 1809

BELOW **XX.** The bridge over the Agueda River, Barba del Puerco, Portugal

BOTTOM **XXI.** Memorial to Lieutenant Colonel Charles Bevan in the British Cemetery, Elvas, Portugal

IV

LIEUT COL CHARLES BEVAN,
4TH OR KING'S OWN REGT

THIS STONE IS ERECTED TO THE MEMORY OF CHARLES BEVAN, LATE LIEUT. COL. OF THE 4TH OR KING'S OWN REGT, WITH THE INTENTION OF RECORDING HIS VIRTUES. THEY ARE DEEPLY ENGRAVEN ON THE HEARTS OF THOSE WHO KNEW HIM AND WILL EVER LIVE IN THEIR REMEMBRANCE.

A STONE WITH THIS INSCRIPTION WAS ERECTED OVER THE GRAVE OF COL BEVAN IN PORTALEGRE CASTLE WHERE HE WAS BURIED ON 11 JULY 1811. THAT STONE HAVING BEEN REMOVED WHEN A ROAD WAS BUILT THERE, THIS REPLACEMENT IS PLACED BY HIS DESCENDANTS TO HONOUR THE MEMORY OF AN OFFICER WHO PUT REGIMENTAL HONOUR BEFORE HIS OWN LIFE. ERECTED ON BEHALF OF ANN COLFER (D 1980) AND SARA CAVALEIRO, DAUGHTERS OF MAJOR JAMES BEVAN WHO CARRIED CHARLES SWORD DURING HIS OWN SERVICE IN THE KING'S OWN 1913-1935 AND OF MRS. R. STAFFORD, HUGH STAFFORD, MARGARET SMITH AND DIANA THOMAS AND THEIR CHILDREN.

WILLIAM COLFER CB, 14 OCTOBER 2000

ABOVE **XXII.** Lieutenant General David 'Dado' Elazar

BELOW LEFT **XXIII.** Marquis Joseph François Dupleix

BELOW RIGHT **XXIV.** Lieutenant General Roméo Dallaire OC CMM GOQ MSC CD

initial assault was carried out by a Japanese regiment, its parent division was moving swiftly up behind. 'In view of these considerations,' Hutton said, 'it is quite clear that a decision to hold Moulmein any longer would almost certainly have involved the loss of the garrison and possibly have hastened the fall of Rangoon.'

Wavell was infuriated and, on a visit to the 2nd Burma Brigade on 6 February, told the commanders to take back all they had lost. Hutton, reacting to this exhortation, insisted that Martaban and the line of the Salween River should now be held, despite Smyth's anxiety to get back to the Bilin River line. No ground was to be given up, 'however the Division was to be dispersed in depth so as to be able to deal with enemy infiltration'. Wavell reinforced this by demanding that 17th Division defend with mobile and offensive action and vigorously counter-attack enemy incursions.

On 8 February, Smyth warned Hutton of a significant problem: 'In September I had rather a bad operation for anal fissure and piles which wasn't too well done. I went back to work too soon and had a go of acute nervous dyspepsia (most unpleasant thing) for which the doctors advised at least a month's leave. ... The wound only stopped bleeding 10 days ago and is still discharging.' On 11 February, the ADMS (senior medical officer) Lieutenant Colonel Mackenzie examined him and while agreeing that he was quite fit to carry on, recommended that he should be given two months leave as early as he could be spared. Neither Hutton nor, of course, Wavell, saw these results as Lieutenant Colonel Mackenzie was made a prisoner of war by the Japanese just before the Sittang Bridge was blown.

On 9 February, the Japanese infiltrated across the Salween, threatening to cut off the British in Martaban. When Smyth reported to Hutton that while he still had 48th Brigade in reserve, of the 16th and 46th Brigades only one battalion, the King's Own Yorkshire Light Infantry, was in a fit state to fight, his request to withdraw was granted. Again a difficult withdrawal, in contact, was made and the long subsequent march, with little or no food, was going to be an unpleasant foretaste of things to come. The Western mindset still could not get round the fact that the Japanese were not tied to roads. The British therefore anticipated enemy thrusts on main supply routes and then were nastily surprised by being enveloped from the flank or from behind.

Sure enough, on 11 February the Japanese took out Pa-an after a fierce battle with 46th Brigade, in particular the 7/10th Baluch Regiment, who fought bravely. The Salween was no longer an effective line of defence and Smyth sent Brigadier 'Punch' Cowan, his chief of staff, back to Rangoon to persuade Hutton of his fears of being outflanked from the north and to gain permission to hold the line of the Bilin River while making preparations to withdraw to a defensive position on the Sittang. Hutton, though still dead against further withdrawal, reluctantly gave Smyth permission to retire to the Bilin when he thought it necessary. On 13 February, Hutton signalled Wavell, 'We have every intention of fighting it out EAST of R. SITTANG but it is possible that exhaustion of troops available and continued infiltration may eventually drive us back to R. SITTANG. ... Most immediate need is for more battalions of any kind.'

On 15 February, Smyth ordered what remained of his division to concentrate behind the Bilin. Hutton thought this precipitate and told Smyth so; however, it was quite clear there was little alternative. Wavell's response to Hutton was typical: 'I do not know what considerations caused withdrawal behind BILIN R without further fighting. I have every confidence in judgement and fighting spirit of you and SMYTH but bear in mind that continual withdrawal as experience of Malaya showed, is most damaging to morale of troops especially Indian troops. Time can often be gained as effectively and less expensively by bold counter-offensive. This especially so against Japanese.'

In any event, the Bilin was no obstacle and was virtually only a 'report line' – a mark on a map where everyone knew where they were. But it did give a small chance to Smyth to get his troops together in some sort of semblance of a fighting force having broken contact with the Japanese. It did not last long and on 16 February the full might of the Japanese 33rd and 55th Divisions was launched against Smyth on the Bilin.

Hutton's insistence on no withdrawal from the Bilin position without his express permission reduced the time to get back to the Sittang River to such an extent that there was now no chance of establishing a major bridgehead. It is certainly true that the Japanese were held on the Bilin for four days but at the expense of exhausting the British units. By the evening of 18 February, Smyth's men were on their chin straps and

Hutton finally realised how critical the situation was. Hutton reported to Wavell that not only could he not hold the Bilin but he also now had doubts about the line of the Sittang. If so, the evacuation of Rangoon would become a distinct possibility.

Hutton visited Smyth on 19 February and told him to withdraw to the Sittang when necessary. Smyth wasted no time and set the withdrawal in motion. On return to his headquarters, Hutton received yet another unwelcome signal from Wavell dated the 21st: 'Why on earth should resistance on SITTANG River collapse. Are you not still successfully holding BILIN River. You have at least four good brigades, no signs that the enemy is much if at all superior and you have had little if any air attack to face. Armoured brigade should arrive today. What is the matter that these sudden pessimistic reports are given', and one from Smyth of the 22nd: 'SITREP at 1400. Heavy fighting going on EAST side of SITTANG RIVER. Enemy shelling our bridgehead with quite heavy guns and appears to be attacking strongly. So far have only got 1/4 GR over complete but oddments of other bns are trickling in. Situation appears to be serious. Have no communications either 16 Inf Bde or 46 Inf Bde but they are obviously very strongly engaged.'

Meanwhile, back in Java, Wavell was completely out of touch, sending more intemperate signals to Hutton.

Desperately trying to break contact with the Japanese, exhausted British units fell back in various states of disarray. The three brigades were trying to get back to the bridge over the river at Mokpalin by a single dusty and potholed track that was only tarmacked to Kyaikto. Communication by radio was ineffective and messengers got lost or killed. To make matters even worse, on 21 February the retreating force was bombed and strafed by its own air force. No inquiry was held at the time and despite some slippery explanations there is little doubt that the RAF made an error. In an attempt to run as orderly a withdrawal as possible, Smyth ordered 46th Brigade to cover the other two going back. Its commander, Ekin, was appalled as he felt the best course was for his men to go flat out for the bridge and establish protection around it to ensure the safe crossing of the remainder of the division. Smyth rejected the suggestion and clung to the plan he had made.

To make matters worse, Smyth allowed the division 24 hours' rest in the Kyaikto area rather than pushing on to the bridge at best speed. No doubt this was from the best of motives to rest his utterly exhausted troops but it gave the Japanese additional time to reach the bridge first. Indeed, they did so and kept up sporadic attacks by their leading troops on the two small hills overlooking the bridge on the eastern side. The Japanese were now in a position to bring direct, let alone observed artillery and mortar, fire down onto those trying to cross the bridge.

Of all the astonishing signals Wavell sent to Hutton, the following, sent on the 21st, must rank the most extraordinary: 'You should draw up at once plans for counter offensive with Armoured Brigade and all available troops. If at all possible Sittang River must be re-crossed and counter offensive made east of the river. In any event plans must be made to hit enemy and hit him hard if he succeeds in crossing. He will go back quick in face of determined attack. Have your organized armoured train for railway.'

By 22 February, divisional headquarters and the 48th Brigade had begun to cross the bridge, but that evening the brigade was still not complete. Both the 16th and 46th Brigades were still making their difficult way towards Mokpalin. The bridge itself, which was built to run a railway line, had been planked over to take wheeled vehicles. Inevitably, a lorry got stuck and another couple of hours were wasted trying to extricate it. Early on the 23rd, Smyth signalled Hutton: 'Now clear that bulk of division have ceased to exist. Have so far only got over bridge two formed bns [battalions] but odd troops continue to arrive. Obvious that bulk of tpt [transport] have been lost. Am still holding bridge but must blow very early hour today when it is considered that all who can do so have crossed.'

At dawn on the 23rd, Brigadier Noel Hugh-Jones, commanding the protection force, realised that he could not hold off the enemy for much longer. He spoke to Cowan at Smyth's headquarters, who sought permission from Smyth to blow the demolitions on the bridge. In Smyth's mind there was simply no alternative; if the bridge was blown, two-thirds of the division would be stranded on the far side. If it was not blown, a Japanese division would capture it and march straight for Rangoon, leaving its follow-up division to kill or capture the remnants of the 17th Division. He accepted the lesser of these two devastating evils and at 5.30 a.m. the bridge was blown and so damaged as to prevent any troops or vehicles getting across it.

Two brigades, the 16th and 46th, under command of Brigadier 'Jonah' Jones, were now isolated. Jones decided to order withdrawal to the river and for people to save themselves how they could. Many were killed by the Japanese then or subsequently, some managed to swim or raft across, some were captured and some broke out north and crossed the river higher up. Both brigade commanders actually swam the river themselves. The Japanese wasted no time in trying to round up the British remnants and broke off their attacks that night. They took another fortnight to make a road from Kyaikto and bring up bridging equipment. They then moved north on the eastern bank of the Sittang and easily crossed at Kunzeik.

Then the recriminations started.

On 25 February, Smyth wrote to Hutton, 'The medical board held on me on 11.2.42, whilst agreeing that I was quite fit to carry on, recommended that I should be given two months leave as early as I could be spared. As my division has now been so much reduced in numbers and will not be fit for anything in the way of active offensive operations for some time, I am writing to ask if I could have that leave as early as you could spare me.'

No doubt Wavell approved Hutton's following signal before it was sent:

PERSONAL FOR MILITARY SECRETARY FROM HUTTON.
Ref my D/O re SMYTH he has now asked in writing for two months leave as soon as he can be spared. Medical authorities report him fit. I visited him yesterday and he appeared well and cheerful. I made no suggestion that he was to blame for recent reverses. This is not the moment to spare people to proceed on leave and I must assume that he has lost confidence in his ability to command and should be relieved. Propose to appoint COWAN and despatch SMYTH to India forthwith. Wire approval.

On 1 March, Smyth was informed that he was granted a month's leave in India and Punch Cowan was to take over command of the 17th Division. Hutton himself had already been told by Wavell that he was to be replaced by General Alexander but, humiliatingly, to act as his chief of staff. Smyth travelled in Wavell's aircraft with him to India. During the whole journey Wavell completely ignored him and when he met Alexander at Calcutta, he cut Smyth out of the briefing he gave Alexander. It is difficult to understand, when he had with him a divisional commander who had had first-hand experience of fighting the Japanese, why he decided not to include him in the discussions. Furthermore, Smyth was told Wavell would travel on to Delhi alone and he was to follow. Smyth's kit was dumped on the tarmac and Wavell strode past him to board his plane, completely ignoring him. He never spoke to him again. For a man of Wavell's quality and character, who was so widely admired, it was an astonishing, and disgraceful, performance.

The day after he arrived in Delhi, Smyth was informed that Wavell had ordered him to relinquish his acting rank of major general and be retired from the army forthwith. He was also required to put his reasons in writing why he had applied for leave when his division was in action. Additionally, he was to explain why he had proceeded to Burma when he was unfit in that he was suffering from the effects of an operation that had not fully healed. Wavell was seemingly immune to his and others' protests at this treatment and Smyth's health deteriorated even more. On 6 June a medical board found him to be suffering from paroxysmal tachycardia, the after-effects of a fissure operation, acute dyspepsia and malaria. He was given a further three months' sick leave and downgraded as not fit for active service. He was retired with the honorary rank of brigadier.

Historians still debate the disaster at the Sittang Bridge: was it Smyth's fault that two-thirds of his division were stranded on the enemy bank or was it also a series of misjudgements by others that contributed to the catastrophe? Smyth was certainly held to blame at the time and relieved of command and sacked from the army. Both Hutton and Wavell ultimately were relieved of theirs, but not directly and they kept their honour. For those at the very sharp end, like John Randle – commanding a weak company of the 7/10th Baluchi Regiment who had seen seven of the thirteen officers in his battalion and 500 men lost a week before

– the bridge demolition, which resulted in another 100 men killed or captured, was something he, very understandably, blamed on the man who in his eyes was responsible: Smyth. Smyth's family today say that he never forgave Hutton and Wavell. Like many of these things, there is not a simple answer. A number of charges can, therefore, be laid against Smyth, Hutton and Wavell.

Dealing, then, with Smyth first. The criticisms are that he failed to: establish a strong bridgehead on the Sittang to protect the bridge from sudden attack, including by airborne forces; protect the vital demolition firing party and engineers putting in their explosives; and develop sufficient area defence to allow incoming troops freedom from attack as they were approaching an inevitable bottleneck. Additionally, was it Smyth's responsibility to ensure the decking was placed on the bridge to enable motor transport to use what was a railway, in time to pass his division through? Smyth accepted the bridge and its problems were part of the divisional plan and responsibility. But should it have been? We know Smyth was ordered to fight well forward and the bridge was, certainly initially, well to his rear. In modern operations the bridge, a choke point on a main supply route, would have been a major factor in the large overall plan. Hutton fully realised its importance (the direct Japanese route into Rangoon) and should have made its protection very much, if not his specific responsibility, then in his interests. He had travelled over it himself a number of times and should have realised how weak the defence was. He did 'advise' Smyth that it required adequate protection and did provide a company of the Duke of Wellington's on the west bank. Brigadier Roger Ekin, commanding 46th Brigade, suggested that his brigade should leave the Bilin battle, in advance of the rest of the division, and go back and deploy as the bridgehead protection. Smyth refused this, requiring Ekin's brigade to cover the withdrawal of the other two brigades.

The second criticism is that having been given the clearance to withdraw by Hutton, on 19 February, Smyth took too long and lacked the urgency to get his formation back and over the bridge before the Japanese reached it. There were invidious comparisons with the speed of the Japanese against the British. We have seen above how and why the Japanese were so much faster through the jungle but they were also helped by a radio intercept giving uncrypted orders for the withdrawal.

They now had information that they might have had to fight for, and made full use of it by making a dash for the bridge. Brigadier Thompson, Smyth's chief administrative staff officer said, 'But the final stupidity was making you stand those four days on the Bilin which was no defensive position but only a coordinating line. That really did upset the apple cart. It completely exhausted the troops, resulted in heavy casualties which we found it difficult to evacuate, and stretched the transport and supply services to the limit at a time when we could have been getting transport back. However you knew this as well as I did.' Smyth knew, more than most because he had pressed for it from the start, of the need to get back over the Sittang. To accuse him of taking his time, once released, is very difficult to understand.

The major criticism, of course, is that Smyth blew the bridge too early. The fact is that the Japanese wanted the bridge intact to get to Rangoon as soon as they could. Having virtually destroyed the 17th Division before they even got to the bridge, very little was going to stop them except its destruction. Had they wished to destroy it to prevent the 17th Division withdrawing over it, they could have done so relatively easily, at least to stop wheeled traffic, using their air force. Smyth was highly conscious that had he not had the bridge blown when he did, it would have been captured within the hour. The bridge guard was under direct Japanese fire and the bridge was, in any event, impassable because of that. Cowan wrote to Smyth:

> There was no option on the information given to you and the appre-
> ciation of the Commander on the spot, Noel Hugh-Jones. You
> will remember that Hugh-Jones had a conference with Lentaigne
> and Edwardes [battalion commanders], and it was their considered
> opinion that the bridge should be blown because they did not con-
> sider the troops would 'stand up' to a Jap attack of any intensity.
> Furthermore, they considered that all officers and other ranks who
> could get over the bridge had already done so. All this informa-
> tion was given to me over the telephone by an officer deputed by
> Hugh-Jones, as the latter had gone forward to arrange for an evacua-
> tion of the bridgehead troops. Who the officer was I have never been
> able to find out.

While Smyth has also been criticised for being in his headquarters some 5 miles away, he was in touch with Hugh-Jones and had discussed the operation with him in the bridgehead area that day. Curiously, given the immediate difficulties, Smyth had been summoned to a conference with Hutton that morning, rather than Hutton coming to him, which is what should have happened.

The final, and most devastating criticism, because it is entirely accurate and indefensible, is that Smyth was an ill man. He had the appalling anal fissure, which is somewhat akin to an open boil in the back passage, which failed to heal. At times he could barely sit and was kept going with strychnine injections. However tough and competent a commander is, if he is in pain or has nagging physical worries, it inevitably affects his judgement. Had he not had this, he might, for instance, have felt much more inclined to be more robust with Hutton and through him, Wavell, to get his division back earlier. He should not have put up with an order (forward defence) that he knew to be wrong. We know that he was quite prepared to argue with his superior, and that was in his character. What was not in character was acceding to a bad order. Where the charge sticks, is that he knew he was ill before taking command. With his original division, he thought he had six months' training, which would have given him time to recover. Then he switched divisions and went straight into battle. He should have bowed out then and not bluffed the doctors. However, for a man of his ambition and character, forgoing command of a division going into action was something he just could not do. The last word comes from Attiqur Rehman, adjutant of 4/12th Frontier Force Regiment: 'It was quite wrong for Jacky [*sic*] Smyth to command when he was so ill. Everyone knew that he was a very brave soldier but unless a divisional commander, especially in the jungle, is 100 per cent fit, I think it is very unfair on his troops.'

On 27 December 1941, Lieutenant General Thomas Hutton arrived to take command of the army in Burma having been chief of staff in India. Wavell had sacked his predecessor. Hutton was, by nature, an administrator rather than a field commander. Wavell, having been appalled by what he found in Burma in terms of preparedness to fight a war, needed a Hutton to sort it out. He thought he had time before the Japanese attacked. Clearly, he did not envisage Hutton being, in effect, the corps commander with two divisions under him. Hutton, of course, had no experience at command at this level and was not supported by a properly effective headquarters, a long way from the scene of action in Rangoon. The Burma Army headquarters was unkindly described as a '2nd class District HQ in India'. He became fixated by the danger, quite rightly, to Rangoon and used his not inconsiderable administrative powers to backload materiel north out of the city for the evacuation he anticipated. Had he not done so it might have been a different story for his successor, Alexander, but he was there to command the army and give Smyth, and others, formation level orders to halt the Japanese onslaught. His solution was forward defence, to delay the Japanese to give time for reinforcements to arrive in Rangoon and the Chinese to come in from the north. It was militarily fatal, as we have seen, and Hutton simply did not understand this. In a letter to the official historian, he wrote, 'It should have been obvious to Smyth that unless he delayed the enemy as much as possible, he would not be able to stage a counter-attack before they arrived at the approaches of Rangoon and had over-run the air-raid warning system. Besides the state of training of his troops was such that the prospect of successful counter-attack the first time they went into action would not be very favourable.'

Hutton's real error was not to allow the commander on the spot, Smyth, to make the immediate decisions within an overall directive. His insistence on holding the line of the Bilin for so long against Smyth's advice was instrumental in the Sittang disaster. He simply failed to listen to Cowan on his visit to his headquarters on 12 February to plead for the withdrawal behind the Sittang without delay. Smyth withdrew to the Bilin without permission on 14 February and received a rocket for doing so. Stressed and shaken from his aircraft crash, Hutton visited Smyth on the 16th and was adamant that there was to be no further withdrawal without his express agreement.

Hutton was loyal to his chief, Wavell, and it was not in his nature to argue with him. Not only was it physically difficult anyway with signals subject to long delays between Rangoon and Java, but also Wavell was not an easy man to understand and interpret, with his interminable silences. His extraordinary out-of-touch demands and querulous telegrams did not help Hutton's difficulties.

Wavell was not particularly sympathetic:

I don't want to enter into a long controversy about the Burma campaign. I was quite wrong, as I have stated in my despatch, in my
estimate of what the Japanese would and could do; and did not expect
them to advance as soon or as rapidly against Burma. But I cannot
accept your contention that you were right throughout or consistent
in your attitude. I have examined again the whole series of telegrams
and could show by chapter and verse that you varied from normal
to extreme pessimism and back again with the most remarkable sud-
denness. I looked up all the telegrams again and could quote them
but do not wish to waste time and paper ... I think you had a most
extraordinary difficult job in Burma and were very unlucky, but I
cannot accept that your appreciation of the situation was invariably
correct, or that your handling was always correct ... I still think,
however, that but for the disaster on the Sittang river we stood a
very good chance of holding him. I think I over-estimated the training and to some extent the fighting qualities of the troops, and for
the commanders. Smythe [sic] was certainly a great disappointment.

Wavell's initial problem was that he totally underestimated the
Japanese. Taffy Davies, Hutton's chief of staff, wrote to Smyth:

Wavell had the idea that the Jap was the same sort of chap as the
Italian. He would never face the truth that the Jap was, in 1942, just
about the best infantry soldier in the world in his own selected area
of operations. Wavell's attitude in this matter undoubtedly affected
Hutton who was brusquely urged to get cracking and smash these
third class Jap invaders by adopting the offensive and regaining all
the territory that had been lost initially in the first Jap inroads into
Burma early in 1942.

On top of that he wildly overestimated the abilities of the British
troops and the Indian and Burmese forces. Given the complete absence
of any worthwhile intelligence, he could be forgiven for not anticipating
the lines of Japanese attacks and, perhaps, their speed and aggression,

but after the fall of Singapore there was no excuse. However, he was a seasoned general with an enormous amount of experience and he should have realised how weak and ineffectual his forces were. He was the sort of man who could tell instantly by talking to commanders and soldiers, and seeing for himself how capable they were, what they would be like in battle. He was tired, adrift and out of touch. He said himself,

> I admit I did not at this time consider the threat to Burma serious. I overestimated the natural difficulties of the wooded hills on the Burmese frontier. Nor did I realise the unreliable quality of the Burmese units, nor the lack of training of the British and Indian troops. I was certainly guilty of an error of judgement in minimizing the danger to Burma, but it is doubtful whether, even if I had appreciated it thoroughly, I could have done much to help Burma.

He could have done a lot to help by understanding the fatality of the forward defence, listening to Smyth and sanctioning a well-organised defence behind the Sittang. Instead, he just raged at Hutton from Java, 2,000 miles away.

In the end, far too late, he realised Hutton was not the man for the job and replaced him with Alexander. Wavell had signalled Winston Churchill on 18 February 1942:

> Leaders of real drive and inspiration are few. I looked for one for Malaya and Singapore and could not find him. Hutton has plenty of determination behind quiet manner and will never get rattled but lacks power of personal inspiration. At time I selected him reorganisation of whole of military machine in Burma was imperative I knew he would do this excellently and considered also he would be resolute and skilful commander. I have no reason to think otherwise but agree that Alexander's forceful personality might act as a stimulus to troops. Dorman-Smith when I last visited Rangoon spoke well of Hutton and said he had impressed his Ministers.

He certainly changed his mind with the fall of Rangoon. Again, a general of his experience should have demanded the right man (Alexander) and not put up with second best. He must have realised how inadequately set up the army headquarters in Burma was.

But did the ultimate responsibility go deeper than all that? In a letter to Smyth in 1955, Davies wrote,

> The presence of the Arch Angel Gabriel would not have influenced the final result in the circumstances in which we fought that campaign. You were just very unlucky to find yourself with a collection of formations quite untrained and unfitted for jungle warfare, with inadequate transport and air support. Burma was thrown at India, an unwanted and uncared for baby, the day after Japan entered the war. Surely therefore the state of Burma's defence, its lack of all modern arms and equipment, its reliance on out-of-date aircraft and complete absence of any intelligence organisation, from which we suffered terribly, all through the campaign, must be laid at the door of the War Office.

Jackie Smyth had been beaten by the Japanese, broken to full colonel by Wavell and was now severely ill. Then, on 7 April 1944, his eldest son John was killed leading his company at Kohima. It would have finished lesser men. However, he pulled himself up with drive and fortitude, supported by his wife, Frances. He became a military correspondent for the Kemsley Newspapers and, towards the end of the war, took up political life. In 1950, he was elected to Parliament. As an MP he was in an influential position to give great help to the Far Eastern Prisoners of War Federation (10,000 British prisoners had died in Japanese captivity) about which, not surprisingly, he felt very strongly. Returning to the back benches after a ministerial appointment, he served some twenty-one years in politics and was rewarded with a baronetcy. Writing and his interest in many ex-Service matters, particularly the Victoria Cross and George Cross Association, of which he was founder and chairman, later president, dominated the rest of his life. He died on 26 April 1983, in his own words a happy man: 'I remain as I began – an incurable optimist.'

However, deep down he never forgave Wavell and Hutton, as he wrote in his memor, *Milestones*: 'I suddenly began to see that a scapegoat

would be required for the Burma disaster and it would be very convenient for General Wavell and Hutton if I could be made out to be the villain
of the piece and removed from the scene altogether.'

Another divisional commander who suffered from vague orders
and inadequate superior command was Lieutenant General Sir Charles
Warren, the casualty of the Battle of Spion Kop in 1900.

EIGHT

Lieutenant General Sir Charles Warren GCMG KCB

'Scapegoat-in-Chief of the Army in South Africa'

January 1900

The Battle of Spion Kop, on 24/25 January 1900, in the Second Boer War was one that should not have happened and, when it did, should have been won by the British. General Sir Redvers Buller, commander of the British forces in Natal, his confidence drained by a series of defeats in December 1899 and early January 1900, put Lieutenant General Sir Charles Warren, GOC 5th Division, in charge of a wide sweep round from the west, having crossed the Tugela River, in an attempt to relieve Ladysmith. Instead of a wide outflanking movement, Warren attempted a more direct route, which necessitated taking Spion Kop, a hill that, at 1,400 feet, dominated the approach. After a climb by night, the British found themselves on what they thought was the summit. As dawn rose and the mist evaporated, they discovered they were badly positioned and exposed to merciless Boer fire. Instead of hanging on into the night, being reinforced and then attacking the small kopjes overlooking their positions, a decision was made for a premature withdrawal leaving the Boers, to their surprise, in command of the hill.

Scapegoats abounded. Initially, Colonel Thorneycroft, who had ordered the withdrawal, having personally fought tenaciously on the summit all day, was roundly blamed. Clearly, he was too far down the seniority list to be censured for a disaster of this magnitude, so Warren, the commander on the spot, was held responsible. Buller, who had delegated – quite improperly – command to Warren but could not resist interfering, by judicious handling of his dispatches managed to condemn Warren, who had no opportunity to defend himself until two years later.

Warren undoubtedly made mistakes, but it was Buller who should have commanded properly and, when the operation failed, taken the full blame himself instead of making Warren the scapegoat.

The end of the nineteenth century saw a culmination of conflict in South Africa between the British Government and the Afrikaners. For a number of years there was an uneasy and ambivalent relationship between the two. In 1843, Britain annexed Natal but later recognised the independence of the Transvaal and Orange Free State. However, with the aim of creating a South African Federation, the British annexed the Transvaal in 1877. The Boers revolted and, under Kruger's leadership, inflicted significant and embarrassing humiliation on the British Army. After the Boer victory at Majuba on 27 February 1881, peace was negotiated, giving the Afrikaners relative independence, with restrictions on external treaty-making and establishing vague guarantees over European residence rights.

In 1887, the discovery of the largest goldfield in the world in the Transvaal significantly changed the situation. Thousands of British settlers, known as uitlanders, emigrated from Cape Colony into the Transvaal. They rapidly outnumbered the Boers in the mining areas, although remained an overall minority in the Transvaal. The Afrikaners, nervous and resentful of the uitlanders' presence, denied them voting rights and heavily taxed the gold industry. In response, there was pressure from the uitlanders and British mine owners to overthrow the Boer Government. The failure to gain improved rights for the settlers was used to justify an increase in military power in the Cape, with British colonial leaders appearing to favour annexation of the Boer republics.

In 1897, Sir Alfred Milner became the British high commissioner in Cape Colony. His instructions were to seek a peaceful resolution to the problems of the region, but within a year he had become convinced that war was necessary. Paul Kruger was, at the beginning of 1898, re-elected president of the South African Republic for another five-year term, thus ending Milner's hopes that more moderate Afrikaner political forces would gain control of the country and ease restrictions on the uitlanders. Kruger regarded the uitlanders as a threat to his nation because, if given the vote, their numbers might soon give them control. The re-election of Kruger also led to increased uitlander agitation, which helped convince Milner that force was necessary to resolve the dispute. British Colonial Secretary Joseph Chamberlain and mining syndicate owners were firmly behind Milner. Confident that the Boers would be quickly defeated, they attempted to precipitate a war. Earlier, in 1895, Cecil Rhodes had backed an armed incursion into the Transvaal Republic, the Jameson Raid, which failed spectacularly. It has been suggested that Chamberlain certainly knew more about the raid than he was prepared to admit, but there is no evidence to prove it. The German Kaiser had sent a note of support to Kruger, which caused outrage in the United Kingdom and neatly deflected some awkward questions about the Jameson Raid.

President Steyn of the Orange Free State invited Milner and Kruger to attend a conference in Bloemfontein on 29 May 1899, but negotiations broke down. In September 1899, Chamberlain sent an ultimatum demanding full equality for British citizens resident in the Transvaal. Kruger, believing war was inevitable, simultaneously issued his own ultimatum. This gave the British forty-eight hours to withdraw all their troops from his borders, otherwise the Transvaal, allied with the Orange Free State, would be at war. Both ultimatums were rejected and war was declared on 11 October.

Initially, the advantage seemed to be with the Boers, for the British at that stage had relatively few troops in South Africa. There was a suggestion that had the Boers driven into Cape Colony, seized the ports and stirred up support from Cape Afrikaners, it would have been an immediate success. It was actually irrelevant because the Boers chose, instead, to besiege Mafeking, Kimberley and Ladysmith. In Britain, both Commander-in-Chief Lord Wolseley and Buller, commanding the 1st Army Corps at Aldershot and commander-in-chief designate for Cape Colony and Natal, urged the massive strengthening of the South African garrison before war began. In Natal, the country was such that if the Boers invaded in force, the garrison at Ladysmith, high in the Drakensberg Mountains, would be difficult to relieve. Consequently, Wolseley and Buller advocated a defensive line along the Tugela River, believing that the main theatre of operations would be the open land west of the Drakensberg. On 29 October 1899, Buller arrived in Cape Town to take over as commander-in-chief. He moved his headquarters to Natal and left operations in the Cape Colony to subordinates.

———

By the mid 1890s, Britain was so stretched with overseas commitments that there were only two corps and a cavalry division available to deploy for a war on the South African scale. The army was badly funded, below strength and short of supplies. Nevertheless, the technology of war had reached new heights: Maxim machine guns (later to become the Vickers in the First World War), breech-loading field guns, high-powered magazine-fed rifles and smokeless powder were now in service. British military tactics, however, had not made the same advances. Solid straight lines of order and discipline and volleys fired on command had not radically changed since the Crimean War. With insignificant opposition, little had been learned from native wars in the intervening years. Artillery, unprotected by gun shields, unlimbered in the open and gunner officers had little idea of how to provide indirect fire or overhead cover. Amateurish officers lacked training to equip them for modern warfare and recruits from the cities were incapable of observation, judging distance and had no eye for ground. Only an eighth of the force was mounted. Communication depended on heliograph, when the sun was out, signalling flags on a clear day and in line of sight or unreliable telegraph.

Frontal attacks in line were standard, and individual fire and movement were alien concepts; this was fatal over open ground against an accurate-shooting enemy. Maps were poor and inaccurate, and reconnaissance, whether in depth by cavalry or close-in by specially trained soldiers, was something yet to be learned the hard way. Fighting by night, even by today's standards with superb night-vision devices and radio communication, is always one of the most difficult assault phases of battle. The British thus confined themselves, probably sensibly, solely to approach marches by night and dawn attacks. Defensive tactics were virtually unknown, except for digging shallow trenches in iron-like ground and raising 'schanzes' or rock parapets (later called 'sangars' in other parts of the world). Intelligence was hard to come by and relied on locals whose motives could be questionable. Lumbering ox-drawn supply lines were vulnerable to ambush and slowed down any quick tactical moves, as well as being easily spotted by the enemy. Inadequate medical arrangements and health provision meant that of the overall 22,000 casualties, 16,000 died from disease.

Against the British were men defending their own property, country and way of life. Formed into ad hoc 'commandos' of between 500 and 2,000 men, the Boers were loosely disciplined and commanded by elected leaders. They wore no uniform and understood, from stalking game, the art of camouflage and concealment and had a good eye for ground. From infancy they rode well and were used to the harsh conditions and climate of their country. All their infantry were mounted. They were armed with modern five-shot, smokeless, magazine-fed Mauser rifles and Creusot heavy artillery. Accurate shooting was second nature and when properly controlled and disciplined was devastating at long ranges. When outnumbered, they would dismount, fire off some rounds, remount and ride away. Strategy tended to be more about opportunism and was not always carefully thought through. Tactics at a lower level relied on their instinctive eye for the lie of the land and their familiarity with the bush, the rivers and the kopjes. Morale was sometimes fragile and remembering they were merely volunteers, it was easy to slip away when the going got tough. However, they were a formidable and determined guerrilla force.

General Sir Redvers Buller has been described as a superb major, a mediocre colonel and an abysmally poor general. To his troops, though, he looked like a 'proper' general: he was large, well covered, had an air of authority, a certain charisma and, of course, a VC. He looked after his own physical well-being, but also ensured the good administration of his soldiery. While this is always appreciated by soldiers of their leaders, it can lead to a loss of speedy initiative and risk-taking. Given what disasters he put his soldiers through, it is extraordinary that he remained so popular. His critics say he was bereft of imagination, reserved, uncommunicative and lacked the intuition of a successful commander. He lacked self-confidence. He was irresolute and indecisive. This led him to appointing subordinates to take control in the hope that if things went wrong, no blame would attach itself to him. A scapegoat would then, hopefully, readily appear. While his personal courage was not in doubt, his moral courage was significantly lacking.

Instead of taking out Bloemfontein and Pretoria – the centres of Boer rebellion – and leaving hundreds of enemy ineffectively tied up besieging Mafeking, Kimberley and Ladysmith, he became mesmerised by badly informed public opinion and his own muddle-headedness in raising the sieges of those towns as a priority. The 'Black Week' of the defeats of Stormberg, Magersfontein and Colenso from 10 to 15 December 1899, when the British lost 2,776 killed, wounded or captured, appalled the population at home. Lord Lansdowne, Secretary of State for War, understandably replaced Buller as commander-in-chief (C-in-C) with Field Marshal Lord Roberts. Instead of sacking Buller, however, Roberts made him GOC Natal Field Force with instructions to relieve Ladysmith. On 6 January 1900, Buller complained to Lansdowne of his treatment and his resentment of Roberts's appointment. Lansdowne riposted by quoting Buller's telegram of 20 December accepting the situation. Lansdowne wrote to Roberts, 'What a strange mortal he is! He took the news of your appointment like a gentleman when it first reached him, but his second thoughts far from being best are tinged with envy, hatred, malice and uncharitableness.'

Colonel Ian Hamilton, besieged in Ladysmith, wrote in his diary on 17 December 1899 when the news of Buller's failure at Colenso reached them, 'Apparently our great General is inclined to chuck up the sponge – goes so far indeed as to recommend us to fire away all our ammunition and make the best terms we can.'[1]

By any standards, the appointment of Lieutenant General Sir Charles Warren, aged 59, to command the 5th Division in 1899 for service in South Africa was a curious one. Not only that, as Buller's second in command, he was Buller's heir apparent if anything should happen to him, thus making him a 'heartbeat away' from C-in-C South Africa.

---

[1] This refers to Buller's No. 88 cipher of 16 December 1899 to Major General Sir George White in Ladysmith. 'I tried Colenso yesterday, but failed; the enemy is too strong for my force, except with siege operations, and those will take one full month to prepare. Can you last so long? If not, how many days can you give me in which to take up defensive positions? After which I suggest your firing away as much ammunition as you can, and making best terms you can. I can remain here if you have alternative suggestion, but, unaided, I cannot break in. I find my infantry cannot fight more than ten miles from camp, and then only if water can be got, and it is scarce here.'

Warren had retired from the army in 1886 to become commissioner of the Metropolitan Police. He was plagued with disagreements and animosity among the police themselves and he quarrelled with the Home Secretary and a number of colleagues. His time was marked by the Jack the Ripper scandals and he was blamed for the police's inability to arrest the killer. He resigned in November 1888. Surprisingly, he rejoined the army and was posted to Singapore where, again, he argued with the Home Secretary. His final appointment was GOC Thames District and he then retired for a second time. His critics said that he was obsessive, obstinate, self-opinionated and bad-tempered.

The public, however, who saw disaster looming in South Africa, hailed him as the hero who would save the day – after all, he had had considerable experience in that country. In 1876, he had been appointed special commissioner to survey the boundary between Griqualand West and the Orange Free State. In the Transkei War, 1877–8, he commanded the Diamond Fields Horse and was badly injured at Perie Bush. This was when he first met Buller, who was then commanding the Frontier Light Horse, and they subsequently became firm friends. He was then appointed special commissioner to investigate 'native questions' in Bechuanaland. In 1879, he became administrator of Griqualand West. In December 1884, Warren, as a major general, commanded the military expedition to Bechuanaland to maintain British sovereignty in the region. The campaign was a success and Warren developed strong views as to how effective operations should be conducted in that part of the world, not only against natives but also against the Boers.

He was not an easy man and his detractors would accuse him of being irresolute and overcautious but there were many who saw his experience and knowledge of the area as the answer. On arrival in Cape Town, Warren received a letter from Wolseley, dated 6 December 1899:

You will have found a telegram awaiting your arrival at Cape Town informing you that in the event of any accident overtaking Sir Redvers Buller you are to take *supreme* command in South Africa. A Dormant Commission goes out to you by this post.

I look to Sir Redvers Buller and to you to put an end to this folly. Our men and Regimental Officers have done splendidly. Our

Generals so far have been our weak point. I am very anxious to push
on good Colonels, so please let me know the names of those whom
you think promising. If you have time please let me hear from you
now and then, and write your own views freely on everything. May
God bless you is the devout prayer of yours very sincerely.

WOLSELEY.

The scene was set.

Having been badly mauled at Colenso, Buller reverted to his original plan
of a wide sweep to the west, crossing the Tugela at Potgieter's Drift, penetrating the hopefully lightly held hills overlooking the river and moving
on Ladysmith in an arc from the west. On 8 January, he was reinforced by
the 5th Division under Warren. Between Buller's army and Ladysmith lay
not only the rain-swollen Tugela River with only about four or five passable fords or drifts, but also a range of kopjes through which there were
few practical routes. The Boers had long seen that the Tugela was their
main defensive obstacle to Buller's attempts to relieve Ladysmith and had
spent months preparing defensive positions along the northern bank with
trenches dug by black labourers, to be occupied later when the British
axes of advance were identified. Fast riding scouts would easily be able to
spot the lumbering British columns, enabling their commanders to react
quickly. Surprise was an asset Buller did not possess.

However, when Buller saw the situation from his headquarters on
Mount Alice, which overlooks Potgieter's Drift, the danger of attempting
to force the river at that point became obvious. The route he had hoped to
take after crossing here was clearly dominated by the high ground of Vaal
Krantz and Doornkop, and the Brakfontein ridge to the north-east, round
to the west overlooked by Spion Kop. Warren wrote in his diary, 'I did not
like it. It was exposed to gunfire from three-quarters of a circle, to which
we could not effectually reply, and it was exposed to rifle fire from unseen
riflemen at 2,000 yards. Could there be a worse line of advance?'

On 13 January, Buller cabled the War Office that, having found the
Potgieter's Drift route impracticable, he proposed to send Warren across
at Trickhardt's Drift some 5 miles higher up the river. His idea was to

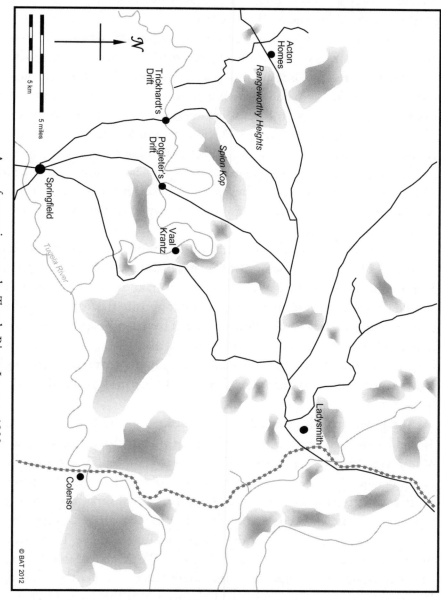

Area of operations on the Tugela River, January 1900

© BAT 2012

hold the enemy frontally while effecting a flanking attack; there was nothing wrong with this as long as surprise and speed of the indirect attacking force was maintained, having identified that that was where the weakest point of the enemy defence lay.

Warren was not told of this plan until 15 January when he received Buller's 'secret orders'. The key paragraph read: 'You will of course act as circumstances require, but my idea is that you should continue through-out, refusing your right and throwing your left forward till you gain the open plain north of Spion Kop. Once there you will command the rear of the position facing Potgieter's Drift, and I think render it untenable.' (Later there was much made of the fact that these orders were 'secret' as though this, in some way, justified non-publication until much later. This, of course, is nonsense. They were only secret for the time it took to carry them out. Once the operation was complete there was no need, obviously, for any secrecy.)

Warren left Springfield at 5 a.m. on 15 January to reconnoitre the crossings. He reported back to Buller that it was feasible but that Spion Kop ought to be taken at once. If he was to take Bastion Hill first, he should cross the river a further 3 miles up, opposite Bastion Hill, rather than crossing at Trickhardt's Drift followed by a 3-mile approach march under the eye of the enemy. The question really was, had the enemy long-range guns, with sufficient ammunition, to cover the crossing? Intelligence suggested that they had but Buller was inclined to dis-believe it.

While Warren with some 2,300 mounted troops, 12,000 infantry and 36 field guns was approaching Trickhardt's Drift, 9,000 troops under Major General Neville Lyttelton had already started, and during the night, occupied a position on the north side of the river near Potgieter's Drift with two battalions and some howitzers as a diversion and to sup-port Warren's attack. At dawn on the 17th, Warren managed to erect two pontoons and trestle-work bridges over the Tugela above Trickhardt's Drift and establish Major General Fitzroy Hart's and Major General Edward Woodgate's brigades on the north bank to cover the crossing. But it was not until the evening of 18 January that the entire force with its 15-mile administrative tail was established on the north side of the river. Buller had put Warren in command of the force but retained his complete staff, leaving Warren with just his own divisional staff to deal with a large mixed arms group, then sat back to watch. Nevertheless, that did not stop Buller interfering with Woodgate's dispositions. Later Warren was criticised for taking so long to pass his division over the river but he had plenty of good reasons for doing so, not least, he maintained, getting his inexperienced men used to light contact with the enemy.

Mounted troops under Major General The Earl of Dundonald were sent out at midday to reconnoitre north-westwards to a depth of about 10 miles. That afternoon his leading troopers came upon a Boer commando at Acton Homes, which they dealt with and reported the contact. The reporting was hazy and Warren assumed they were in trouble, and it was not until the next morning, after reinforcements had been sent out, that Warren heard from Dundonald that, in fact, all was well. Dundonald, doing exactly what cavalry medium reconnaissance is designed for, had found a possible lightly held route and expected Warren to move his main force in the Acton Homes direction. Nevertheless, he was reprimanded by Warren for going too far without protection and support, and failing to remember that Warren's mission was to link up with Buller after the latter had crossed Potgieter's Drift in force, not go off on some frolic of his own. His troops were pulled back to guard the column.

The plodding British columns gave the Boers ample time to identify their direction and by 19 January, when Warren had reached Venter's Spruit 3 miles from Trickhardt's Drift, they were occupying a line from Vaal Krantz to the Rangeworthy Heights. This included the vital ground of Green Hill, Spion Kop, the Twin Peaks and Bastion Hill. Warren had two possible routes – one running by Fairview north from Trickhardt's Drift between Green Hill and Three Tree Hill, and the other 8 miles longer via Acton Homes, earlier identified by Dundonald. Warren rejected the latter as being too long, coupled with some intelligence that the Boers were reinforcing Acton Homes. Roberts later criticised Warren for not taking the Acton Homes route in obedience to Buller's orders of 'refusing your right and throwing your left forward'. But, of course, Buller's orders were vague and never specified that Warren should adopt that particular route.

Warren decided to consolidate his position near Trickhardt's Drift, await resupply and prepare to take ground to establish good artillery fire bases to cover his attacks on likely enemy main positions – what he called 'special arrangements'. With the benefit of hindsight, Buller wrote later that he thought 'things were not going well' and that he ought to have resumed command himself. At the time he did nothing. Major General Francis Clery was ordered to direct the operation.

Early on 20 January, Clery, with one brigade supported by artillery, advanced up the re-entrant that leads from the Tugela towards the east end of the Rangeworthy Heights and positioned his guns halfway up the valley on Three Tree Hill. Hart, with a brigade of five battalions, was directed to occupy the southern crest running from Three Tree Hill to Bastion Hill. Initially, he overcame the forward Boer positions but found himself dominated by enemy on higher ground. He was ordered by Clery to hold his present position. On the 21st, Major General Henry Hildyard, with the mounted troops under his command, on his own initiative or Buller's interference is not clear, seized Bastion Hill, thus securing Hart's left on the crest. So far, so good. Warren had done what he had been told and refused his right and thrown his left forward. He now threatened the Boer right which, although covered the frontage, lacked depth. He considered, if he had reinforcements, the possibility of cutting off the retreat of some Free State Boers who were heading home westwards but Buller was anxious that he would overextend his front and be liable to counter-attack.

On 22 January, Buller discussed future options with Warren. Warren was determined to push on up the Fairview Road. Sending Warren a reinforcement of Major General John Talbot Coke's brigade and some howitzers, Buller left him to it without giving him any further orders. Warren decided that as Spion Kop dominated the Fairview Road, it would have to be taken before progress could be made. Spion Kop is the highest ground in the area from which both machine gun and artillery can dominate the other hills and approaches through them. From various spurs it rises to a plateau, overlooked in turn by the small kopjes of Conical Hill to the north-west and Aloe Knoll in the north-east. So, with the approval of his chief subordinates, Warren resolved to seize Spion Kop that night. The attack, however, was postponed for twenty-four hours to allow the ground to be reconnoitred. Unfortunately, this gave the Boers more time to get their guns into position.

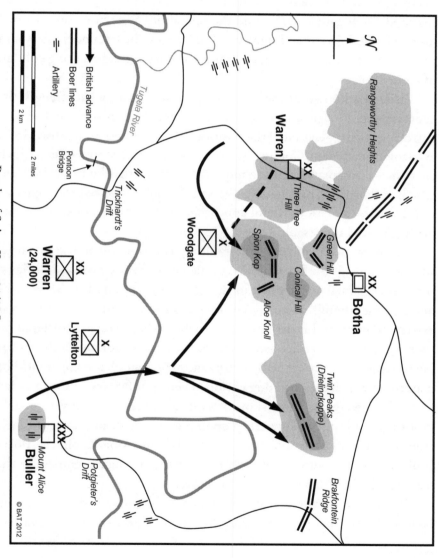

Battle of Spion Kop, 24/25 January 1900

© BAT 2012

On the morning of 23 January, Buller again saw Warren to press him to make an attack on the Boer right, but finding that the orders for the assault on Spion Kop had already been issued, said nothing. However, he made it quite clear that if Warren did not take some immediate action, his troops would have to be withdrawn south of the Tugela. Buller then required Woodgate to command the operation. Warren merely divided his command into left and right attacking forces, the left under Clery and the right under Coke. Woodgate was to command the assaulting column of Coke's force.

Little was known of the Spion Kop ground or in what strength the enemy were. No ground reconnaissance had been made nor had any patrols or scouts penetrated the position. There was no local information available. Lieutenant Colonel Thorneycroft, the 20 stone, 6 feet 2 inch charismatic commander of the mounted infantry that he had raised and who bore his name, had, in daylight, sensibly identified by telescope various features to mark the night approach. On that basis alone, Woodgate made him lead the assault.

At 6 p.m. on 23 January, the assaulting troops set off and, after a brief skirmish, saw off the Boer lightly manned observation post and, as dawn rose on 24 January in a thick mist, the British appeared to be in command of the summit. Instinctively, they began to dig in. The ground was extremely hard, and little more than shallow shell scrapes, bolstered by rock parapets, could be constructed. As the mist evaporated in the morning sun, the exposure of the British position became all too apparent. The plateau on which they had dug in sloped gently at first, then abruptly fell away. They were 200 yards short of a line to cover any enemy approach. Not only could the enemy creep up unseen in the dead ground to their front but also, with troops on Conical Hill and Aloe Knoll, the Boers could bring fire onto the British positions, particularly enfilading the trenches the British had started to prepare.

The Boers, however, had been taken by surprise and alarm set in. Deneys Reitz[2] reported that they had a message that the British had

---

2 Deneys Reitz was one of the more interesting characters in the Boer War. He subsequently wrote about his experiences in *Commando: A Boer Journal of the Boer War*, which became an important source not only because it is very well written, but also because he was present at virtually every major battle. Later, during the First

'made a night attack and had captured Spion Kop. This was most serious, for if the hill went the entire Tugela line would go with it, and we could hardly bring ourselves to believe the news.' They soon sorted themselves out, drafted in reinforcements and, with their guns on Green Hill and Twin Peaks, brought down devastating fire onto the exposed British defensive line. Spion Kop was vital ground to the Boers and they were determined not to lose it.

Woodgate was mortally wounded and command fell on Colonel Malby Crofton. The British naval guns on Mount Alice and at Potgieter's Drift opened fire on Aloe Knoll and on Twin Peaks. A field battery on Three Tree Hill shelled the open ground on which the enemy were advancing. However, this did not prevent panic starting to rise among the British. Muddled and unclear signals were sent by heliograph or signalling flags to those below. A despairing message was sent by Crofton reporting Woodgate's death and pleading for reinforcements: 'Reinforce at once or all is lost. General dead.' Warren responded that there must be no surrender, and that Coke was on his way up with help.

Warren, Lyttelton and Buller were too far away to be able to know what was happening. Lyttelton's naval guns engaging Aloe Knoll were twice silenced by a message from Warren, who was under the impression that the whole of the ridge from the Twin Peaks to the main position on Spion Kop was held by the British. A thrust made earlier in the day by Lyttelton towards Brakfontein was stopped by Buller, who was unwilling to engage the enemy in that direction.

By midday the situation on Spion Kop had become perilous. Reinforcements had arrived but were immediately subjected to intense rifle and machine-gun fire. No definite orders had been given to Clery, who was on the southern crest of the Rangeworthy Heights, except that he was to 'use his discretion about opening fire against the enemy to his front, with a view to creating a diversion'. He did nothing.

Buller, who was 4 miles away on Mount Alice, decided that the troops on Spion Kop needed a 'fighting man' to take control and suggested Thorneycroft assume command on the summit with the local rank

---

World War, he commanded the 1st Battalion, Royal Scots Fusiliers, on the Western Front until he was severely wounded early in 1918.

of brigadier general. Warren assumed this to be an order and issued the command. There were several officers present senior to Thorneycroft and it was a number of hours before the appointment was made known, particularly to those like Coke who were most affected. The latter, who was now on the south-west spur, was unaware of it, and without communicating with Thorneycroft, sent a message to Warren at 12.50 p.m., which was not delivered till 2.20 p.m., that as the summit was crowded and the defence was steady, he had no need of further reinforcements. Meanwhile, Thorneycroft was rallying his men and fighting with great personal courage.

At 3.50 p.m., Coke, who was still on the south-west spur and therefore not in direct touch with Thorneycroft, informed Warren that the enemy was being gradually cleared from the summit and that he had been reinforced with the Scottish Rifles from Potgieter's Drift by Lyttelton, whom Warren, after receiving Crofton's despairing message, had ordered forward. Despite warning messages from Thorneycroft, to which he paid little attention, Warren was reasonably optimistic. He hoped during the night to place some naval guns on the plateau, was confident that water was available on the summit and had reinforcements readily available.

Lyttelton, having realised that Spion Kop was now full of troops, on his own initiative dispatched the King's Royal Rifles towards the Boer position on the Twin Peaks. Ignoring Buller's messages of recall, the battalion achieved great success, routing the Boers and digging themselves in by 5 p.m. The right flank of Spion Kop was therefore secure and the Boers thrown into panicky confusion. Sadly, Buller, nervous about spreading his forces too thinly and without really knowing what was happening on Spion Kop, peremptorily recalled the battalion.

On Spion Kop, Coke believed that Colonel Hill, who had come up with a reinforcement soon after midday and was next in seniority to Crofton, was in command on the summit. He thought that Crofton had been wounded and neither saw Thorneycroft nor knew until the following day that Warren had given him the local rank of brigadier general at Buller's suggestion. Thorneycroft only held the local rank of lieutenant colonel. There were two colonels senior to him there as well as a major general, so he found it difficult to know where he stood. He had no orders from Coke, he had no idea Twin Peaks had been taken and he was incapable of signalling to Warren. He therefore had no inkling of what was in the minds of his commanders.

The men on the summit were, by now, utterly exhausted by fear, fatigue, hunger, thirst and exposure not only to enemy fire but also scorching sun. Ammunition was running short. At 5.50 p.m., Coke reported 'that the situation is extremely critical' and that the men 'would not stand another day's shelling … Please give orders, and should you wish me to withdraw cover retirement from Connaught's Hill,' but it was two hours before the message reached Warren. At 6.30, Thorneycroft reported the situation critical and that if casualties 'go on occurring at present rate I shall barely hold out the night'. This message did not reach Warren until the following morning. Warren, confused by what was going on on the summit, ordered Coke to come down to consult him. Coke tried to obtain permission by signal lamp to stay where he was, but no oil could be obtained for it, so regarding the order as imperative, he came down from Spion Kop at 9.30 p.m., leaving, as he thought, Hill in command. For four hours he floundered around looking for Warren's headquarters, which because it had come under artillery fire had moved from its earlier position.

It was not only the British, however, who were confused. 'There was a growing scarcity of ammunition, and some of the guns made longish pauses in their firing. Hope of victory was very faint. The sun sank, and a quarter of an hour later it was dark. Firing ceased and the Boers, in spite of their orders to remain on the plateau, sneaked away to refresh themselves in the laager. I do not believe there were four (untouched) Boers left on the hill an hour after sunset,' went one enemy report. Lieutenant Otto Schwikkard, an indefatigable local officer in Warren's headquarters, infiltrated the Boer lines by moonlight and found many enemy dead and wounded and that there had been a significant withdrawal by the Boers. But by then, of course, it was too late for the British to do anything about it.

Ignorant of all this, Warren's troops felt isolated and forgotten. Morale reached rock bottom. After a day's non-stop fighting and with the additional responsibility of command, Thorneycroft's nerve finally went and, without knowing what assistance was being planned or what support he could expect during the night, decided that the only option was to withdraw and wrote the following dispatch shortly after the battle:

1. The superiority of the Boer artillery, inasmuch as their guns were placed in such positions as to prevent our artillery fire being brought to bear on them from the lower slopes near camp, or indeed from any other place.

2. By my not knowing what steps were being taken to supply me in the morning with guns, other than the mountain battery which, in my opinion, could not have lived under the long-range fire of the Boer artillery, and their close-range rifle fire.

3. By the total absence of water and provisions.

4. By the difficulty of entrenching on the top of hill, to make trench in any way cover from artillery fire with the few spades at my disposal, the ground being so full of rocks.

5. Finally, I did not see how the hill could be held unless the Boer artillery was silenced, and this was impossible.

Hill, who was still on Spion Kop eleven hours after Thorneycroft's appointment as brigadier general, believed that he was in command and tried to stop the flow of troops, maintaining that there was no authority for the withdrawal. Nevertheless, Thorneycroft's order stayed and the retreat continued by soldiers who were, frankly, glad to do so. Thorneycroft eventually received Warren's message to hold on at 10.30 p.m. By now it was far too late and Thorneycroft was well on his way down. At 2 a.m. both Coke and Thorneycroft stumbled, exhausted, into Warren's headquarters. At 2.30 Warren frantically signalled Buller, giving him the news of the evacuation and seeking immediate orders.

At first light on 25 January, the Boers found to their astonishment that the British had left and Spion Kop was theirs.

Buller did not arrive at Warren's headquarters until sometime between 5 a.m. and 6 a.m., and was given three options by Warren; first, to reoccupy the summit covered by guns now in position; second, attack on the left with ready troops; or, third, retire as wagons can be moved at a moment's notice.

Buller decided to withdraw south of the Tugela and assumed the direct command of his forces, which on 27 January were once more in exactly the same position as they had been ten days before. The British had lost 1,500 men killed, wounded or captured. On 27 January, Buller issued the following statement to the press:

> General Woodgate who commanded at the summit being wounded, the officer who succeeded him decided on the night of the 24th and 25th to abandon the position, and did so before daylight 25th. I reached General Warren's camp at 5 a.m. 25th, and decided that a second attack on Spion Kop would be useless and the enemy's right was too strong to force it. I accordingly decided to withdraw the force south of the Tugela and try some other part. ... The fact that the force could withdraw from actual touch (in cases the lines were less than 1,000 yards apart) with the enemy, in the perfect manner it did, is I think sufficient evidence of the morale of the troops ... [and]... proof that the enemy had been taught to respect our soldiers' fighting powers.

Now the recriminations started. A series of dispatches were sent to Lord Lansdowne, the Secretary of State for War, immediately after the Spion Kop action. They were expurgated and published during the Parliamentary Easter Recess on 17 April 1900. The full editions, notably Buller's dispatch annotated 'not necessarily for publication' and his 'secret orders' to Warren of 15 January, were not made public until April 1902. In his dispatch dated 13 February 1900, Field Marshal Lord Roberts, commander-in-chief, did not mince his words, and two paragraphs, in particular, are worth reading:

> In his note on Sir Charles Warren's report, accompanying despatch of 30th January 1900, Sir Redvers Buller expresses a very adverse opinion on the manner in which Sir Charles Warren carried out the instructions he had received. Without a knowledge of the country and circumstances it is difficult to say whether the delay, misdirection, and want of control, of which Sir Redvers Buller complains, were altogether avoidable; but, in any case, if he considered that his orders were not being properly given effect to, it appears to me that it was his duty to intervene as soon as he had reason to believe that the success of the operations was being endangered. This, indeed,

is admitted by Sir Redvers Buller himself, whose explanation of his non-interference can hardly be accepted as adequate. A most important enterprise was being attempted, and no personal considerations should have deterred the officer in chief command from insisting on its being conducted in the manner which, in his opinion, would lead to the attainment of the object in view, with the least possible loss on our side.

The attempt to relieve Ladysmith, described in these despatches, was well devised, and I agree with Sir Redvers Buller in thinking that it ought to have succeeded. That it failed may, in some measure, be due to the difficulties of the ground and the commanding positions held by the enemy – probably also to errors of judgment and want of administrative capacity on the part of Sir Charles Warren. But whatever faults Sir Charles Warren may have committed, the failure must also be ascribed to the disinclination of the officer in supreme command to assert his authority and see that what he thought best was done, and also to the unwarrantable and needless assumption of responsibility by a subordinate officer.

Enclosed with it was Buller's dispatch to the Secretary of State of 30 January. In it he explains how he reassumed command:

On the night of the 23rd, General Warren attacked Spion Kop, which operation he has made the subject of a special report. On the morning of the 25th, finding that Spion Kop had been abandoned in the night, I decided to withdraw General Warren's force; the troops had been continuously engaged for a week, in circumstances entailing considerable hardships, there had been very heavy losses on Spion Kop. General Warren's dispositions had mixed up all the brigades, and the positions he held were dangerously insecure. I consequently assumed the command.

Why he thought he should have, at any stage, *not* been in command is symptomatic of his muddled thinking. Of course, he had given orders to Warren for a specific part of the overall operation but he, Buller, remained in command. Warren's dispatch of 29 January was enclosed with it. He outlines Buller's directive and explains the difficulties. He goes on to show that Buller, ostensibly not in command, cannot resist the temptation to interfere in the detail.

Buller additionally forwarded a report to the Secretary of State endorsed 'not necessarily for publication' dated 30 January 1900. It, together with Thorneycroft's and Coke's dispatches, was not made public until March 1902. What did 'not necessarily' mean? Was it for publication or not? Effectively, it was a mealy-mouthed statement putting the onus on someone else as to whether it should be published at the time or not. In it, he conclusively blames Warren, finishing up:

> He seems to me a man who can do well what he can do himself, but who cannot command, as he can use neither his Staff nor subordinates. I can never employ him again on an independent command. On the 19th I ought to have assumed command myself; I saw that things were not going well – indeed, every one saw that. I blame myself now for not having done so. I did not, because I thought that if I did I should discredit General Warren in the estimation of the troops; and that if I were shot, and he had to withdraw across the Tugela, and they had lost confidence in him, the consequences might be very serious.

Indeed, a paragraph worthy of the most accomplished modern spin doctor – blame someone else and avoid the blame for not doing something oneself.

Buller did not have the moral courage to confront Warren with his criticisms until his 'confidential' dispatch was made public later on. What he tried to do was blame Warren without the inconvenience and embarrassment of Warren being able to defend himself. Since his orders to Warren were not revealed until then either, no one actually knew what Warren had been told to do. Roberts's dispatch, even from a distance and relatively soon after the event, was quite clear that both Buller and Warren had been inadequate; nevertheless, Buller was in charge and the whole operation was his responsibilty. In 1902 a book was printed entitled *Sir Charles Warren and Spion Kop: A Vindication* – the writer is unknown. It very firmly put Warren's side of the story.

Then in 1903 a Royal Commission was set up to inquire into the military preparations and conduct of the war in South Africa. It was extremely thorough and took a great deal of evidence, notably from Buller and Warren.

It is extraordinary that having written what he did Buller did not sack Warren. Perhaps he was useful to have around in case things went wrong again, which indeed they did. Making yet another effort to get through to Ladysmith, Buller was again forced to withdraw back over the Tugela at Vaal Krantz. Not for nothing did he earn the sobriquet of 'Sir Reverse Buller' and 'the Ferryman of the Tugela'. Buller did relieve Ladysmith but his own commanders found it difficult to forgive his flaws. Although he goes down in history, mainly due to Leo Amery's *Times History*, as an incompetent general, he remained popular with his troops and, indeed, the population at home. However, he ended on a high note with success at the Battle of Belfast in August 1900, which was the last sizeable set-piece battle of the campaign. That October he sailed for England and a hero's welcome. He resumed his job at Aldershot.

Roberts now put into motion his long-felt antagonism towards Buller. An anonymous letter (undoubtedly from Amery) was written to *The Times* exposing Buller's telegram to General Sir George White in Ladysmith telling him to fire off his ammunition and make terms with the Boers. Buller publicly and intemperately responded at a lunch on 10 October 1901. The adjutant general wrote to him on 16 October demanding his resignation. He refused and was summarily dismissed on half pay. His request for a court martial to clear his name and an interview with the King was rejected. There remained a good deal of sympathy for him, however, and he retired to a quiet life in the West Country where he died on 4 June 1908.

Warren had played a significant part in the relief operations for Ladysmith but he was barely mentioned in Buller's subsequent dispatches and, to his fury, nor were his staff, both in the 5th divisional headquarters and 4th and 6th Brigades.

After Ladysmith's relief, Warren's division was subjected to order, counter-order and disorder while Roberts and Buller argued about force levels. Warren himself was dispatched to be the military governor of Griqualand West, which was part of Cape Colony north of the Orange

River, a region, of course, he knew well. Of his farewell interview with Buller, Warren recorded:

> He [Buller] was at the time smarting under Lord Roberts's rebuke about Spion Kop, and he made out it was all my fault. I told him he was quite wrong, and that I hoped he would some day realize how much he had misjudged me. The curious point is that though we both spoke in very strong terms, yet we remained in the best of humours. ... I had saved his reputation; I had made it possible for him to relieve Ladysmith, and yet he had forgotten all this ... when I read later his unkind reflections in the Spion Kop despatches of the 30th January I always expected, even to the last, that he would one day say that he had retracted them.

Warren certainly saw himself, to use his words, as 'The Scapegoat-in-Chief of the Army in South Africa'. Even so, he bore Buller no personal animosity and returned to England in August 1900. Although passed over for any decoration or award, on 24 February 1904 he was promoted to full general and later the colonel commandant of the Royal Engineers. He died on 21 January 1927.

Buller could be seen as a scapegoat and, indeed, commentators say that his enforced resignation in 1901 was a sop to the public dissatisfaction with the way the subsequent guerrilla war in South Africa was going, and blame had to be levelled somewhere. It was militarily and politically expedient to maintain that the guerrilla war was a direct result of Buller's earlier incompetence. However, he *was* incompetent, possibly not so much as to cause the problems over the later guerrilla war, but to follow the losses of 'Black Week' with Colenso, Spion Kop and Vaal Krantz was hardly a success story.

Warren, with hindsight, could have done better at Spion Kop; he should have taken the wider route to the west and left Spion Kop alone, but having decided to take Spion Kop, he should have ensured the command and control and communication systems were coordinated, and then found out exactly what was happening on the summit for himself and made plans to reinforce and attack the Boers, who had effectively given up. Buller, however, was wrong to let him take all the blame; Buller was in command, he had the ability and wherewithal to sort it out and when he did interfere, it was to the detriment of the operation. By standards of the time and, indeed, today, what is difficult to forgive is the way in which he failed to accept any of the blame himself and laid it all at Warren's door. By his manipulation of the publication of his critical dispatch and orders to Warren, and his evidence before the commission, it is beyond any doubt that, in the modern vernacular, he well and truly shafted Warren.

Bringing the story nearer to our own times, we next examine the dismissal of a brigade commander in the Korean War in 1951. Brigadier George Taylor was sacked after the Battle of Maryang San but reinstated on appeal to the Army Council. Was he a scapegoat? That will be up to the reader to decide.

NINE

Brigadier George Taylor

DSO and Bar

The Battle of Maryang San

October 1951

'Am writing these notes in a special aircraft. Felt very important when it was sent until I remembered that the last special aircraft was to remove a Brigade Commander who was getting the sack!' Thus wrote Brigadier William Pike in a letter home from Korea on 10 November 1951. He was commander of the 1st Commonwealth Division artillery and had escorted Brigadier Taylor to Major General Cassels for his final interview, from which he did not return.

After the Second World War, Korea, a Japanese colony since 1910, was to be occupied north of the 38th parallel by Soviet Russia. The South would be under United States administration. In the North, the Soviets backed a Stalinist regime under Kim Il-sung and created the North Korean People's Army, equipped with Russian tanks and artillery. The American-trained South Korean Army was limited to a lightly armed gendarmerie, with no tanks or combat aircraft and only a small amount of field artillery. After several years of frontier incidents along the 38th parallel, the Republic of Korea was invaded by the North Korean People's Army on 25 June 1950.

As the North Koreans swept south, overwhelming all opposition, the US successfully called on the United Nations Security Council to invoke the United Nations Charter and label the North Koreans the aggressors. Member states were urged to send military assistance. American troops were immediately deployed to stiffen the resolve of the South Koreans.

The British responded similarly with ships of the Far East Fleet. The North Koreans advanced rapidly south, aiming to take the vital port of Pusan. American troops initially fared badly against the North Koreans, but General Walton Walker, commanding the Eighth United States Army, managed to hold the Pusan perimeter securely enough to allow reinforcements to arrive. In August 1950, the first British troops – the 1st Battalion The Middlesex Regiment and 1st Battalion The Argyll and Sutherland Highlanders – landed at Pusan and were immediately sent into action.

In mid September, General MacArthur, in a spectacular indirect approach, landed two divisions behind enemy lines at the port of Inchon. The landing was a decisive victory, and X (US) Corps quickly overcame the few defenders and threatened to trap the main North Korean army in the south. MacArthur recaptured Seoul, the capital of South Korea, and the North Koreans, virtually cut off, rapidly retreated northwards. A few weeks later, following the landing at Inchon, UN forces broke out of the Pusan bridgehead and quickly advanced north. Joined by the 3rd Battalion The Royal Australian Regiment, the British units formed the 27th British Commonwealth Brigade and took part in the pursuit of the enemy into North Korea. Meanwhile, a strong brigade had been mobilised in England and several thousand reservists were recalled to active service. The 29th Brigade set sail in October 1950, reaching Korea a month later.

The Eighth (US) Army, with the South Koreans, drove up the western side of Korea and captured Pyongyang in October. By the end of the month, the North Korean army was rapidly disintegrating and the UN took 135,000 prisoners. MacArthur ordered pursuit across the 38th parallel and deep into North Korea. As UN forces drew near the Manchurian border, there were strong indications that Communist China would intervene to defend its area of influence. The Chinese, with some justification, did not trust MacArthur to stop on the Yalu River, the border between North Korea and China. Indeed, many in the West thought that spreading the war to China would be necessary and that since North Korean troops were being supplied from bases in China, they should be attacked. In October, MacArthur met President Harry Truman to persuade him that a massive UN effort would conclude the war by Christmas.

No sooner had this offensive been launched in November than the Chinese strongly reacted by invading North Korea on a massive scale. The 27th Brigade held them off from their positions on the river Chongchon but the Chinese broke through elsewhere. In freezing conditions, the UN forces carried out a fighting retreat across extremely difficult terrain. On 25 December 1950, the Chinese entered South Korea and in early January they captured Seoul. The 27th Brigade was now joined by the 29th Brigade, comprising the 1st Battalions, The Royal Northumberland Fusiliers, The Gloucestershire Regiment (Glosters) and The Royal Ulster Rifles, together with the tanks of the 8th King's Royal Irish Hussars and the guns of the 45th Field Regiment Royal Artillery. The two brigades acted as a rearguard until a defensive line was established on the river Han. The UN forces withdrew in disorder and, by New Year 1951, were defending a line well to the south of Seoul. Morale sank to a dangerous level but the new US commander, General Ridgway, revived spirits and, encouraging his army, advanced slowly north. In March 1951, a UN counter-offensive pushed the Chinese back and recaptured Seoul. As winter cleared, the UN forces dug in close to the 38th parallel and in early spring advanced a few miles north in order to create a buffer in front of Seoul. On 22 April, the Chinese counter-attacked, aiming to break through to the South Korean capital. They were held by the 27th Brigade near Kapyong and by the 29th Brigade on the Imjin River, where the last stand by the Glosters helped to break the Chinese advance but resulted in heavy casualties. The UN line held, then moved north again, the position stabilising in the general area of the 38th parallel.

Armistice negotiations began at Kaesong in July 1951. Largely static fighting then followed. British troops were deployed on a rotational basis, defending hill positions and carrying out patrols. However, set-piece operations did from time to time occur, as both sides sought to control key areas of terrain and win a success that might improve their negotiating position. On 28 July, the 1st Commonwealth Division, comprising the 28th Commonwealth Brigade, 29th Brigade and 25th Canadian Brigade, was formed under the command of Major General James Cassels.

Cassels was an inspired selection. He had fought during the Second World War in north-west Europe, being awarded a DSO for his leadership of a brigade in operations around Le Havre, the Ardennes, the Reichswald, the crossing of the Rhine and the advance into northern Germany. After the war, he commanded the 6th Airborne Division in counter-insurgency operations in Palestine. As a major general, he was appointed Chief United Kingdom Liaison Officer in Melbourne, Australia, in December 1949. With a tall, commanding presence, 'Gentleman Jim' got on easily with his Australian colleagues and soldiers, often through his love of and skill at cricket.

Despite his natural good manners, he found the Americans in Korea difficult, mainly through the differences in planning and procedures. Often the poor relation, his division lacked numbers of men, serviceable equipment and robust transport, much of which dated from the last war. Thus he was forced to rely on American largesse and boost his numbers with South Koreans. His relations with corps commander Lieutenant General John W. 'Iron Mike' O'Daniel were uneasy. Cassels once described him as a '"Two-Gun Patton" type … always wanting to undertake foolhardy stunts which had no serious military purpose. … On many occasions I was ordered, without any warning, to do things which I considered militarily unsound and for which there was no apparent reason. … I am being harassed and ordered by Corps to produce a prisoner every third day, regardless of cost. As we know quite well what enemy divisions are in front of us I cannot see the point in this and have said so.' On 4 September 1951, O'Daniel addressed his divisional commanders and staff in the following terms, 'Everyone must continue to be alert, sharp. Men must be made to eat, sleep, live "killing" so as to be able to destroy this barbaric, cunning enemy whose wish is to "distribute poverty". This enemy will bring us down to his level if he can.' O'Daniel was later reassigned to a less stressful appointment.

It was vital to deny the enemy access to ground strategically important to the armistice talks. Cassels's orders were to 'restore international peace and security in the area'. To do this he decided to establish patrol bases on the far side of the Imjin River. Once he had secured the crossings, he moved the division across and established defensive positions from which he could dominate no-man's-land with patrols. Unfortunately, the Chinese 191st Division was able to maintain observation not only over the crossings and no-man's-land but also all along the front held by the

US I Corps. It became essential therefore to occupy the entire area up to and including the line of ridges from which the Chinese could overlook the area. This ridgeline contained two formidable hills – Kowang San at 355 metres (1,165 feet) and Maryang San at 317 metres (1,040 feet). To take these objectives, Operation Commando was planned with some urgency.

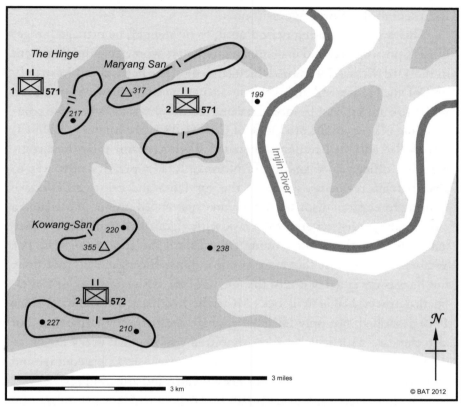

Enemy positions overlooking the Imjin River, October 1951

But what of the man who was to not only lead his brigade in this operation but also be sacked as a result? George Taylor was born on 17 September 1905, the fourth of six sons of Colonel Thomas Taylor. In 1929 he was commissioned in the West Yorkshire Regiment, then stationed in Northern Ireland. Taylor went with the West Yorks to the Caribbean, then Egypt and on to Quetta, where a massive earthquake occurred in May 1935. Throughout the 1930s Taylor, very fast for his bulk, played rugby for the army, for Lancashire and finally for the Barbarians, which brought him an England trial. At the outbreak of war in 1939, he joined the BEF in France. In 1940 he became embroiled in the ill-fated Norwegian operation. He was a staff officer in 1942 in Madagascar with the Combined Operations Reserve Force, which was soon sent to the North-West Frontier.

This was a frustrating period until, to his delight, he managed to get himself posted as second in command to the 1st Worcestershire Regiment in the 43rd Wessex Division, which landed on the beaches in Normandy on D-Day. He was still in his thirties, experienced but never having been under fire until then. His moment came after four weeks, when two commanding officers of the 5th Duke of Cornwall's Light Infantry (5 DCLI) were killed and the battalion decimated. Taylor became their third commanding officer since landing in Normandy. His priority now was to absorb reinforcements, galvanise the survivors and create an effective fighting force from disorder. Taylor, an experienced trainer of men and a charismatic leader, set about the task with vigour and panache. He then led 5 DCLI with an outstanding record until the end of the war. The Wessex Division lost thirty-six commanding officers during that time, but he was never a day out of the line until the Armistice. Taylor's intelligence officer, David Willcocks MC, who had been with 5 DCLI since 1940 described 'not only his great courage and inspiring leadership, but also the care with which we reconnoitred and planned every attack or defensive engagement, in order to minimise casualties ... his courage and concern called forth in all ranks a deep loyalty and affection'.

The first Tiger tank ever to fall into British hands was captured by 5 DCLI in one of Taylor's initial night battles, conducted with cunning after careful daylight reconnaissance. German self-propelled guns, tanks and personnel fell into 5 DCLI hands. Taylor was awarded an immediate DSO and began to acquire a reputation for coolness under extreme stress, and for communicating that coolness to his men. Taylor's second immediate DSO came through his actions in Arnhem in September. Working furiously to close the gap between its own column and the beleaguered parachutists, 5 DCLI ultimately linked up with the Polish Parachute Brigade, after being infiltrated by German Tiger tanks. Despite this, the Battalion managed to supply the Poles with much-needed rations, ammunition, petrol and medical stores.

Taylor was a man of drive and daring rather than caution but knew what he could ask of his men, and they responded to that. Interestingly, this was not just confined to his own battalion – his fellow commanding officers also held him in high regard and had great respect for him. His delightful autobiography of his wartime experiences, *Infantry Colonel*, demonstrates a straightforward, uncomplicated man with a love of soldiering and a deep respect for his men.

In 1950 Taylor was promoted temporary brigadier to command the 28th Infantry Brigade in Hong Kong; from there, in April 1951, he took the brigade to Korea where it became the 28th Commonwealth Brigade in the 1st Commonwealth Division. General Sir Brian Horrocks, Taylor's old corps commander in the drive for the Arnhem bridges back in 1944, wrote to him on 17 July on being told of Taylor's promotion to command the brigade, 'I can think of no better choice, as nobody knows more about the sharp end of the battlefield than you.' The brigade then consisted of the 1st King's Shropshire Light Infantry (1 KSLI) (Lieutenant Colonel Barlow), the 1st King's Own Scottish Borderers (1 KOSB) (Lieutenant Colonel MacDonald) and the 3rd Royal Australian Regiment (3 RAR) (Lieutenant Colonel Hassett).

Taylor had an unusual relationship with Field Marshal Sir William Slim, then Chief of the Imperial General Staff, with whom he exchanged personal letters. Nowadays, senior officers might find it irksome to the chain of command for a commanding officer to write directly to the chief but no harm was done and Bill Slim, of course, being very much a 'front line' soldier himself probably relished the direct and unvarnished reports from the fighting edge. However, it might be relevant to what happened later. The following is an extract from a letter Taylor wrote to him on 18 May 1951:

My Dear Field Marshal,

I took over the Commonwealth Brigade in the closing stages of the Kapyong battle, when the 27th saved the day for the 9th Corps.

My two Battalions, 1 KOSB and 1 KSLI, have joined us from Hong Kong and we are now 28th British Commonwealth Brigade.

Both Battalions are finding their feet and morale is high, and they will soon be as good, or even better, than the fine 3 Royal Australian Battalion, who fought like tigers in the last action (One Section killed 55 Chinese).

We are under command 24 Division and get on well with the Americans, but there is something the matter with them. They have as an Army lost confidence in themselves and it is rather pathetic to see the trust and confidence they have in our two small Brigades. Van Fleet seems a good man and a sound General, and there are other good fighting men in the ranks, but not enough. We seldom get a 'Warning Order' and they have little conception of the time and space factor. They are apt also often to be 'Yes men' and they do not query unsound orders from above.

As regards ourselves, these are some of the conclusions I've rapidly come to:

1. No unit should be asked to serve more than nine months in this theatre, or an individual more than a year.
2. Carriers are of little use, they are always having track trouble. The Jeep and trailer is the answer for this boulder strewn country.
3. (a) The Sten is too unreliable to trust men's lives to. The Australian Owen's gun is a much better weapon.
    (b) We require in defence an extra 4 Brens per company to meet the Mass Night Attacks. This is based on the Australians experience, who have extra weapons.
4. I require a Deputy Commander. I am fairly fit and robust, but the physical strain, not to mention the mental side, is very great. I insist on seeing the forward companies and the ground in some detail. This means a lot of hill climbing, even though one tries to cut this down by flying in a light plane or helicopter. He should be on the young side, under 40, have been a Commanding Officer in World War II.
5. Half of our transport inherited from 27 Brigade is in a very poor condition owing to hard usage.

We expect to fight a big battle in a few days time. There are signs of the enemy's approach. He is about 10–20 miles to the north. I'm confident that the Brigade will do well. I am getting the Battalions to go in for night patrolling which people seem afraid of doing. With skill and luck hope to catch the mass night attacks forming up, with our artillery. The enemy put in a strong attack last night on the US Regt on our right.

With every good wish

Yours most sincerely

George Taylor

Field Marshal Sir William J. Slim GCB. GBE. DSO. MC.
Chief of the Imperial General Staff
The War Office

P.S. Please do not from the above remarks consider I'm Anti-American, far from it, my personal relations with them are good. In spite of expressing my opinions in an outspoken way, where operational matters are in dispute. We must as two Nations stick together. Aubrey Coad who arrives home early June would give you valuable information about the Korean campaign.

Characteristically, on 31 May, Slim replied: 'I have heard excellent reports of your Brigade and am glad all goes well', with assurances that he would take up Taylor's points.

To return to Operation Commando, Cassels's plan was to carry out the attack with the Commonwealth and Canadian Brigades, each reinforced with a battalion from the 29th Brigade, the remainder of which was to be kept in reserve. The Commonwealth Brigade would lead the assault on the northern flank to take the ridgeline including Kowang San (Point 355) on D day (3 October). The following day, the Canadians would take the lower-lying hills overlooking the Sami-chon valley. By having two phases, Cassels could support both brigades on each day with the complete divisional artillery. On D+3, both brigades would secure the remaining features which, for the Commonwealth Brigade, included Maryang San (Point 317). The Brigade was to be reinforced for Operation Commando by elements of the 8th King's Royal Irish Hussars (8 H) (Lieutenant Colonel Sir William Lowther) in Centurion tanks and the 1st Royal Northumberland Fusiliers (1 RNF) (Lieutenant Col Speer). Indirect fire support was to be provided by the 16th Regiment, Royal New Zealand Artillery (16 RNZA) (Lieutenant Colonel Moodie).

In outline, Taylor's brigade would take Points 210 (689 feet) to 355 on D day, with 1 KSLI on the left, 1 KOSB centre and 3 RAR on the right. On D+1, they would take Point 317.

On what was to become, as described by Professor Robert O'Neill, the official historian of Australia's involvement in the Korean War, probably the greatest single feat of the Australian Army during the Korean War, it is instructive to hear the views of the Commanding Officer (CO) of 3 RAR prior to the attack:

> I thought the Brigade plan was good tactically, if ambitious. I kept my reservations to myself as there was no point in disturbing others. Not so my fellow battalion commanders.
>
> In later years the Brigade Commander told me that each had separately protested, one claiming that the Brigade would suffer a thousand casualties. I thought the Brigade Commander to be an experienced infantryman and skilled tactician. If he set ambitious tasks then one had the comfort of knowing that he knew what it was all about and would not ask for anything that he was not prepared to do himself.
>
> This is a good illustration of the isolation of command. The Brigadier had been told to take 355 (Little Gibraltar) and 317 (Maryang San). He had given his plan. Nobody came up with anything different. He had two concerned COs. The third, myself, was still a 'new boy', still under scrutiny. In the event, the matter was sorted out with the British COs. I was not involved.

At first light on 3 October, 1 KSLI moved to secure the ridgeline between Points 210 and 227 (745 feet). The battalion initially made good progress but their supporting tanks trailed behind due to the difficult going. Taylor told them to push on without them; they were always considered a bonus anyway. By the end of the day they had covered 12,000 yards in twelve hours. Taylor was disappointed but told them to go firm and complete their tasks the following day. In the centre, 1 KOSB was not so lucky in trying to capture two intermediate features to cover the eventual assault on Kowang San. This resulted in one of its companies having to withdraw in order to resume the attack later in the day. Well forward as was his style, Taylor visited both commanding officers in their command posts to give them direction and encouragement. Additionally, he managed to speak twice to Cassels on the telephone but not over the radio. By the evening the south-west spur of Kowang San had been captured and 1 KOSB was able to reorganise and rest before continuing the next day. 3 RAR had set off at three o'clock in the morning to capture Point 199 (653 feet) as a preliminary to assaulting Maryang San on 5 October. It took five hours to go 3 miles but success was achieved when it deployed its reserve company and could then support the KOSB attack on Kowang San with its heavy machine guns. The accompanying Centurions of 8 H could bring fire to bear on the two 220 Points (722 feet).

Taylor issued clear orders for operations on 4 October by signal at 6.20 that evening. But Kowang San was still in the hands of the enemy by D+1, making life difficult for the Canadian Brigade, so, at Taylor's request, Cassels delayed their start time by five hours to enable his artillery to continue to support the Commonwealth Brigade in its final push onto its objective. Under pressure of time, Taylor ordered 3 RAR to take the twin Points of 220 on 4 October to assist 1 KOSB in its attack on Kowang San. This was not popular. Hassett wanted to preserve his battalion's energies for the attack on Maryang San on 5 October, which he knew was going to be a struggle. However, he did not want to approach Maryang San with Point 355 still occupied by the Chinese artillery observation posts, which could bring fire down on his assault troops. So at three in the afternoon on 4 October, the Australians advanced to the north-east to the first of the two 220 Points and, having taken that, moved onto the second.

Meanwhile, one company of 1 KOSB had pushed up the spur south-west of Kowang San by first light on 4 October. Unknown to them, the Australians having successfully dealt with Points 220 had established themselves on the eastern slope of Kowang San and cleared the enemy from there by 1215. So, although not entirely planned like that, the outcome was a highly successful pincer movement. 1 KSLI had taken Point 210 by 1010 hours and Point 227 by the evening. Taylor thought it was slow but said, 'after the battle I let the cloak of victory obscure this stickiness'. The Commonwealth Brigade's occupation of Kowang San (Point 355) was now complete. At the same time, the Canadian Brigade had a relatively easy time in the Sami-chon valley.

Maryang San (Point 317), as everyone anticipated, was going to be a very difficult task. The feature was steep, riddled with spurs and ravines and false crests. The Chinese had dug themselves in well, making much use of reverse slope positions, in order to catch their enemy coming over the crest. They had considerable artillery and mortar support and were known to have brought up large quantities of ammunition. This, clearly, was going to be too much for one battalion, so Taylor reinforced 3 RAR with 1 RNF.

Dawn on 5 October was heavy with mist, making direction-finding difficult, and life was made more stressful by unreliable radios. The two leading companies of 3 RAR came under heavy effective fire and, at one stage, when he could get through to his commanding officer, one company commander had to admit he was lost. Hassett realised the threat to his men and reinforced with his reserve company. This enabled the exhausted battalion to get onto a feature about 1,000 yards east of the objective, which finally fell to the Australians at five in the evening.

The Chinese were still in possession of the south-west spur, however, and forced 1 RNF back under heavy fire onto its original start line, carrying its casualties with it. Consequently, the men had to reorganise themselves and Taylor ordered them to take Point 217 (712 feet) on 6 October. He then instructed Speer to pass one company through 3 RAR and exploit to the head of Point 217 spur from the north. The commanding officer realised this would mean a very difficult approach through deep gullies and ravines and raised his objections. Taylor accepted his view and the order was rescinded.

The Chinese put in strong counter-attacks onto the Australian positions on 6 October and early the following morning Hassett ordered an attack on the Hinge, a feature directly above Point 217. This achieved success, with heavy artillery and tank support, by 0920 hours. One Australian was heard to comment, 'I'll never be rude about Gunners again.' Possession of the Hinge was vital – without it the Chinese would not be able to recapture Maryang San.

1 RNF again had a go at Point 217 but was forced back without success, sustaining heavy casualties when caught in the open once the mist cleared. While the least effective of the battalions in the brigade in this particular operation, the Fusiliers had been in Korea a long time and were on the point of going home which may have made them, understandably, more cautious. Nevertheless, they had, although repulsed, occupied a significant number of Chinese for two days, who, without their attacks, would have been deployed elsewhere. On 9 October, 1 KOSB relieved the weary 3 RAR on Maryang San and then realised the Chinese had abandoned Point 217, so sent a company to occupy it. The final tally was 58 killed and 257 wounded against the Chinese of 474 killed, 241 wounded and 93 taken prisoner.

Operation Commando had been extremely hard-fought and was a great success. Taylor was rightly proud of his troops and issued a congratulatory letter on 9 October to all ranks of the brigade. This was endorsed by the American corps commander in a fulsome letter to Cassels. Like many battles though, as time goes on, it has become forgotten. American commentators do not mention it and some British historians reduce it to a mere footnote. For the Australians however, it became the Battle of Maryang San and a significant battle honour that has gone down in legend and a lesson in how to fight this sort of war. The commanding officer of 3 RAR, Frank Hassett, was awarded an immediate DSO in the field and much later became the Australian Chief of the General Staff.

On 22 October, both the American corps commander and divisional commander, Cassels, visited Taylor's headquarters. Was there any indication from either of them that they were in any way dissatisfied with Taylor after what was, by any standards, a resounding victory? Yet, on 25 October, Brigadier Taylor was relieved of his command and replaced by Lieutenant Colonel MacDonald, CO 1 KOSB. MacDonald was not even a full colonel, let alone a brigadier. The Australians were sorry to see 'this fine soldier fall victim to the intrigues and undermining of a few British officers within the Brigade. ... This unforeseen change of command could not have come at a worse time for the Brigade.' Maryang San was shortly recaptured by the Chinese. To add insult to their disgust over the loss of what they had fought so hard for, the Australians learnt that the new brigade commander had issued a Special Order of the Day, effusively praising his old battalion, the KOSB, without a mention of anyone else.

What prompted Cassels to make this emergency appointment with no reference to the Army Board or Military Secretary's department? If the problem (of Taylor continuing in command) necessitated this immediate action, why did Cassels not put Brigadier Pike, the highly experienced artillery commander, in to command the brigade? Pike had all the confidence of the Commonwealth allies and, although a gunner, that did not preclude him from commanding an infantry brigade.

Then, as now, an officer receives an annual confidential report, initiated by his immediate superior and then commented on by the next rank up. It grades the officer, comments on his performance and recommends him for promotion, or not, and future employment. He sees it and initials it. When an officer is removed from his appointment for misconduct or inadequacy, an interim 'adverse' report is raised. The officer can appeal against this right up to Army Council level. Unsurprisingly, this is what happened here. On 24 October, Major General Cassels wrote the following adverse report on Taylor:

When I first visited 28 British Commonwealth Brigade in May '51 I found Brig Taylor in the middle of a battle. It struck me at the time that he did not have real control of his battalions and his plan and explanations were somewhat vague. It was also clear that his Brigade H.Q. was not a happy one. However as I was not his commander at the time I said nothing. When I assumed operational command of the Division on 28 July '51, 28 Bde was in a static defence role and the only operations were patrols and small raids over the IMJIN. Therefore, during this period, I had no opportunity of judging whether my previous impressions were right. At the same time, I still got the feeling that he was vague in his plans and, though he may have known exactly what he wanted, he could not clearly explain it. I could not pick a specific instance and therefore did not talk to him about it.

It was not until October that I really had a chance to see him in action when his brigade took part in a divisional attack. The brigade played its part extremely well but I felt at the time, and have since had confirmation of this, that this was due to the coordination and planning of three first-class battalion commanders aided by an excellent Brigade Major and Field Regiment commander. Brig. Taylor did not really make or coordinate the plan and, in the battle, he spent far too much time out of touch with the big picture and his H.Q., and interfered with the battalion commanders. Meanwhile the Brigade was virtually being commanded by the Bde Major and the gunner C.O.

After the battle it was quite clear that all was not well in the Brigade and many rumours came to my ears which I have now investigated. I have found that the three battalion commanders, the affiliated Field Regt. C.O. and many other officers have no confidence in Brig. Taylor as a brigade commander. From all I have heard and from my own impressions I confirm this. In my opinion he is militarily stupid but at the same time he is vain and either pays no attention to advice or brushes it aside. He lacks forethought and, though personally very brave, is liable to make illogical and unthinking decisions in a crisis. He is determined and knows what he wants to do but cannot produce clear and intelligible plans or orders to his subordinates who have to guess what he wants. I consider he is not capable of commanding a brigade.

I wish to emphasise that he is a most gallant, sincere and good-hearted officer who is well liked by everybody. Nevertheless he has not got the characteristics required in a brigade commander and I must reluctantly recommend he be replaced.

This was supported by the Australian Lieutenant General Sir Horace Robertson, the Commander-in-Chief British Commonwealth Forces in Korea, in a letter of 30 October:

A very gallant officer with plenty of drive, enthusiasm and likeable qualities. In view of his previous record, had there been another

Division available, I must have considered posting him there for confirmation of this report. I feel and I felt before the Division was formed that a very gallant and forceful Battalion Commander had been moved past his sphere but I was careful not to prejudice the Division Commander as I wanted him to decide for himself. The type of operations at present in progress in Korea demands a careful and skilled planner in all grades of command, for there is scope for and need for good planning and manoeuvre with carefully worked out co-operation of all arms. Without all this disaster is almost inevitable and casualties can be overwhelming. I believe that Brigadier Taylor's qualities might enable him to command a brigade in trench warfare where plans in meticulous detail were made at Army and Corps level, but I do not consider he has the planning capacity to command a brigade in any war of manoeuvre.

He is a staunch man, afraid of nothing and would die gallantly rather than give up an inch of ground to the enemy, and his personal example to the rank and file would be inspiring. However, I am convinced the Division Commander took the right decision.

Taylor initialled the report on 25 October and forwarded an appeal to the Army Board through the Military Secretary. Cassels then commented on the appeal on 28 November:

I would like to make clear the circumstances immediately prior to my decision to write an adverse report on Brig Taylor. Immediately after the battle I naturally congratulated Brig Taylor and his brigade having won it, but some time later it came to my ears, NOT through RA channels, that all was not well and that the three infantry COs were not happy. This was most disturbing news but, as the COs themselves had not said anything, I had no positive proof one way or the other. I was considering what to do when, the next morning, Lt Col Moodie, OC 16 NZ Fd Regt, saw Commander Royal Artillery [Brigadier William Pike] and told him categorically that he knew that the three infantry COs had no confidence in their Brigadier and were even contemplating asking that they should be relieved of their commands. The CRA, naturally and rightly, told me.

It seemed to me that the first thing I had to establish was whether Lt Col Moodie's statement was, in fact, correct. After considerable thought I ordered the CRA to go and see Lt Cols MacDonald and Barlow and find out. He did this and brought back full confirmation of Lt Col Moodie's statement.

It was then clear that either the Brigadier or the COs would have to go. I did not think that any useful purpose would be served by 'putting the cards on the table' with Brig Taylor as, whatever happened at any such discussion, the result would still have been that one or the others must go.

On the other hand, if the CRA had found that Moodie's allegations were quite wrong then I would of course have told Brig Taylor of all the facts and would have removed Moodie. In this case I maintain that Brig Taylor's stock would have risen with his COs and not fallen as he suggests.

I had a high opinion of the COs and, as stated in my report, I already had my doubts of Brig Taylor's capacity to command a brigade. I therefore decided that he must go and, as the current state of affairs was obviously unsatisfactory, that it must be done quickly. After personally talking to Lt Cols MacDonald and Barlow to confirm what I heard, I wrote an adverse report on Brig Taylor.

Since Brig Taylor has left I have taken particular pains to confirm all I said in his report because I wanted to be quite certain that I was not doing him an injustice. My inquiries included a discussion with Lt Col Hassett, OC 3 RAR, to whom I had not previously spoken on this subject. I regret to say that everything has been fully confirmed, and there is nothing in Brig Taylor's appeal which causes me to change my opinion.

The papers now went the rounds of three Army Council members: the Adjutant General (AG), Vice Chief of the Imperial General Staff (VCIGS) and the Quartermaster General (QMG). They commented:

Clearly the removal of this officer from Command of 28 British Commonwealth Brigade must be confirmed.

The more I read the case, however, the less I am certain as to why the Divisional Commander relieved Brigadier Taylor of his Command. Taylor's background is excellent and his record as a soldier should have made him in every way fit to Command his Brigade. The Brigade which he, Taylor, has trained and commanded for some time appears to have put up a first-class performance in its first major action in Korea, and as Taylor was in command during this action, to him must go the major share of the credit.

His methods may not have appealed to General Cassels but they would seem to have been effective.

Apart from all this I am not entirely happy in regard to General Cassels' handling of the case. I should have thought that the simple and correct approach was for Cassels to have told Taylor of what he, Cassels, thought Taylor was doing wrong and to have told him to put it right. If after a reasonable trial Taylor failed to put it right then there would have been a case for removal.

It is impossible not to feel that some clash of personalities has been at any rate a contributory cause to the incident.

I consider that the report should stand and the appeal fail insofar as it is against that report, but that Brigadier Taylor should be given Command of another brigade (not in Korea) at the earliest possible date.

17 Dec 51   General Sir John Crocker AG

I agree with AG's view. I suggest that he should, if possible, be appointed to command a Regular brigade, where he will have an opportunity of proving his worth.

20 Dec 51   Lieutenant General Sir Nevil Brownjohn VCIGS

I agree with AG's minute but not the last paragraph. I am very unhappy at the way Cassels has handled this case. Quite apart from the fact that he says he had misgivings, unsupported by any specific instances, in May 1951, it seems to me inconceivable that during, anyway the first day and perhaps the whole of an important engagement a Div Comdr should only speak to his leading Brigadier <u>on the phone</u>. Cassels ought to visit his Brigadiers during a battle, and doubly so if he suspects their abilities. I deduce this from [the papers], and from the absence of any mention of a visit. Here, apparently, Cassels thought the Brigade HQ were 'unhappy' over a period of some five months (even though he states that the Brigadier is 'good hearted and liked by everybody'), and yet he did nothing about it.

You cannot handle, and dismiss, Brigadiers on rumours, hearsay and enquiries. You must go and see for yourself.

I know Brigadier Taylor very well indeed. He is the finest type of fighting soldier – and that type will always repay a little 'stringing along' from their more intellectual seniors.

Clearly, his removal from command of 28th Brigade must be confirmed, and to that extent the appeal must fail. But I believe that the circumstances of his removal demand that the report should be expunged from his record. He should be given command of a Regular Brigade.

21 Dec 51   General Sir Ivor Thomas QMG

As there was disagreement between the members, the Military Secretary forwarded the papers to the Deputy Chief of the Imperial General Staff (DCIGS) and the senior civil servant on the Army Board, the Permanent Under Secretary (PUS). The DCIGS agreed with the last paragraph of the QMG's note, without further comment and the PUS minuted the following:

I restrict my remarks to the point which is not agreed, i.e. whether the report should stand or be expunged.

In a case of this kind, I cannot see how the report can be effectively expunged even if it were considered desirable to do so. The officer has been removed from command and if his records do not show why, they will be incomplete. It is hardly in the officer's interest that the facts recorded in the Report should not go on record. Indeed I personally regard the report with the discussion of it that has followed as on balance to his credit and I do not agree that it should be washed out.

Generally I have assumed that a report which is an honest expression of opinion ought to stand even though we do not agree with it; and that we only expunge records which are untrue or grossly unfair.

1 Jan 52   Sir George Turner PUS

In cases of disagreement such as this, the Military Secretary forwards the papers to the Secretary of State for War (in this case, Sir Anthony Head) for a decision. Here, the Miliary Secretary reminded him that there were two issues: the officer's future employment and whether or not the adverse report should be expunged from his record. He also added that Sir Anthony Head might like to discuss the case with the CIGS, 'who knows about this case' before giving a final decision. Sir Anthony Head responded, on 23 January, that Taylor should be given another brigade and the report should not be expunged, and Taylor was informed by letter on 28 January. Taylor was subsequently appointed to command the 49th Infantry Brigade, which went on to deal successfully with the Mau Mau in Kenya.

Clearly, in the view of Army Council members, Taylor had been badly and unfairly handled by Cassels and, although the report remained on his record, they saw to it that his career was not ruined. Indeed, after retirement he became a sought-after lecturer on leadership in battle to up and coming army officers. His subject covered his experiences in the Second World War rather than Korea.

So why did this happen? If Taylor was a scapegoat, who was to gain? First of all, Cassels. He behaved uncharacteristically badly in his handling of Taylor. He acted against all the conventions of warning an officer as to his future conduct by sacking him without any prior indication of dissatisfaction. There is no record that he even spoke to him about it, let alone gave a formal, recorded rebuke, which should have happened. He failed to give proper reasons for doing so and his response to the challenge in Taylor's appeal was weak and relied on hearsay, rumour and innuendo. He utterly misunderstood and misjudged Hassett, who, if anyone, would have made his views abundantly clear if he thought Taylor was inadequate. Cassels only spoke to Hassett *after* he had sacked Taylor. Cassels's last paragraph of his response to Taylor's reaction is simply not true.

In a letter to Taylor on 14 May 1987, Hassett wrote:

I thought we got on well together and I was very sorry when we said goodbye. To have to leave when the Brigade had just achieved a resounding success was a shattering experience for you.

The Brigade plan for Operation Commando was a very good one. Moreover, the Brigade and Divisional support given my Battalion was excellent. Most noteworthy were the artillery and tank support (which you controlled) and the supply trains bringing up ammunition and carrying out the casualties. Had the attack failed, you would have been blamed. Since it succeeded brilliantly, you must get the credit.

I think one of your senior officers was very ambitious. Perhaps that was part of the trouble.

I shall watch out for any information about anyone making allegations about you and speak up for you, if it is necessary.

On 12 June 1991, Hassett wrote to Captain Eaton who was writing a history of 3 RAR:

The Korean chapters are quite the best I have read so far. I was particularly pleased to note they demonstrated well the tactical skill of Brigadier Taylor. Of course, the whole Divisional action was extremely well planned and executed. The timing of the attacks in series so as to make maximum fire support available to battalions at any given time, is one example. As a battalion commander it was comforting to go into an attack with the knowledge that over 120 guns and mortars, as well as tanks, were in support and that any administrative or other back up would be quickly forthcoming. I particularly appreciated the senior commanders being well forward, fully in touch with progress of the battle and able to make the right decisions quickly.

I also suggested, and I understand it is agreed, that the History include the comment 'George Taylor was a most able tactician'.

Hassett then wrote to Taylor on 27 February 1992:

> Here is the 3RAR version of the battle of Maryang San by Lt Col
> Breen, drawn on Eaton's writings.
>   There is criticism of some British units, the KOSB in particular.
> Much of this flows from the KOSB having MacDonald as its CO.
> He disliked Australians, a sentiment they returned in full measure. I
> consider him a poor CO and a worse Brigade Commander.
>   I have taken pains to ensure that your own part in Commando is
> recognised as a valuable contribution from an experienced and able
> commander. This may be some belated consolation for the harsh
> treatment given you and the enormous hurt you must have felt. Of
> course, it is a 3RAR view as seen by junior officers and soldiers.
> Always forthright, they have called the shots as they saw them!
> Mostly, they were not in a position to appreciate the enormous sup-
> port the Battalion was given at the Brigade and Divisional level. I
> recognised it and have said so.

When Taylor returned to England, he was given lunch at the House
of Lords by his old friend General Horrocks, now Black Rod, who was
dumbfounded when he learned what had happened. Horrocks told him
that Cassels, as a brigadier before the Rhine crossing, was at the point of
being sacked but his divisional commander was killed by a mortar bomb
and Cassels was saved.

Cassels was not the sort of man to enhance his own career by stepping on the necks of others. He did not need to; he had a good record,
was eminently capable and went on to great things later, including
becoming Chief of the General Staff. Was he frightened of a rebellion
by his battalion commanders? Were they anxious that Taylor was too
robust for them? Peace talks had already started so no one wanted to
expend life unnecessarily at this stage. Hassett was the star but, contrary to what Cassels thought, he had no problem with Taylor. With the
possibly inadequate and unpopular New Zealand artillery commander,
Moodie, did Cassels fear a falling out among the Commonwealth allies?
Cohesion was important, particularly under intense American scrutiny.
Cassels found the Americans difficult yet had to rely on them for much

materiel. They would have been quick to drive a wedge into the fledgling Commonwealth Division if they thought it was not up to it.

Cassels then made MacDonald the brigade commander. Was it he who fomented disloyalty and distrust among his fellow commanding officers to further his own ambitions? Hassett had no time for him but he did appear to achieve that ambition, if that is what it was, by commanding a brigade as a lieutenant colonel. Barlow was a pessimist and possibly thought he would have an easier ride under a softer brigadier. He had to be pushed and prodded, so would have been no friend of Taylor's. Possibly he resented Taylor's earlier criticisms. Speer was at the end of the road, having completed a gruelling tour with his battalion in Korea. They had not done well on the operation and all he would have wanted was to return home as intact as possible; not for him a possibly gung-ho brigade commander.

Clearly, a key figure was Brigadier William Pike, the divisional Commander Royal Artillery. He was a fine officer and would have undoubtedly been Cassels's closest confidant. As we have seen, he was charged by Cassels to find out what was going on and then escorted Taylor to Cassels for his final interview. Sadly, the family papers, well researched by his son, Hew, in his excellent *From the Front Line* are silent on the matter.

So there was a nasty brew in the cauldron and Taylor was thrown out. Whether he satisfies the definition of a scapegoat as the price to be paid for the cohesion of the 1st Commonwealth Division, or was more the victim of some disruptive disloyalty by his subordinates and blatant mishandling by his commander, we shall probably never know. If, however, he was a scapegoat, there must have been another or others to benefit.

'*Cui bono?*'[1] Cassels possibly; easier for him to sack a brigadier than all the commanding officers, if that was the alternative? Or was it to demonstrate his strength in the face of the Americans? The commanding officers? Taylor was not popular, except with the Australians, so they would have been glad to see him go. MacDonald? He certainly boosted his career by Taylor's dismissal but Regimental Headquarters of the

---

[1] 'Who benefits?' Lucius Cassius

KOSB was unable to throw any light. What is not in doubt, as agreed by the Army Council, was that Taylor was wrongly dismissed. If he was not a scapegoat, then why? The reader must decide.

The weight of responsibility on the shoulders of the battalion commander is enormous. Only he can make the decision where to move his men and when. His superiors can give him orders to do so, but he has to make them work. In the next chapter, Lieutenant Colonel Bevan receives orders, but very late – they are so delayed, in fact, that he arrives at his objective too late to catch the French. But should he have moved earlier? What were the problems in doing so and would it have made a difference?

TEN

Lieutenant Colonel Charles Bevan

Scapegoat of the Peninsula

July 1811

On 8 July 1811, Lieutenant Colonel Charles Bevan, commanding the 4th of Foot, died of fever in the town of Portalegre on the border between Portugal and Spain. On the 11th, his funeral took place with full military honours. The officers of the battalion attended, with a firing party of four captains, eight subalterns and 300 rank and file, under command of Major Tanner, the second in command. His grave was bricked over and a stone placed at the head bearing this description:

This stone is erected to the Memory of Charles Bevan Esqre,
Late Lt. Col of the 4th or King's Own Regt.
With the intention of recording his virtues.
They are deeply engraved on the hearts and minds of all
who knew him.

Sadly, this was a complete fabrication. There is no trace of his grave or headstone in Portalegre, Portugal. There is no record in local documents and no residual memory handed down to present-day inhabitants. It was a complete cover-up, the truth of which was not revealed until 1843.

The Peninsula War, which lasted from 1808 to 1814, was only part of the twenty-year struggle against Napoleon but an important aspect of it, to the extent that Bonaparte famously described it as the 'Spanish ulcer'. For him, indeed, that is what it turned out to be.

Essential to the British effort, as in many conflicts before and since, was control of the sea. Not only was this vital to protect our shores and guard the resupply chain for the troops in the Iberian Peninsula, but it also enabled Britain to attack the French outlying territories with impunity. In 1800, Britain effectively stood alone and on the defensive. Napoleon had set out to conquer the Middle East and, though halted in Egypt, he was still paramount throughout Europe. Indeed, from 1803 to 1805 there was a serious threat of invasion as Napoleon had assembled a shipping armada in the Channel ports with a ground force of some 160,000 troops, quite capable of mounting a seaborne assault.

However, frustrated by his inability to control the Channel sufficiently to achieve this, he decided to cripple Britain's economy by forbidding any European country over which he had control or influence from trading with it. Portugal, a maritime nation with close ties to Britain, refused to comply, and Napoleon sent Marshal Junot with 28,000 men through Spain to Portugal to teach it a lesson. The French reached Lisbon in November 1807.

In the spring of the following year, 75,000 Frenchmen invaded Spain. Joseph, Napoleon's brother, was placed on the throne. The populations of both Portugal and Spain were enraged and rose against the invader, asking Britain for help. Overestimating the extent and effectiveness of the rebellion, the government agreed to become involved.

The small Spanish Army was badly trained and unpredictable but contained many brave men and officers. Time and again in the coming years their troops would try to take on Napoleon's armies and generally they were routed; only on a few occasions were they successful. However, a more effective erosion of the French effort was achieved by guerrillas who conducted what was to become a classic of that kind of warfare: hit and run with small bands, constantly harassing rearguards and supply lines and, effectively, tying down troops who were badly needed elsewhere. The Spanish became such masters of this kind of combat that, it was said, it took the French 200 cavalry to guard a vital messenger and 1,000 men to ensure the safety of a general travelling round the country.

An essential factor in Wellington's strategy was that he had the support of the local population whereas the French had to be constantly on their guard against marauding bands and received no local supplies without seizing them and no local intelligence. Even if entering a town or village without being attacked, their troops were largely met with sullen non-cooperation.

Britain's naval superiority now came to the fore. It allowed the government to send a force to assist the Portuguese and Spaniards in August 1808, withdraw it from Corunna a few months later, and then replace it in April 1809. Throughout, this meant that in the coming campaign Wellington could maintain a first-class commissariat, ensuring his troops, by the standards of the day, were properly fed and armed. He also insisted his quartermasters paid for local provisions, which the French were unable or unwilling to do. This was critical to winning the 'hearts and minds' of the population.

At the same time, Wellington preserved his army by taking few risks in the early years and fighting only when the odds were favourable by ensuring the French were never able to concentrate large numbers against him. He broke the French ciphers, had a network of agents and so often therefore had better information than the French generals themselves. Although maps were poor, good sketches were drawn and much of the ground had been ridden over a number of times before a battle was actually fought there. So cover from view and concealed approaches ('dead ground') were marked down and remembered.

In August 1808, the British, under Sir Arthur Wellesley, as he then was, landed 80 miles north of Lisbon. Wellesley immediately set about plans to evict the French from Portugal. However, he learned that as a mere 39-year-old he was to be superseded by a couple of senior, and elderly, generals – the 58-year-old Sir Hew Dalrymple and 53-year-old Sir Harry Burrard, neither of whom had recent operational experience. It was a political move, and the sort which was to land Wellington with some incompetent commanders for much of the time. He had to accept the decision but hoped to oust the French before his seniors could arrive. He had some early success at Roliça and Vimeiro before Burrard arrived and put a damper on further exploitation of these achievements. Nevertheless, it was a nasty surprise for the French who were not used to failure.

The controversial Convention of Cintra was signed between the British and French in August. In it the French agreed to withdraw from

Portugal and return to France. However, what infuriated those at home were the clauses that stipulated the French were to be returned home in British ships and they were allowed to keep the booty they had looted from the Portuguese. The generals, including Wellesley, were arraigned before a Court of Inquiry accused of incompetence. Dalrymple was sacked and Burrard retired. Luckily, Wellesley was cleared but was not immediately given another command.

In Wellesley's absence, Lieutenant General Sir John Moore was ordered to advance into Spain and drive the French back over the Pyrenees. At the same time, Napoleon himself entered the fray and took command, determined to sort out the British. After a certain amount of difficulty in putting his reinforcements together, Moore realised that he was to be trapped between two large French armies under Napoleon and Marshal Nicolas Soult, so, to the disgust of his troops, withdrew to Corunna from where, Dunkirk-like, they could be evacuated. The retreat was an exhausting and very tough three weeks of constant rear-guard actions against the harrying French, but they never lost a gun or a set of Colours.

Napoleon, realising he was not going to be able to cut the British off, left for Paris with better things to do and relinquished the pursuit to Soult. Moore and his bedraggled troops finally made it into Corunna in January 1809 to find no shipping awaited them. They turned and fought their pursuers so successfully that they were actually forcing them back when Moore was killed and the momentum faded. Boats arrived and 19,000 men were successfully embarked and sailed for England to fight another day. It was the nadir of British hope and expectation. Political morale at home was low and the population thoroughly dissatisfied. The French were now back in northern Portugal and in strength in Spain, although Lisbon itself was unoccupied, where there were still some British troops. Additionally, southern Spain was still not entirely subjugated.

Wellesley, however, was optimistic and put forward a plan to occupy Portugal, from where he could launch a campaign into Spain. The grateful British government endorsed his ideas with alacrity and he sailed for Portugal, landing in Lisbon in April 1809. Wellesley had reshaped and reorganised the army and began to restructure the Portuguese Army under British officers. He realised that, with the three French armies a long way apart, he could take them out piecemeal if he moved quickly; if they were allowed to join together they would present an insuperable force. With lightning speed, Wellesley crossed the river Douro and drove Soult's army of 20,000 men into full retreat out of Portugal and back into Spain, with the loss of all their baggage.

Wellesley now entered a difficult time with his Spanish allies, some of whose generals resented him and his relative youth. By July, Wellesley set up a defensive position north of Talavera. Although, on paper, he outnumbered the French, he was dependent on the Spaniards whom he simply did not trust. Talavera was a ferocious battle over two days with the British losing over 5,000, and the Spanish 1,200, against the French 7,000. It was a significant, but only tactical, victory for the British, with the French withdrawing towards Madrid, but they had fought themselves to a standstill, run out of supplies and were too exhausted to follow up. Wellesley deservedly became Viscount Wellington.

Wellington always kept in his mind the safety of Portugal behind him for resupply lines and seaborne protection, either for reinforcement, repositioning along the coast or for Corunna-type evacuation if necessary. So he was constantly anxious not to be cut off from his routes back. Despite their setback at Talavera, the French remained a serious threat and clearly Soult wanted to cut Wellington off from the Portuguese lifeline for the same reasons Wellington wanted to preserve it. Consequently, Wellington reconnoitred defensive positions north and west of Lisbon, which became known as the Lines of Torres Vedras. Work began immediately and secrecy was such that the French failed to discover them until they arrived a year later.

Soured by the difficulties of cooperating with the Spanish, Wellington refused to collaborate with them in any military operation for the remainder of 1809 and in December he withdrew back across the border into Portugal to settle down for the winter. Very little happened the following year until, in the autumn, the French invaded Portugal for the third time. Wellington, though, had not wasted his time; reorganisation and streamlining of his forces took place, particularly incorporating the Portuguese, contingency plans were made and potential battle positions reconnoitred and intelligence was quietly gathered. He even reached agreement with the Portuguese Government over a scorched earth policy.

There are three main approach routes into Portugal from the east. The central one was least likely to be used and Wellington left that to General William Beresford to protect. The southern ran through Badajoz in Spain and Elvas in Portugal to Lisbon and was the most direct. The northern, and most likely, was through Ciudad Rodrigo in Spain to Almeida in Portugal. These fortresses were in Allied hands. He took personal control of the northern route, leaving 'Daddy' Hill, one of his most trusted generals, to guard the southern corridor.

The French were now in a better position to reinforce the Peninsula, having made peace with the Austrians. Masséna, one of Napoleon's ablest generals, was ordered to drive the British out but, even though he was given overall command, he still had to receive instructions from Paris, which because of the time delay stifled initiative. However, in July and August both Ciudad Rodrigo and Almeida fell to the French, but it was not to go all their way. Wellington had long planned his defence on the Bussaco Ridge and, in September, soundly defeated Masséna's assaults. It was a tactical victory in which, for the first time, the Portuguese troops played a significant part. Rather than pursuing the French, he stuck to his original plan and withdrew in good order to the Lines of Torres Vedras. From there, Wellington could take on Masséna's renewed attacks on his own terms. Masséna had been unaware of the strength, or even existence, of the Lines and very soon gave up but not as quickly as Wellington had hoped. The rapid fall of Almeida meant that the French had advanced much faster than expected and so the scorched earth policy proved less effective than it should have been. There was nothing Masséna could do that winter, so he withdrew, losing some 25,000 to disease and starvation. The die was set and the French never again were in a position to drive the British into the sea.

In the south, the British in Cadiz had been happily tying down a considerable force of French who were besieging them. It was decided in March 1811, though, to make a daring breakout by sea, with an Anglo-Spanish force, land behind the French besiegers and attack them. The Spanish failed in their part of the operation, leaving the British outnumbered and isolated at Barrosa, but with a bold counter-attack they succeeded in defeating the enemy.

Meanwhile, in the north, Wellington was closely pursuing the weak and demoralised French, who had now withdrawn back into Spain leaving a garrison in the Portuguese fortress of Almeida. Unfortunately, Soult had captured Badajoz, so both main lines into Spain were now in the hands of the enemy. Wellington ordered Beresford to besiege Badajoz but, realistically, there was little chance of success with Soult threatening him from the south. Masséna, having regrouped much more swiftly than anticipated, now pushed westwards from Ciudad Rodrigo to relieve the blockaded Almeida. Wellington set up his defence around Fuentes de Oñoro on ground he knew well. The French were beaten off in a battle over three days. But then came the French garrison escape from Almeida: 'the most disgraceful military event that has yet occurred to us', stormed Wellington.

We now turn to the main player in this disaster. Charles Bevan was born in 1778 into a well-to-do middle-class family. He had a happy family life with a brother and two sisters. Luckily for historians, he was also an assiduous letter writer. In 1795, he purchased a commission in the 37th Regiment of Foot (later the Hampshire Regiment). This was common practice at the time but advance was also by immediate promotion on the battlefield through some act of bravery or literally filling dead men's shoes after a campaign when vacancies occurred. Hence there was never any lack of volunteers for the 'Forlorn Hope' – the spearhead of any assault when survival by itself was pretty much a guarantee of promotion. It also helped to have the eye/ear of a senior and influential general who could often nudge things in the right direction. Bevan was very aware of this. His first overseas posting, by now a lieutenant, was to Gibraltar, where he remained for three and a half years. After a period with his regiment, he was made aide-de-camp (ADC) to Lieutenant General William Grinfield. While he would have missed some of the excitements his contemporaries were having at the time, he would have been noticed by important people his general was meeting and it would have done his career no harm.

In March 1800, no doubt itching to see action, he bought himself a vacancy as a captain in the 28th Regiment of Foot (later the Gloucestershire Regiment). While these line regiments perhaps lacked a little of the glamour of the green-jacketed light infantry, such as Harry Smith's famous 95th (later the Rifle Brigade after Waterloo) or the Foot Guards, they were very steady regiments with dependable NCOs and countrymen in the ranks. Later, of course, in the reforms of 1881, they were to be based on counties and deliberately recruited from them. Bevan was blessed in his new regiment with an outstanding commanding officer in the person of Lieutenant Colonel Edward Paget, fourth son of Lord Uxbridge, who was to have a very successful later career and, indeed, influence over Bevan's. For a time he served in Minorca with the regiment as the island was again in British hands. It had been lost in 1756 through Admiral Byng's failure (see Chapter 3) but had been returned to Britain under the terms of the Treaty of Paris in 1763 following the Seven Years War. Ceded back to Spain in 1783 by the Treaty of Versailles, Britain invaded yet again in 1798 (the 28th were in this action) and resumed occupation of this important base controlling the Mediterranean Sea. Bevan was now, at last, to get his first taste of action.

Napoleon had invaded Egypt in 1798, not only to help control the eastern Mediterranean and establish a colony but also to provide a corridor and main supply route into India with the eventual aim of annihilating the British there. However, the virtual destruction of his fleet at the Battle of the Nile curtailed these aspirations and, instead, he set about making himself ruler of Egypt in his characteristic egotistical style. Meeting strong resistance, and with Turkey and Russia now taking the field against France, Napoleon returned home to the chagrin of his troops left behind. A British force commanded by Lord Abercromby had been ordered to the Mediterranean in May 1800. He captured Malta and, in October that year, it was planned to use his army to expel the French from Egypt. The British, supported by a small Ottoman army, would land on the Egyptian coast. A second, larger Ottoman army would invade through Palestine, while a third British force, made up of troops from India and reinforced from Britain, would land on the Red Sea coast and march down the Nile to Cairo.

Abercromby's force arrived at Aboukir Bay, where a determined assault commanded by Sir John Moore succeeded in establishing a beachhead. Bevan was in the assault force and was severely wounded together with his commanding officer, Edward Paget. The Battle of Alexandria took place in March and by the end of April the main British Army, combined with the Ottomans, advanced on Cairo. They reached the city in June, and after a short siege the French surrendered. General Hutchinson, who had replaced Abercromby, defeated the remaining French in Alexandria and the occupation of Egypt was over. Bevan recovered from his wounds and took command of the Light Company of the battalion, a specific honour, no doubt in recognition of his performance in the invasion. The 28th left for home towards the end of 1802 but not before its men were given the distinction of wearing a smaller version of their cap badge on the back of their headdress. They had been attacked by the French cavalry during the battle before Alexandria on 21 March 1801. They were in line and there being no time to form square, the commanding officer ordered the rear rank to 'Right about face' and they succeeded in beating off the enemy. Such is the stuff of regimental tradition.

Paget became a brigade commander in October 1803 and, recognising Bevan's quality, made him his brigade major. This position is, in essence, the chief executive of the brigade and, as such, is the senior staff officer. Then, as now, it is a sought-after job by those looking for high-grade employment and with an eye on promotion. The brigade, with both battalions of the 28th under command, was stationed in Fermoy, north of Cork in Ireland. Before this, Bevan had met his future wife, Mary, the daughter of Admiral Dacres. From his letters to her, he was clearly deeply in love and they were engaged in 1804. Although Mary's letters to him have not survived, there is much in his that reflects her words to him and clearly they have considerable rapport.

He finishes a letter to her of 27 May 1804, 'I am very anxious to compare your picture with yourself, as on a more intimate acquaintance with it I begin to fancy it very like – my dearest love! I have a thousand things to say to you and plans to propose – which if realised!! But it is impossible to write on these subjects as I fear my imagination, perhaps too ardent, may lead me to hope what, for your dear sake must not be – I hardly need tell you what this is – Now, how can I ever part with you.'

Paget then commanded a brigade in Folkestone, taking Bevan with him. The threat of French invasion was very real so Bevan was unable to get away to visit his fiancée in Plymouth. However, his ambitions were being met by his purchase of a majority in the same regiment. This, no doubt, put him in a good light with his future father-in-law, and Mary and he were married in December 1804. Return to regimental duty meant rejoining his battalion in Ireland with his new wife.

Early wedded bliss was, however, not to last long. A coalition (the third) between Britain, Austria, Prussia and Russia sought to defeat Napoleon on the Continent. The French, having given up the idea of invading England, now concentrated on Central Europe. Lord Cathcart, commander-in-chief in Ireland, was ordered to command an expedition to Hanover. Paget's brigade, with the 28th including Bevan under command, arrived near Bremen in late 1805 to be part of the force to expel the French from Hanover and recover northern occupied territory. It was a relatively half-hearted operation, let down by the Prussians who made peace with the French in January 1806, leaving the British no option but to re-embark for England soon afterwards. Napoleon's victories at Ulm and Austerlitz could hardly have helped British morale. William Pitt produced one of his most famous quotes at the time: 'Roll up that map [of Europe], it will not be wanted these ten years'. Nelson, however, had completed the Royal Navy's mastery of the sea at Trafalgar in October 1805, which gave some comfort.

Bevan was now reunited with his family and at regimental duty in Colchester. However, even when on manoeuvres, Bevan would take every opportunity to write to his wife. On 24 June 1807, he wrote, 'We still remain, my beloved Mary, in uncertainty as to the period of our embarkation but we have received orders to practise some particular things relating principally to Continental Service. … I am very well only my unfortunate Face is quite skinned by the sun. We have every morning Field Day for about 3 hours in the heat of the day. But it will soon get seasoned and then I shall do very well.'

In July 1807, there were two Treaties of Tilsit between the French and, firstly, Russia and, secondly, Prussia, thereby isolating Britain, with its sole ally Sweden, even further. Denmark, at the time not formally allied to any power, had a considerable navy. Britain was concerned that Napoleon would occupy Denmark, seize its shipping and force it to close the Baltic, vital to Britain for ships' naval stores material and access to Sweden. Additionally, Britain was uneasy about the Danes' loyalty having failed to persuade them into an alliance. Consequently, a naval force, with a land element embarked under Lord Cathcart, was put to sea to monitor the Danish fleet.

On 16 August, the troops were landed, unopposed, north of Copenhagen. Bevan's regiment took part in the relatively low-level operations against the Danes. It was difficult for the British really to regard the Danish as foes and the actions were not pressed home with the customary vigour. However, Cathcart was forced to bombard Copenhagen city as it refused to surrender and much unnecessary destruction resulted. A military success, having neutralised the Danish Navy, but a diplomatic failure as it, unsurprisingly, drove the Danes into the arms of the French. Nevertheless, the Swedes remained implacably anti-Napoleon and refused his demands to close the Baltic ports. Bevan and his regiment returned home hardly to a heroes' welcome.

The consequence was that Finland, then part of Sweden, was invaded by Russia, while Prussia and Denmark declared war on Sweden. Britain, thoroughly alarmed that Napoleon might take advantage of this and launch an attack on Sweden through Denmark, decided to send an expeditionary force to Sweden under Sir John Moore. The aim of this undertaking was not entirely clear except, perhaps, to demonstrate solidarity with the Swedes, but it was not an operation of war. To Bevan's delight, his regiment, also interestingly in the same brigade as the 4th Regiment of Foot, was again under Edward Paget, by now a divisional commander. The force set sail in May 1808 but lay idle for weeks, cooped up in their transport ships anchored off the Swedish coast. The whole expedition was a muddle and complete waste of time and resources. The Swedish king had insane ideas of how the British force was to be used and Sir John Moore, though summoned to Stockholm for 'consultations', was having none of it.

In a letter to Mary of 2 June 1808, Bevan tells her he had been ill but, on recovery, managed to go ashore with Paget's ADC and see some of the country. Rumours were rife, even that the force was to sail for Buenos Aires. The fleet, however, returned to Spithead in July but, to everyone's frustration and disappointment, no one was allowed to disembark (imagine the uproar nowadays!) and fresh orders were issued for the force to sail direct for Portugal. The Peninsula War had started.

Bevan was a great admirer of Sir John Moore, having seen how he trained his troops when they were stationed not far away in Kent in 1804. So now, being under his command in Portugal must have been very heartening. There have been observations that his letters to Mary contained elements of moaning and a suspicion of depression. However, this is not untypical of soldiers stationed far from home, critical of the way they think the war is being run, exasperation with their leaders or, simply, missing their wives and families. It is fortunate that so many letters and accounts were written at this time, not only by officers but also by many rank and file as well. Much of their content echoes Bevan's, so not too much should be made of it.

Still in the 28th Regiment of Foot and, to his continuing exasperation, a major ('Thirty years old & alas! Still a Major'), Bevan's battalion was at full strength and well regarded by Moore. They were all keen to chase the French out of Spain. There was much optimism and self-confidence but the reality was that they knew very little of Spain and even less about French strengths and dispositions. Bevan and his men faced some hard marching and by November were in Ciudad Rodrigo, which he appeared to like, then later in Salamanca, which he didn't. Being unaware, like much of the army, of the difficult choices facing Moore, Bevan was keen to be on the move to face the French and, in December 1808, happily, started to move north-east. However, after a small-scale victory when Bevan was in reserve in Paget's division, Moore decided to pull back to avoid entrapment. Thus began the long slog back to Corunna.

Sadly, there is no evidence of what happened to Bevan during the retreat. Understandably, he cannot have had time to write to Mary, or, if he did, the few letters that he would have been able to write have not survived. We do know his battalion was in the Reserve Division, which meant that it would often find itself fighting rearguard actions against the pursuing French. This is not an attractive operation even by today's standards – trying to protect the rear of a withdrawing force but judging the exact moment to break clean from the enemy oneself. Even the great 'Black Bob' Craufurd would make a mess of such a manoeuvre with his famous Light Division on the Côa in July of 1810. Embarkation from Corunna under continual French pressure was difficult but successful for Bevan and the 28th, who reached England in January 1809 in a pretty poor state.

Soon after this major setback, the British again sent an expeditionary force to the Continent, this time to the Scheldt in Holland in 1809. This was the biggest amphibious operation of the Napoleonic war with some 40,000 men embarked. The short distances enabled such a large force to be deployed and supplied. Scheldt was a key strategic objective with the hope that its capture would have an impact on Napoleon's attack on the Austrians as well as take out the docks at Antwerp. Bevan, now back to his normal form, left with his battalion on 28 July. The voyage was made with agreeable companions, reasonable food and interesting discussion. Little did they know what awaited them. The Walcheren Expedition was one of the most ignominious military episodes of the time. The intention was to assist the Austrians, now allies, against Napoleon by forcing him to look north. The immediate aim was to destroy the French fleet in Flushing. However, before the British even landed, the Austrians had been beaten at Wagram and were out of the war. Nevertheless, the British went ashore and captured Flushing only to find that the French fleet had been moved out of harm's way to Antwerp. Severe sickness in the form of a kind of malaria set in, decimating the British ranks. Over 4,000 troops died, of which only 106 did so in combat. The residual effect of Walcheren fever was to persist in the battalions that had been exposed to it throughout the rest of the war. The force was withdrawn in September.

For Bevan any actual fighting was low level and desultory – he drew a fairly indecipherable map of the islands for Mary, which survives today. Luckily, he was not affected by the fever and returned, despairing of the leadership, on 16 September. However, a new dawn was awaiting him. A vacancy in command occurred in the 2nd Battalion of the 4th Foot and in 1810, Bevan was appointed commanding officer, having gained his lieutenancy-colonelcy by purchase. He had served alongside the 4th a number of times when in the 28th, and so would have known a number of the officers and been known by them. This was all to the good.

In February 1810, Bevan and his battalion set sail from Portsmouth, they thought for Portugal, but they did not know their destination at that stage. They arrived in Gibraltar after a very rough passage, including one ship running ashore in northern Spain and its occupants being captured by the French. To Bevan's disappointment his battalion was ordered to occupy the Spanish enclave of Ceuta on Africa's north coast, opposite Gibraltar. This was important to ensure that the French could not disrupt the passage of shipping through the Strait of Gibraltar. Nevertheless, for a commanding officer looking forward to commanding his battalion in action, this dull garrison task was very unwelcome. Life, for Bevan, became one long grind of administration; his quartermaster had been captured with the boat running ashore in the storm, his adjutant was ill with fever and his paymaster was in Gibraltar. He didn't like the Spanish inhabitants whom he found idle and work-shy. Interestingly, he could happily speak French but no Spanish, unlike Harry Smith who, of course, found it very advantageous (particularly having married a Spanish girl). He didn't like the social scene, having to entertain or the pretensions of the exiled Spanish nobility. The solitary life of command, financial concerns and the separation from his family played into his dark, self-pitying moods – what he called his 'Blue Devils'.

In September 1810, he received the news he had been waiting for. The commanding officer of the 1st Battalion, 4th Foot, Lieutenant Colonel Wynch, had been selected for promotion and Bevan was appointed in his place. He hoped, therefore, to return to England where the battalion was stationed. However, by November, the battalion had been posted to Lisbon. In December, Wynch moved on and Bevan left for Portugal, and the battalion, as soon as he could. The only disadvantage was that he did not have an intervening break in which to visit his family.

He arrived in Lisbon in January 1811 after a fifteen-day voyage from Gibraltar in a slow and dirty Portuguese ship, and then, to his intense frustration, was held in quarantine for another eleven days. To cap it all, the first thing he had to do ashore was arrange the funeral of Colonel Wynch, his predecessor, who had died from fever. Now in Portugal, he was also anxious to meet up with his brother-in-law (married to his wife's sister, Eleanor) Jim Paterson, who was serving in his old regiment, the 28th. The 4th were presently in the 5th Division, which was being held in the Lisbon and Torres Vedras area. It is easy to understand Bevan's distaste for this rear-area establishment – full of resupply materiel, leaderless reinforcements, sick and malingerers and those trying their best to avoid the dangers of being in action. He was also worried about a lack of money, no doubt because of the expense of equipping himself properly for his new status. To add to the gloom, the useless General Erskine took over command of the division from a sick predecessor. It is difficult today to understand, sometimes, how and why Wellington put up with low-grade generals such as Erskine and Brent Spencer. One can only assume that quality at that level was scarce, reinforced by some of them having political power and influence at home to maintain their positions. Allied to this there were very few who had experience of handling large bodies of troops in battle.

By early spring 1811, Masséna had had enough of sitting in front of the Lines of Torres Vedras and, with starvation and sickness daily reducing his force, decided to withdraw back into Spain. Wellington seized the chance to pursue him. Sadly, due to the absence on leave of the redoubtable 'Black Bob' Craufurd, Erskine was transferred to command the Light Division. Comments of those in the elite regiments of the 95th and 52nd were predictable. Needless to say, when he had the chance of trapping the French at Casa Nova in March, Erskine made a nonsense and the 52nd were badly cut off and suffered unnecessary casualties.

Bevan and the 4th were not involved in any action but plodded on in the morale-raising knowledge that they were chasing a fleeing enemy. He did, however, manage to write a number of letters home that were full of the things typical of soldiers down the ages: separation from family, physical discomfort, lack of good food and boots, iniquities of the commissariat, tiresome fatigues and low standards and behaviour of the enemy. His battalion was also suffering. It had landed in Portugal in October 1810 with the strength of about 1,000 men but the exertions of campaigning in the field had renewed the effects of Walcheren fever. It would shortly be reduced to only 600 men.

By April, Masséna had taken up a defensive position on the line of the Côa River and Wellington was determined to force a crossing at Sabugal. Bridges then, as now, were important factors in any operation and particularly so when the rivers in Portugal and Spain were often unfordable and many ran through steep ravines. With thick fog descending, two of the sensible divisional commanders decided to delay; not so Erskine, who ordered his men forward across the river without any idea of where the French were or in what strength. Near disaster was averted only by the bravery and courage of the British soldiers who found themselves facing overwhelming enemy numbers with the river at their back. Masséna, however, continued his retreat into Spain and, leaving General Antoine Brennier to garrison the town of Almeida, withdrew to Salamanca to plan further offensives. Bevan, who had only actually seen action in Egypt and to a lesser extent on the retreat to Corunna, must have been wondering when he was going to have a chance to command his battalion under fire.

The Battle of Fuentes de Oñoro, which took place in early May, was one of Wellington's 'worse scrapes' and, he confessed that had Napoleon been there, he would have been beaten. Nevertheless, it was a success by a narrow margin, with many casualties on both sides. Masséna, whose aim had been to relieve the besieged Almeida, failed and he was subsequently removed from command. No doubt to his fury, Bevan was not involved in the battle, Erskine's 5th Division barely featuring. Was Erskine not to be trusted after his two previous debacles?

The French garrison at Almeida was now isolated and impossible to replenish, so Masséna determined that it should break out. Governor Brennier's instructions were to evacuate the fort by night and head for the French lines in a north-easterly direction, crossing the bridge over the Agueda River at Barba del Puerco. The road and the bridge itself were built by the Romans in the 1st century BC. It was designed for foot and mule traffic rather than wheeled vehicles. It is about 165 feet long, 15 feet wide and 66 feet high. The road on the western side drops down some 755 feet from the level of the plateau above down the ravine to the river. At the final approach down by the bridge the drop is almost vertical. The original road surface is largely still in place. The bridge (now named Puerto Seguro), even today, remains a masterpiece of construction.

The responsibility for blockading Almeida fell to Major General Campbell's 6th Division. The 5th Division, in support under Erskine, was given clear deployment instructions on 9 May. This included the directive to place a battalion 2 or 3 miles beyond Fort Conception and deploy picquets over various rivulets. The battalion was Bevan's 4th Foot, positioned some 6–8 miles to the east of Almeida and approximately 8–10 miles from the Barba del Puerco bridge. The trap was set for the escaping French. Or was it?

Wellington ordered a Distribution of the Army (Operation Order) on 10 May, in writing, via the quartermaster general, in which a battalion from

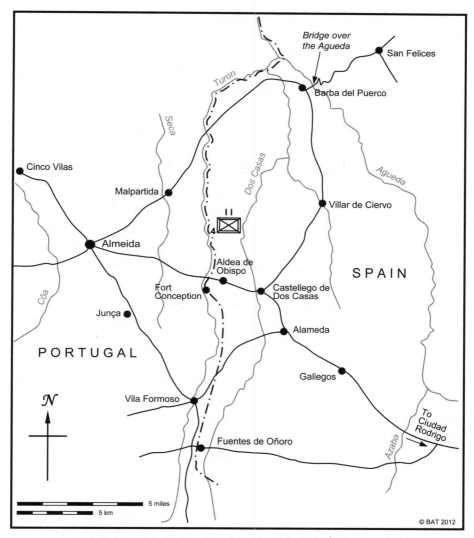

Escape of the French from Almeida, 10/11 May 1811

Erskine's division was to deploy, specifically, to the Barba del Puerco bridge
to guard it. This would be perfectly understandable, given the importance
of the bridge. Indeed, it would be inconceivable that it should remain
unguarded. It is unlikely he would specify which battalion (although he
says he ordered the 4th when discussing the matter with Stanhope in 1836.
At the same time he admits that no one can agree as to the exact time the

Battle of Waterloo began, so his memory is not 100 per cent). The battalion would be a matter for Erskine or one of his subordinate brigade commanders to nominate. Again, there are differences as to the time the 10 May order reached Erskine, but the generally accepted view is that it was around four o'clock in the afternoon; indeed, Wellington says exactly that in his dispatch to Lord Liverpool on 15 May 1811.

Most commentators believe that Erskine certainly failed to react immediately and the order to the 4th to proceed to the bridge was not issued until midnight or thereabouts. Again, although even eyewitness accounts in history are not always totally reliable, there is absolutely nothing to suggest that the order *was* issued immediately. Edward Pakenham, who was present and a pretty reliable witness, says Erskine put the order in his pocket and forgot about it. Given Erskine's myopia, fondness for drink and general inadequacy of which there *is* much evidence, it is not difficult to believe.

Assuming that Bevan did receive his orders at midnight, why did he not react immediately? He was a competent professional soldier who would have easily grasped the importance of getting to the bridge as quickly as possible. A good battalion, even at rest, can start moving within the hour. He could have been at the bridge by 3 or 4 a.m. There has been much speculation since. It ranges from Bevan thinking that he should keep his men in their present position (to oppose enemy he thought were in his area and merely send a patrol to the Barba del Puerco bridge), to waiting for dawn in order to find his way in the light, or waiting for guides to show him the way. Another conjecture is that he was advised by his subordinate officers not to start until daybreak. Bevan was hardly the man to pay attention to that if he thought otherwise. Whatever the explanation, none of it really holds water to excuse Bevan's delay. He knew the importance of the mission and there was no reason not to get going at once. It has been argued that there was no intelligence that the French were *actually* on the move that night and therefore it might have been sensible for Bevan to wait for dawn. However, in terms of getting a guard to the bridge as soon as possible for the eventuality of a French breakout *at any time*, this is difficult to sustain.

General Brennier was an experienced and resourceful officer. He was in no doubt how difficult it was to extract some 1,400 of his troops from the town and make it safely to the French Army now in the Ciudad Rodrigo area. He also needed to destroy as much as he could in Almeida that could be of use to the allies, including, in particular, his guns, which he could not take with him. At 11.30 p.m., Brennier's men silently left the town in two columns. They made their first contact with elements of the British cordon just as their demolitions in Almeida started to go off, confusing and disorientating their opponents. Brennier had planned indirect routes and deliberately did not use local guides in order to preserve utmost secrecy. Nevertheless, his rear, with his baggage, and flanks were harassed by the British. Despite that, the two columns reached the west bank of the Agueda at dawn in good order and to their intense joy and surprise found the bridge unguarded. The French had sent troops from General Jean Reynier's II Corps to set up a bridgehead the other side of Barba del Puerco to protect Brennier's crossing.

It is difficult, even by the standards of the time, to understand how Brennier could have evaded the allied cordon and picquets. The British knew he had to evacuate Almeida and knew the only course open to him was to rejoin the main army by travelling eastwards and cross by a number of bridges over the Agueda with Barba del Puerco the most likely. Campbell had the whole of his 6th Division, augmented by a Portuguese independent infantry brigade and a cavalry brigade, to prevent this. Indifference and apathy seemed to reign.

There were, however, exceptions to this and some resolute and determined well-led troops did manage to attack parts of the French columns, but they were uncoordinated and lacked the strength and information to prevent the columns reaching the bridge. As Brennier's men arrived at the bridge and started to cross, the 36th Regiment of Foot, joined now by Bevan's 4th, caught up with them. But it was too late. There then followed a frenzied, confused action with British and French tumbling down into the ravine and courageous assaults across the bridge being met with devastating covering fire from the French bridgehead the other side of the river. For Brennier, it was a success against considerable odds. Out of his 1,400 men, he lost 360 killed and wounded and another 200 taken prisoner.

As a postscript, many years later Wellington was discussing with Earl Stanhope the benefit or otherwise of sacking a town that failed to give in to its besiegers. 'I had some intimation of General Brennier's purpose' he said, 'to blow up the place and retire, and I sent him word that if he did, he and every man we could catch should have no quarter. It is contrary to the laws of nations; and troops so conducting themselves are not entitled to consider themselves prisoners of war.'

'It was, then, very brave of General Brennier to venture?' queried Stanhope.

'Why, if it had come to the point, I dare say I should not have done it. But Brennier had another motive. I had seen him before: I had taken him prisoner at Vimiera [sic]. Before he was exchanged he came to me in London, told me he was in difficulty, and I lent him £500. I dare say he thought if I had taken him prisoner I should have made him pay me. I have never seen him since. I heard no more of the money.'

So, now the explanations and excuses. Wellington was understandably infuriated. Both Campbell's and Erskine's reports embroidered the truth. Campbell's dispatch asserting that he had destroyed or captured the greater part of the garrison was blatantly untrue and Erskine's excuse that the 4th had lost their way to Barba del Puerco was equally false. Wellington himself exaggerated the real facts by reporting that had the 4th reached the bridge earlier, Brennier would have surrendered. Given the strength of the French bridgehead on the eastern side of the river, this is highly unlikely.

Harry Smith of the 95th Regiment was pretty clear: 'Now occurred the dreadful disaster of the escape of the French garrison of Almeida. I shall never forget the mortification of our soldiers or the admiration of our officers of the brilliancy of such an attempt, the odds being a hundred to one against success. My long friend Ironmonger [sic], then of the Queen's ... was grievously to blame.' Iremonger was commanding officer of the 2nd Regiment of Foot, who had been particularly inactive when it was reported to him the French had contacted his picquets on their way out of Almeida.

A further point that historians have, to a certain extent, overlooked is, if Bevan had reached the bridge before Brennier, what next? Bevan did not know the ground, whereas Brennier might well have done given the importance of this critical path to his escape. Bevan would have arrived in the dark with the French bridgehead force already in place on the eastern side of the river. His battalion of, say, 400 would be facing Brennier's 1,000 plus, with a strong enemy force at his back. The bridge itself, at the bottom of a very steep ravine, was a difficult position to defend. What were his options? To put a suicidal block of men on the bridge itself? Defend the bridge from the height of the western plateau, with his back to the ravine? Or to ambush the French as they approached from the west? Even by today's standards, not an enviable task for a commanding officer. However, this is not to excuse Bevan's failure to march at midnight; had he done so, whatever the outcome of the battle on the bridge, Brennier would hardly have succeeded as well as he did.

In his letter of 15 May 1811 to his wife, Bevan only fleetingly referred to the Barba del Puerco episode: 'On the 11 we had a skirmish with the garrison of Almeida on their retreat but were unfortunately a little too late to do more than what you will see by the Papers took place – these events is a matter of great annoyance to us all.' Bevan lost the first casualties since he took over command; two killed and one officer and ten other ranks wounded. Being totally unaware of how Wellington was reporting this 'annoyance', Bevan continued with his battalion southwards, still in the 5th Division, to besiege Badajoz. This was abandoned for the time being and the 4th fell back on the town of Portalegre at the end of June.

It was then Bevan discovered, from newspapers now reaching them, how Wellington had portrayed the debacle in his dispatch of 15 May, in which he roundly blamed the whole affair on the 4th for losing its way and being too late to prevent Brennier's escape over the bridge. The report was compounded by a further letter in which Wellington asserted the 4th was much closer to the bridge than it actually was. Bevan was understandably devastated. Not only was his personal honour at stake but so was the reputation of his regiment. His reaction was to request a hearing of his side of the story. It is not clear whether this was a formal inquiry or court martial and there is no documentation to support it either way. However, it must be assumed that Bevan was determined, if not to have himself and his battalion completely exonerated, then to demonstrate that the blame was not entirely theirs and there were others involved.

Wellington was not interested. Many things had gone wrong in the course of the campaign; this was merely one of them. Someone was to blame and it was easiest to fasten it onto Bevan and the 4th without wasting time to discover who else was responsible. In talks with Earl Stanhope many years later, he is very dismissive and comments sourly that, 'It was this blowing up of Almeida [by Brennier] and my waiting to see if it would be prepared, that made me too late for Albuera.' Wellington had a war to run, had moved on and was not concerned with involving himself in what he would have regarded as a relatively minor setback at the time. Present-day commentators label him as insensitive and uncaring but that is a misjudgement. He was a man subject to emotion like many of his contemporaries but he was also a man apart. He was a hard man with a mission. He was the commander-in-chief and had to see things, if not globally, then certainly in the context of the Iberian Peninsula and beating the French generals; wasting time on a lieutenant colonel was not a priority.

In the depths of despair and depression, believing he had failed his men, his family and himself, Bevan shot himself on 8 July at Portalegre.

The army was profoundly shocked. A commanding officer committing suicide is deeply disturbing, not only for the staff and commanders who have to deal with the aftermath but also the soldiers themselves who are so reliant on the robustness of their leaders. A cover-up was therefore put in place. This cover-up was not to protect the army – its people would have known full well the reality – but to shield Bevan's wife, who was told that he had died of fever. We know that the residual effect of Walcheren fever was still being felt and, like his predecessor, Bevan could easily have fallen victim. However, given that in his last letter to her of 4 July he makes no mention of any illness, this must have surprised her. James Dacres, Mary Bevan's brother serving in the Royal Navy, and Jim Paterson of the 28th, married to Mary's sister Eleanor, played significant parts in the plot.

In a letter of 15 October 1811, Dacres, in response to Mary's queries, wrote:

> Bevan had the advice of the Surgeon of the Regiment previous to the violence of the attacks commencing, but no danger was then feared, the violence of the fever rendered him delirious, and when that abated, he was too insensible to speak to anyone or to take any

particular notice, his fever seized him very violently on the evening of the 5th, after he reached Portalegre, accompanied by violent retchings, the Medical people pronounced his disorder to proceed from bile, producing an inflammation on his stomach. He became delirious during the night which lasted with some intermission till the middle of the 7th, after which he continued without any appearance of pain in a kind of stupor till the morning of the 8th, on which his Spirit left the Mortal Mansion; from the time of his illness became so very decided he was never in a state to allow any religious duties being performed, or of entering into any conversation.

Dacres had earlier written to her, on 11 July, telling her of all the funeral arrangements and headstone, etc. Was this too a fabrication by his regiment? Did the funeral and firing party actually take place at all? Was there a headstone really put in place?

Had his suicide been official, Mary would not have received a pension. However, she did so, which shows that the cover-up was also sanctioned at a high level, probably by the Military Secretary at the time, Colonel Torrens. Quite remarkably, no more was heard of this affair for twenty-two years.

On 11 July 1843, Charles Bevan, Bevan's son, now in his thirties, wrote to his uncle, James Dacres:

You are always kindly interested in my brothers and me, that I think no apology necessary in applying to you for information on a subject which has occasioned us, of late, much pain and anxiety.

It has very lately come to my knowledge that my father put an end to his own life, and that this shocking event was mainly attributable to some real or imaginary disgrace brought upon himself and his Corps at the time of the evacuation of Almeida by the French, under General Brennier.

Without troubling you for any detailed account of this affair (which I can get from other sources) I wish you would tell me plainly whether my father was, in the opinion of competent judges, really culpable or not, and whether the circumstances of this melancholy business are such as will bear further enquiries by his sons.

His uncle replied by return, and it is worth reading his letter in its entirety:

What you heard about your dear Father, is too correct, but not the slightest blame was thrown upon his character by military men, or any person who knew the circumstances. The escape of the garrison of Almeida being expected Wellington sent orders to Sir W. Erskine to place the 4th Regiment in a particular position to intercept them. He was asleep, and as they say, drunk, and the dispatch was not opened, or orders sent to the 4th until daylight, when it was too late for them to reach the position in time; but no blame was laid to them, and nothing was thought about it till the Gazette came out from England, in which Lord Wellington said 'owing to the neglect of the 4th Foot, the Garrison made their escape!'

Your father directly applied for a Court Martial or enquiry; which the Duke declined, saying it was 'somebody's fault'. Your father was much hurt, and after repeated refusals of his application to the Duke for justice, and having no particular friend near him, he committed the melancholy act, leaving a note for Paterson who was away, saying he considered his military character tarnished.

The event caused great excitement in the Army, and so much was said by some of the higher officers that a Colonel Cockrane was sent home; some time afterwards Sir W. Erskine when at Lisbon threw himself out of a window in a fit of insanity brought on by drink, and was killed.

Every officer there considered your father a very ill-used man; but he had the most romantic ideas of military honour. In 1809 when Sir Hew Dalrymple came home from Lisbon, he always used to say to me that Sir Hew, if he had a true military feeling, would have shot himself. It is, I believe, still unknown to your Mother. I wished to have broken it to you and your brothers when you went to Oxford, thinking you might have heard it there, but your Grandmother would not allow it, and I was in hopes you would not have heard it. I send you my mother's letter, which, when you have read, burn. That was one of the reasons your Grandmother and Aunts always objected to any of you going into the Army.

Not the slightest slur was ever thrown on your father's character, but in the excitement of an active and bloody campaign the thing was dropt without any notice, by the Horse Guards, the Duke then beginning to be all-powerful. I was in America at the time.

———

Does Bevan therefore fit the criteria of the scapegoat? First of all, was he in any way to blame for his predicament? He was certainly not to blame for receiving his orders much later that he should have done. However, there is no substantial reason for his delay thereafter. He must be, therefore, partially at fault. Who benefited by blaming him? Wellington? It was more of a quick convenience to blame Bevan and then move on. It certainly had no impact on his career or standing, and he was not even mildly censured from England. Indeed, his brother William wrote, 'I think you are now above any Intrigue that can be formed or initiated against you.' Was he, though, a bad selector of subordinates? Erskine, Dalrymple and Brent Spencer should have been sacked long ago. Or was he saddled with them by the Horse Guards? Erskine? Certainly, in his befuddled state, he was to blame. He was clearly inadequate and sought to cover his error by insinuating that Bevan had lost his way, conveniently forgetting he had issued orders late. Campbell and his division? A number of his commanders were lethargic or badly positioned. Campbell undoubtedly should have produced a better plan for stopping Brennier. The latter's escape out of Almeida with 1,400 says it all. Campbell was never given independent command again.

Had there been a proper inquiry, it could have been argued that Bevan was not blameless, but he was unquestionably not wholly responsible for the escape of the French from Almeida and their crossing of the bridge at Barba del Puerco. His memorial, re-constructed by his descendants, now lies in the little British cemetery in the town of Elvas.

A man who has no memorial, and is now forgotten, lived fifty years before Bevan. Dupleix was Robert Clive's French equivalent in India. Had he been supported properly by his government, it might have been a French, rather than a British, Raj. Was he a scapegoat for the French East India Company's inadequacy or did he bring much of his misfortune on himself by his grandiose ideas?

ELEVEN

Marquis Joseph
François Dupleix

Nawab of the Carnatic

August 1754

On 1 August 1754, a French ship, the *Duc de Burgogne*, anchored
in the Pondicherry sound. On board was a senior director of the
Compagnie Française des Indes Orientales ('the Compagnie'). He was
Charles-Robert Godeheu, carrying sealed orders that spelt the end for
the Marquis Joseph François Dupleix, governor of all French possessions in India. Godeheu was to replace Dupleix, if necessary place him
under arrest and return him, and his family, in disgrace, to France. To
give weight to his mission, he was accompanied by 2,000 soldiers. He
was to instigate a comprehensive investigation into Dupleix's accounts
and administration, make peace with the English at virtually any cost and
initiate an exit strategy for the Compagnie from India. How did a man of
Dupleix's power and influence reach such a depth?

Eighteenth-century India was a land of the decaying, and increasingly
impotent, Mughal Empire vainly trying to exert its dying power from
Delhi. Ambitious and arrogant Indian princes took the opportunity to
establish their own power bases safe from interference. Intrigue, nepotism and assassination came as second nature and the establishment of
large, showy but relatively ineffectual armies cowed less powerful neighbours into submission. Punitive extraction of tribute and annexation of
land became normal behaviour.

Relationships with the early colonists from Portugal, the Netherlands,
England and France were uneasy but mutually beneficial when the latter

could produce European goods in exchange for jewellery, spice, indigo and sandalwood, and pay rent for trading bases. European mercenaries were eagerly sought after to train Indian troops and even small detachments of European soldiers could make a difference far exceeding their numerical strength when allied to a prince's army. It was a land of opportunity, not only for the government-backed trading companies but also for individuals escaping the restrictions of life at home to make vast fortunes and live a life of luxury unheard of in Europe. Wealthy *nabobs* returning to England bought their way into Parliament and married off their daughters to impoverished aristocrats inevitably earning the secret envy and disdain of the gentry who despised their behaviour and newfound wealth.

Dupleix's life in India from his arrival in August 1722 until his recall was inextricably woven into the relationship between the Compagnie and the English East India Company. Both were governed by directors at home who were on a loose rein from their governments. Concentrating the latter's minds, and therefore pushing the importance of their Indian possessions into the background, was the long-running sore of the European conflict of the War of the Austrian Succession and the following Seven Years War. This allowed people like Dupleix and Clive to carve their own empires with little interference. Dupleix saw himself as an organiser, administrator and merchant. By inclination, he abhorred the use of force, yet was inevitably sucked into it in his dealings with the wily Indian princes.

The Compagnie had a relatively slow start compared to the Portuguese, Dutch and English equivalents. It was not until 1664 that Colbert, Louis XIV's astute financial minister, realising the wealth being accrued from India by the others, established a company with a capital of 15 million francs and a concession for exclusive trading for fifty years. There were clever clauses in the contract that attracted entrepreneurial spirits. However, failure to establish an initial 'halfway house' in Madagascar led to disappointment and it was not until the end of 1667 that the first trading post was firmly set up in India. After fluctuating fortunes, an area of land of over 100 square miles, with Pondicherry at its core, was leased from the local ruler some 86 miles south of the English settlement of Madras (modern-day Chennai) on the Coromandel Coast.

Despite disinterest from Paris, the small post prospered to such an extent that it provoked the envious Dutch into taking it over. This concentrated the minds of the Government and it was restored to France by treaty. From 1701 it was governed by an officer from the Compagnie designated 'Director-General of all French possessions in India'. By the time of the expiry of the original charter, however, its treasury had reached, yet again, a low ebb. In 1720, the financial crash in France with John Law's Mississippi scheme forced the government into granting perpetual privileges to the Compagnie, in exchange for debt cancellations and allowing it to become a private commercial association independent of the State. The Compagnie, however, never freed itself of financial worry.

As with all distant overseas possessions, survival very often depended entirely on how many ships got through to them and then, in turn, how many safely made the return journey. Hazards of navigation, weather and pirates put them constantly at high risk. The Pondicherry settlement was not exempt and, in 1721, to the great relief of the new governor, there arrived three heavily laden merchantmen, enabling him to settle some critical debts in the region with the profits from the cargo. This was, however, only a brief respite. Due to the ongoing financial problems at home not a single ship was sent for the next three years. Confidence in the Compagnie from the local rulers and traders was slipping away. However, a refinancing of the Compagnie allowed it, from 1723 to 1730, to send three or four ships a year thus, once again pushing it into profit.

In 1735, the very able Benoît Dumas arrived to take over and had considerable success as an administrator. He was able to take advantage of the friendly overtures from the Nawab of the Carnatic and, taking a risk by taking sides against the Nawab's enemies by supplying him with money, gunpowder and warlike stores – in strict contradiction to Compagnie policy – he managed to secure a valuable strategic hold on the coast of Tanjore (now Thanjavur). Such was now the confidence of the local rulers in the French that they readily turned to them for help when the particularly vicious Marathas invaded the south of the Carnatic. Dumas calculated that although he would antagonise the Marathas by siding with his local princes, much benefit would later accrue to Pondicherry on the inevitable withdrawal of the Marathas and the restitution of power to the Carnatic rulers. He made a particular ally of Chunda Sahib, a man who was to be of significance to the French in the coming years.

Dumas faced down the threat from the Marathas and cleverly negotiated their departure to western India. The directors of the Compagnie conveniently forgot their strictures about not giving aid to the princes in return for revenue from land and treated Dumas's operation as a purely commercial transaction. Covered in decorations and laden with gifts and jewels from the grateful rulers, Dumas ended his time in India and returned to France, giving firm direction as to where he considered the best interests of France lay to his successor, Joseph François Dupleix.

But what of their most serious rival, the English East India Company ('the Company')? The Company had been given a monopoly of all English trade throughout Asia by royal grant at its foundation in 1600. Through many ups and downs, it evolved into a commercial concern to match its biggest rival, the Dutch East India Company. Directors, elected annually by the shareholders, ran the Company's operations from its headquarters in London. Towards the end of the seventeenth century, the Company's main effort turned to India. Cheap cotton was imported into Britain in huge quantities. The Company's main settlements in Bombay, Madras and Calcutta were established in the Indian provinces where cotton was readily available. These settlements had evolved from small trading posts into major commercial towns under British jurisdiction as Indian merchants and artisans moved in to do business with the Company and with the British inhabitants. There was considerable local skill in weaving cloth and winding raw silk for little pay. Agricultural implements were cheaply produced and sugar, indigo, saltpetre, spices and opium were readily available. English merchants whose ships made it home reaped enormous profits.

The Company's Indian trade in the first half of the eighteenth century was comfortable and prosperous and even extended to the Persian Gulf, Southeast Asia and East Asia. By 1740, its trade volume was twice as much as the French. The Company was run by businessmen, not adventurers or empire builders; their aim was, like any other commercial company, to make profits for the shareholders. They had no wish to fight either the Indians or their European rivals. Warfare was expensive. Nevertheless, they were, inevitably, drawn into taking sides with rival factions in Indian politics in order to preserve their own integrity and protect their interests. They were forced to create their own militia rather than an army, often officered by completely inexperienced Company men. From time to time,

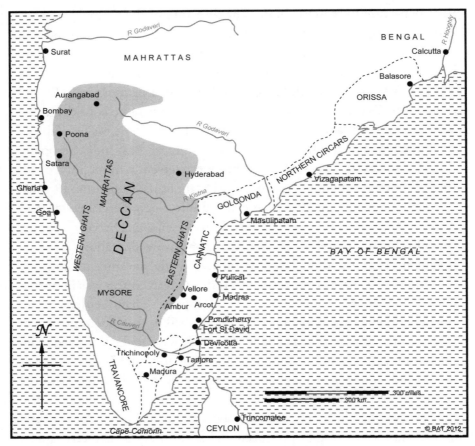

South India, eighteenth century

like the French, in emergency, professional soldiers were sent from the home country. It wasn't until the second half of the century when the more aggressive freebooters arrived and set themselves up as quasi-mercenaries – under the Company's umbrella – that the idea of extensive possessions and, ultimately, an empire came into being.

Early twentieth-century commentators were divided as to whether Dupleix was a self-promoting, arrogant chancer lining his own pockets, disobeying Compagnie instructions and failing to remit any revenue to France, or a visionary who acquired territory and created the start of an empire that, through lack of support from the Compagnie and France, fell to the English. It was certainly convenient, when France could see failure in India as inevitable, to blame Dupleix, return him to France and leave him to die in despair and penury. But how much of that did he bring on himself? Was he really a scapegoat?

Aged 23, Dupleix was packed off to India where he joined the Compagnie, of which his father was a director, in 1720. He soon demonstrated his business qualities by embarking on some private trade of his own, which was, at that time, sanctioned by the Compagnie, and amassing, but also losing, a small fortune. He was posted to Chandannagar in 1731, then a sleepy, run-down outpost in Bengal where, within four years he had revived its prosperity; in his ten years there he trebled the Compagnie's revenues in Bengal. Marked for promotion by Dumas, he succeeded him in Pondicherry in October 1741, taking the oath as governor general of the French possessions in India. Before that, he married the widow of a business partner of his, Vincens, to whom he owed money. (Cynics, at the time, declared this to be a convenient way of settling debts.) Madame Dupleix was a clever, scheming woman, with the ability to speak Tamil, who relished intrigue and was said to have had her own spy network. However, by all accounts she was devoted to her husband, but her mach-inations on his behalf were not always that skilful and some of her own frolics into commerce and business led to disaster.

The War of the Austrian Succession had begun in 1740, when Frederick II of Prussia defeated the Austrians. The fear then was that war would envelop the whole of Europe. France allied herself with Bavaria and Spain and, later, with Saxony and Prussia against Austria. The Austrians were supported by Great Britain, which feared that, if the French were successful in Europe, its commercial and colonial inter-ests would suffer. War between the two was declared in 1744. An uneasy peace of a sort was achieved by the Treaty of Aix-la-Chapelle in October 1748 but there remained the lingering enmity between France and Britain which, effectively, lasted until 1815. While not directly affecting Dupleix or the English in India, it took the concentration of their respective directors off the main effort and certainly removed any hope of prac-tical assistance from their governments. Dupleix was ordered therefore to avoid any armed conflict at all costs and the British were confined to preserving their sea lanes. It was another tiresome dimension in already difficult commercial affairs.

Dupleix was nervous of a British attack on the relatively defenceless Pondicherry either from the sea or overland from Madras. He consequently approached the Nawab of the Carnatic and reminded him of their friendly relationship, particularly during the time of the Maratha invasion, and sought his assistance to persuade the English, also the Nawab's tenants, from attacking any French settlements. The Nawab agreed but also told the English he would forbid the French from attacking them. This clearly could not extend to the sea, however, and in January 1745 some French ships were captured in the Strait of Malacca by the British. This was a blow, not only to the Compagnie but also personally to Dupleix who had a financial interest in the cargo. As far as Dupleix was concerned this annulled his 'agreement' with the Nawab not to attack the English.

Conveniently entering the equation appeared Admiral La Bourdonnais, governor of Bourbon and Mauritius. La Bourdonnais was an energetic professional sailor of considerable quality with extensive sea warfare experience. More of a swashbuckler and privateer, he preferred the swift cutting out operation to lengthy, boring cat and mouse manoeuvres. He had already seen off some ineffectual English shipping and was now anxious to consolidate success and ruin English commerce. Characteristically, on war being declared between Britain and France, he ignored the Compagnie's orders not to engage in a battle. He was just the man to satisfy Dupleix's desire for revenge.

For both Dupleix and La Bourdonnais, the English possession, Madras, was a jewel worth having and its capture had long been in their minds, even to the extent of splitting the cost of the operation between the Compagnie and themselves. Madras, with its fort of St George, was the richest town on the Coromandel Coast with a population of 250,000. However, its defences had been neglected, mainly due to the Company's lack of interest and it relied for protection on the mutual 'understanding' with the French, the Nawab's agreement and its small fleet off the coast. So throughout 1745 the two Frenchmen made preparations – La Bourdonnais fitting out ships and Dupleix assembling stores and receiving intelligence from his wife's spies in Madras.

Uncharacteristically, La Bourdonnais then started to backtrack and put the weight of responsibility in the event of failure onto Dupleix. He also suggested that the destruction of the British fleet was essential before an attack on Madras. Astonishingly their directors were oblivious to what was going on and told La Bourdonnais that a squadron was being sent to him from France and he was to use it to patrol the Bay of Bengal against British shipping. He was to return to Bourbon and Mauritius in mid 1746 and send the squadron back the following year. However, there was a let-out; he could alter the plans in consultation with Dupleix. What more could he ask?

In September, La Bourdonnais sailed for Madras. He landed a force that, after a short bombardment, marched on Fort St George and demanded the surrender of Madras, which quickly gave in. Before he left Pondicherry, Dupleix had suggested to La Bourdonnais that the English be allowed to buy off their attackers with a substantial ransom, the restitution of the captured French ships and an undertaking to observe neutrality east of the Cape of Good Hope for the rest of the war in Europe. La Bourdonnais had not agreed to this and reported that Madras had surrendered unconditionally. Responding to opportunity as ever, Dupleix told him to ignore the ransom option, sack the fort and dismantle its defences with a view to handing it over to the Nawab. La Bourdonnais had no intention of doing any such thing. The prize was his and he was going to make the most of it, personally supervising a systematic plunder. He then came to a private and highly dubious financial agreement with the English governor, Morse, to restore the fort on the payment of a considerable amount of money and hand Madras back to the English after a period of 'parole'. The accusation of accepting bribes was to dog him, justifiably, for the rest of his life.

Dupleix was incandescent; his relationship with the Nawab, who felt he had been duped, was now fragile, he had exhausted the funds in Pondicherry, the treasure in Madras had disappeared, the town itself was being given back to the English and the culprit, La Bourdonnais, was sailing away to Mauritius with his squadron (and loot).

Dupleix swiftly repudiated the agreement La Bourdonnais had made with the English but not before the Nawab, livid with what he considered a breaking of an agreement, sent his son with a considerable force to capture Madras. Dupleix instructed the French occupying Madras to hold it while he sent reinforcements from Pondicherry. With their water cut off, the French made a spirited sortie, driving off the leading elements of the Nawab's army and inflicting a number of casualties with no loss to themselves. Dupleix's relieving force under an efficient Swiss engineer officer called Paradis routed the ambushing Indians in the village of St Tomé. Interestingly, this demonstrated the weakness of the native armies in the face of determined, even if smaller in number, European troops. For the first time, the Europeans realised they no longer needed to be vassals of the Nawab of the Carnatic – their troops, whether as allies or opponents, were extremely strong cards. Entering Madras, Paradis issued a proclamation annulling the ransom treaty made by La Bourdonnais and proceeded to destroy the fortifications. The English were treated as prisoners of war, among whom was Dupleix's future nemesis, the young Robert Clive.

Clearly this had been a very difficult time for Dupleix. He was not a soldier and saw things as a businessman and sought diplomatic solutions to problems. This is what he was best at. He had now been badly let down by La Bourdonnais, alienated the Nawab and lost any good faith with the English. He had been forced to take up arms, not only against the English but also the Nawab. This was not conducive to future good commerce. However, the game had now radically changed with the very visible superiority of the European soldiers over the native armies. Dupleix may not have liked it but it was now a major factor in any assessment of a situation and he was far too astute not to take advantage of this. From this point it has been argued that Dupleix saw India not just as a collection of trading bases but something much bigger – an empire with, of course, him at the head.

A mere 16 miles south of Pondicherry lay Fort St David, an ill-defended and poorly garrisoned English possession. With Madras in his hands, Dupleix only had to take over St David and the Coromandel Coast was his. With his newfound power, he ignored the Nawab and sent an expedition to St David to subdue it. Sadly, it was led by a thoroughly incompetent officer who panicked when the Nawab's army appeared and rushed back to the safety of Pondicherry. A second attack, this time from the sea, was aborted when rough weather intervened. Dupleix realised that with the Nawab siding with the English, taking St David was going to be difficult, so he set about detaching the Nawab from his allegiance and persuaded him that France was the winning side.

This was not difficult as the English were now in dire straits. They were incapable of reinforcing St David from Madras, which was still under French occupancy. Two of their ships coming in, ignorant of the situation, were promptly captured and a third took fright and sailed for Bengal without landing a single soldier. At last, in February, a fourth ship landed twenty recruits and a large sum of silver at St David. However, a fortnight later a French force under the competent Paradis arrived in front of the fort. Had he been a little earlier he would have undoubtedly taken it and the nearby town of Cuddalore but arriving at the same time came two ships under the experienced Admiral Griffin with a hundred European soldiers and native levies, mainly sepoys who were trained in the British fashion. This effectively held the French off without a fight.

In January 1748, a man arrived who was to become fundamental to the success of the British – Stringer Lawrence. Lawrence had joined the English Army in 1727 and was a tough professional soldier having fought at Culloden and Fontenoy. Clive subsequently served under him and they made a formidable pair. The first thing he did, on arrival, was to hang the governor of St David's interpreter, who had been caught spying for the French. Next, he repulsed the final French assault on St David and they were never to try again.

Dupleix now put to his directors three options for the disposal of Madras: the first was to exchange it for Louisbourg in Cape Breton, which had been captured by the English in 1745; second, restore it to the English on payment of a large ransom; or third, hand it over to a local ruler after demolishing the fortifications on the proviso that it could not be handed over to the English. The directors chose the last option and told Dupleix, in the autumn of 1748, to secure territory around Pondicherry that would produce substantial revenue. Dupleix therefore offered Madras to the ruler of the Deccan on that basis.

He now turned his attention to the defence of Pondicherry. As well he might because there had appeared a strong fleet off Pondicherry under the command of Admiral Boscawen. Luckily for Dupleix, Boscawen, with no knowledge of land operations, and his useless military engineers made a series of errors and after a seven weeks' siege, he was forced to give up with a loss of 1,000 men. Sadly, the French lost the excellent Paradis. While there is no evidence of any lack of courage on Dupleix's part, he simply did not have the soldier's instinct or flair. Leadership was foreign to him and he sought to impress with flamboyance rather than real skill. This may have worked with the Indian princes but not with his soldiers. He kept Pondicherry purely due to Boscawen's incompetence but his directors were suitably grateful.

Before negotiations over Madras could be concluded, the peace of Aix-la-Chapelle was reached in Europe, which stipulated that all possessions existing before the war should be returned to their owners. On the face of it that included Madras. Paradoxically though, Dupleix's standing with the native princes remained high: he had seen off Boscawen, St David was pretty ineffectual and Madras, which he had captured, had only gone back to the English because of a treaty in far off Europe.

There was a temptation to believe that now the war was over, the French and English companies could settle down to harmonious rivalry in trade alone. However, the Mughal Emperor died in April 1748 and the dynasty was riven by jealousies and in-fighting. This left the princes to squabble among themselves and seek alliances with their European friends with their powerful armies, which were now looking for something to do. To a certain extent the French were seeking to increase their political influence and power but, for the English, it was an extension and expansion of commerce.

A prime example was the pretender to the kingdom of Tanjore, one Shahojee. He promised the English to make over to them the fort and district of Devicotah, and pay for the expedition, if they would place him on the throne. In modern parlance this was a scam; Shahojee had no supporters in Tanjore and little intention of keeping his side of the bargain. The English, who should have been rather more careful, launched the operation, which resulted in a complete failure due to a storm wrecking their shipping and a pathetic skirmish with little zest against Tanjore troops. The English retired to St David. A second expedition was dispatched, this time under the redoubtable Lawrence. Some hard fighting ensued but before a conclusion could be reached, the chief of Tanjore sued for peace and ceded Devicotah to the English, who promised to control Shahojee.

For the French, it now seemed to be in their interests to pay the ransom for the release of their friend Chunda Sahib, who had been incarcerated by his enemies for seven years. His family, though, had been under Dupleix's protection in Pondicherry and channels of communication had therefore been kept open. It seemed to Dupleix that it would be advantageous to help Chunda Sahib to become Nawab of the Carnatic with his ally, Mozuffer Jung, on the throne of the Deccan, although he strongly distrusted the latter. With a loan of French troops, who did the majority of the fighting, this was achieved and the grateful princes made over some eighty villages to the Compagnie. The French view was that this was purely a mercenary transaction to advance commercial interests; it was not empire building.

There was considerable nervousness in the English camp but they were in no position to remonstrate with Dupleix on account of their own frolic into Tanjore. They were reasonably happy with anyone being the Nawab of the Carnatic as long as he was not under French influence. This certainly ruled out Chunda Sahib. However, they were heartened by the evacuation of Madras by the French under the terms of the Treaty of Aix-La-Chapelle. In October, Boscawen sailed for England thus removing the threat to the French and their allies. One must assume that the Admiralty had rather more pressing need for his services than an obscure settlement far away. (See Chapter 3 for Boscawen's membership of Admiral Byng's court martial). This was the chance Dupleix had been waiting for to quash the other contender for the Carnatic throne, Mahomed Ali, an ally of the English in Trichinopoly. He therefore launched Chunda Sahib and Mozuffer Jung with a strong army bolstered by 800 Europeans. They were, however, distracted and delayed besieging Tanjore in an attempt to extract money to support the large army. A cry for help from the ruler of Tanjore to the English resulted in a derisory body of twenty men being sent to assist. Nothing much happened until the French, becoming bored, carried out an assault themselves and reached terms. However, the news that Nazir Jung, another English ally, was entering the northern Carnatic with an army of 300,000 sent the princes scuttling back to Pondicherry. This army was made even more formidable when Lawrence joined it 15 miles outside Pondicherry with 600 European troops.

One of Dupleix's qualities was that when he was really up against it, he reacted strongly. This was no exception, so he pushed out the maximum force he could muster to confront Nazir Jung's army. To his disgust, on the eve of battle a number of French officers mutinied. The remainder of the army, with Chunda Sahib, retreated back to Pondicherry and Mozuffer Jung was made prisoner. Not to be daunted, Dupleix sought to drive a wedge between Nazir Jung and the English. He succeeded but probably more by Jung's arrogant and demanding behaviour, which drove Lawrence to give up in disgust and remove his men back to St David. Nazir Jung himself headed for Arcot where he lay about in indolence and apathy.

There now followed a series of manoeuvres and skirmishes between the Indian princes and their allies. The former, motivated by greed and ambition, infuriated the latter with their incompetence and lack of moral fibre. Dupleix, with a relatively free hand, was happy to advance funds to his princes whereas the English, under more control from their directors, would not take to the field without an up-front payment. Both quarrelled with their shifty and unreliable allies. Nevertheless, Dupleix had some notable successes, the main one of which was the virtual destruction of Mahomed Ali's army by the French. This made the English allies wonder, again, whether they were on the right side. The French seemed irresistible. Nazir Jung, with many of his men defecting, reached an agreement with Dupleix to cede everything the latter wanted, including the recognition of Chunda Sahib as the Nawab of the Carnatic and the release of Mozuffer Jung.

However, treachery was never far off, even among the French. Dupleix had carefully cultivated disaffection among Nazir Jung's nobles and at the next battle, Nazir Jung was assassinated, his head cut off and laid at the feet of Mozuffer Jung. The latter, now declared the ruler of the Deccan, proceeded with great pomp to Pondicherry to honour his benefactor and brother-in-arms, Dupleix. Considerable amounts of money, jewels and *jagirs* (parcels of land) were distributed.

This was the zenith of Dupleix's power. The Deccan and Carnatic rulers were in his pocket, Mahomed Ali's army had ceased to exist, Nazir Jung was dead, the English had lost Lawrence who had been invalided to England and were left skulking in St David. Mozuffer Jung left for his capital in the Deccan in January 1751, accompanied by a force of 300 Frenchmen and 1,500 sepoys, under command of the very capable Marquis Bussy-Castelnau. The latter was typical of the mercenary soldier of the time: loosely under command of the Compagnie, nevertheless, his object in life was to make a personal fortune. He had to be persuaded to accompany Mozuffer Jung with a considerable amount of money.

Yet again intrigue surfaced and Mozuffer Jung was killed in a skirmish with some of his turncoat nobles. Bussy, a mere captain, suddenly found himself in the role of king-maker as the succession, as in all Indian politics, was far from clear-cut. An acceptable ruler was nominated and Bussy was full of self-congratulation, somewhat to the annoyance of Dupleix, who did not want him getting above himself. Dupleix then launched into some wide-ranging political schemes involving negotiations with Delhi, the ceding of the nawabship of the Carnatic, (disregarding Chunda Sahib's right) and the kingship of Bengal to the ruler of the Deccan. He expressed interest in the Malabar Coast and Goa and began negotiations in respect of the Maldives and Cochin-China. It is not difficult to realise the consternation all this caused to the directors in Paris who could see it leading to war with the English, let alone various Indian princes. They ordered Dupleix to restrict his enterprises to more modest limits and concentrate on running the Carnatic. Dupleix clearly thought the directors out of touch and sent an emissary to Paris to put his case; all he did was sing Dupleix's praises. There were, however, the first stirrings of doubt about Dupleix.

English morale, by contrast, was at its lowest ebb. Saunders, a man of moderate ability and an interferer, became governor of St David, Lawrence left for England, sickened by the in-fighting, and Clive returned to his civilian occupation. Even their ally, Mahomed Ali, made overtures to Dupleix. This did not work and Dupleix dispatched a strong force to oust him from his lair in Trichinopoly. The English were in a real muddle but made one last throw. Earlier Clive had been in command of a small force in Trichinopoly and afterwards returned to Madras to explain the inadequacy of its defence. He suggested that the only way, now, of drawing off the besiegers of Trichinopoly was to take Arcot, the capital of the Carnatic.

To give Saunders his due, he reduced the garrisons of St David and

St George at Madras to the bare minimum to give Clive as much as he could. So, with just over 200 Europeans and 500 sepoys, Clive force-marched to Arcot in the heat of August. On arrival, to their joy, they found Arcot deserted by the enemy and the inhabitants very welcoming. Nevertheless, the defence of Arcot was going to take some doing with his small force; the keep was surrounded by houses giving cover to snipers, the defensive walls were in a state of disrepair and the towers crumbling. The news that Chunda Sahib was sending 2,000 horse to Arcot was worrying. The former garrison of the town was camped a few miles away and, having been reinforced, with increasing confidence, moved up to the walls of the city. As they were asleep on the night of 15 September, Clive launched a sudden and devastating attack on them. This was highly successful, resulting in the enemy bolting and abandoning their camp.

There followed desultory attacks by the enemy on the town, but Clive was able to repair some of his defences. However, news reached him that Raza Sahib, Chunda Sahib's son, was on his way with 4,000 men, including French, and that another 3,000 were reinforcing him. Clive was now down to 120 Europeans and 200 sepoys. On 23 September, the enemy entered the town, forcing Clive and his men to take refuge in the fort. Things were about as grim as they could get. Amazingly, he managed to maintain communications with Saunders through a series of intrepid runners. He told him the only salvation lay in reinforcements. Other Indian elements not involved in the siege of Arcot or Trichinopoly waited to see who was going to win before committing themselves. If Clive lost, southern India would be in French hands for the foreseeable future.

Early in November, the Regent of Mysore persuaded the Marathas to take a hand under their formidable leader, Morari Rao, but they wanted paying first. The reputation of the Marathas was such that the very thought of them appearing on the scene put fear into their enemies. This perhaps prompted Raza Sahib to try to negotiate Clive's surrender, which was rejected out of hand. As a result a very heavy attack, with elephants, was mounted on the fort shortly afterwards. Wave after wave of attackers was driven back but Clive and his men were now nearing the end of their resources. Thankfully, the fight had also gone out of the assaulting troops who had been consistently beaten off. As dawn rose, an exhausted Clive watched as the enemy withdrew, leaving their dead and dying decomposing in the sun. What Clive did not know, which Raza Sahib did, was that reinforcements were arriving from Madras and the fearsome Maratha cavalry was close at hand. It was a significant triumph, which, although Dupleix tried to laugh it off as a mere sideshow, came to show what the English, under Clive, could do. He had held Arcot for fifty days. It was a turning point in the war.

Clive followed this with a number of successes against Raza Sahib, including burning the village of Dupleix Futtehabad, which Dupleix had founded the year before on the spot where Nazir Jung had been murdered. This in itself was not important but was a blow against Dupleix's prestige and a significant public relations exercise when viewed by the Indian princes. Reinforcements now reached St David with the return from England of Stringer Lawrence with the title of commander-in-chief. Together with Clive, he immediately set off for Trichinopoly. (Lawrence and Clive had an extremely warm relationship, to such an extent that, many years later, when Lawrence had not lined his pockets as others had done, Clive looked after him financially.) The expedition was a success, with all the French and the whole of Chunda Sahib's army surrendering. Chunda Sahib was strangled and beheaded – such was the fate of failed chiefs at the time.

Dupleix must now have seen the writing on the wall. Yet he still had the ruler of the Deccan under Bussy's influence, received annual reinforcements from France and proclaimed Chunda Sahib's son Ali Reza Khan, Nawab of the Carnatic. He was not to be daunted. He had a minor success against the English at Gingee then, when 200 Swiss mercenaries in the pay of the English were sent by boat from Madras to reinforce St David, he ambushed them and took them prisoner. This particularly infuriated the English. France and Great Britain were at peace and the code in India was that you only took on the enemy as auxiliaries of the rival native princes. The sea, however, was open season. Added to La Bourdonnais's repudiation of the Madras agreement, the Swiss abduction was classed as international piracy. A seething Lawrence then sailed to St David determined to raise the French blockade. He did so and the French scuttled back to Pondicherry out of Lawrence's reach. However, moving up to Pondicherry, he managed to entice them out. There is disagreement by historians whether the exit was at Dupleix's instigation or

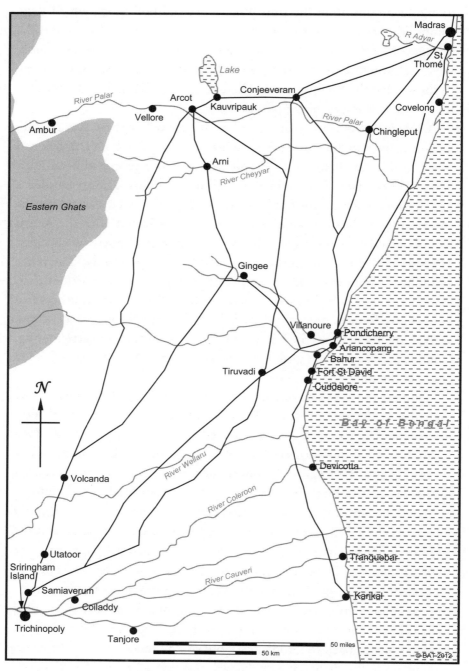

The Carnatic, eighteenth century

the hot-headed French commander. Either way, Lawrence soundly beat them. This was the first time that both contestants revoked the fiction that they only operated as auxiliaries and purely stood against each other. Notwithstanding that, Louis XV made Dupleix a marquis.

Owing to ill health, Clive had to leave for England in 1753. The English Army was, however, in Lawrence's good hands. The same could not be said of the French. Their best, Bussy, was tied up in the Deccan and reinforcements from France under the redoubtable De La Touche sank with all hands before they could reach India. Dupleix was still, though, master of intrigue. Through Bussy's efforts, a grant was obtained that gave Dupleix control of 600 miles of sea coast and revenue of half a million sterling. The Regent of Mysore and the Maratha commander, Morari Rao, had been persuaded to switch sides to the French. With this advantage, it would have been the key moment to settle with the English. They were still defending Trichinopoly, which was cut off from the scantily garrisoned St David. However, they also knew of anti-Dupleix feeling arising in France and were prepared to negotiate terms in Mahomed Ali's name in July 1753. Dupleix was evasive and non-committal.

While Dupleix's directors were perfectly happy for him to acquire extra territory – and therefore increased revenue and trading opportunities – by intrigue and subterfuge, they baulked at his military forays, which seemed to produce disaster after disaster. His lieutenants – Law, Astruc, Brennier and even the Maratha horse – were simply not up to Lawrence, who destroyed them time after time. The shareholders were getting restive and Dupleix was told, in no uncertain terms, that peace was to be negotiated at any price. Interestingly, the English Company had paid dividends of 8 per cent from 1744 to 1748. Since 1745, the French Compagnie had been virtually insolvent: in fifteen months of war, twelve merchantmen had been captured or lost at sea; it owed the government 9 million francs in loans; and after further loans, dividends were paid from the State Treasury.

Dupleix therefore opened negotiations with the English but his preliminary demand that they recognised him as the Nawab of the Carnatic was simply too much to take. The English were not taken in by his bluff that he had, in any case, been granted it by the ruler of the Deccan and, indeed, the Mughal Emperor himself. The decision point therefore lay in what was happening in front of Trichinopoly in October. If Astruc defeated Lawrence outside the walls and then took the city, the English would be forced to negotiate. However, the death knell of the French military sounded with the loss of 200 Europeans, capture of their leader and the retreat of the remainder. The fact that Lawrence did not even bother to follow up the retreating rabble showed what he thought of them.

This, and the fact that Dupleix realised he was going to be made the scapegoat for this series of resounding failures, drove him to open discussions with the English. Bussy had also reported that he was in severe financial difficulties in the Deccan. Commissioners from both sides therefore congregated at Sadras in January 1754 to discuss terms. There were not unreasonable proposals on both sides with the exception of the nawabship of the Carnatic, with the English absolutely refusing to recognise Dupleix and insisting on their man, Mahomed Ali, as the proper ruler. The English even proposed the concession that the nawabship should be declared vacant on condition that Mahomed Ali should be appointed under the protection of the two Companies. To no avail and on this point the meeting broke up after eleven days' argument.

Dupleix cannot really have believed the English would give way and maybe it was just a test to see how far he could get them to go. Perhaps he was waiting for the inevitable break-up of the relationship between Mahomed Ali and the English to pounce? A few days after the conference, the French captured a valuable convoy on its way into Trichinopoly and destroyed 230 of the best English troops. This only hardened the English position. The war lingered on for a further six months but the French were finished: Bussy was in trouble in the north, the soldiers were leaderless and disheartened and the Indian princes, always the fair-weather sailors, could see which way this was going and started to slip from under Dupleix's influence. Even his subordinates were fed up with his arrogance and haughtiness, and his penchant for dressing as an Eastern potentate.

Back in France things were warming up against Dupleix. The Compagnie directors were exasperated by his acquisition of personal wealth, probably exaggerated by rumour, his indifference to their demands, his concealment of important factors and the insolent tone of his letters. One of his friends wrote to him, 'One doesn't write to one's valet as you have written to the Compagnie.' They were upset that they heard news from the English before it reached them from him. By January 1753, they had been without dispatches from Dupleix for twelve months. When letters finally arrived, they made no mention of Arcot in 1751, his adoption of the nawabship of the Carnatic or the reasons for the dispatch of Bussy to the Deccan. The directors complained that they had received no revenue from the sums they had sent out to him. It seemed to them that in pursuit of his political aims, he had completely lost sight of the Compagnie's commercial interests.

The Compagnie decided that Dupleix was the one obstacle to peace and he had to be replaced. Indeed, as early as the autumn of 1751 proposals for his recall had been put before ministers but put into abeyance. There was no doubt that there was also a feeling of personal animosity against Dupleix and a suspicion about his loyalty. They found it difficult to ignore the enormous sums of money that Dupleix and his officers acquired for themselves, particularly when, after Dumas's departure, he had been reminded that acceptance of gifts by French officials from foreign princes was forbidden by Royal Ordinance. The Compagnie had not covered itself in glory in dealing with Dupleix in the early stages of his governorship and was now feeling the cold wind of its shareholders blowing towards it. There was doubt whether the Compagnie would continue to exist at all. The directors needed a scapegoat and it was Dupleix.

In his well-received work on India, *L'Univers Pittoresque* of 1853, Xavier Raymond wrote:

> England has been much admired and often cited for having resolved the great problem of how to govern, at a great distance of 4000 leagues, with some hundreds of civil functionaries and some thousands of soldiers, her immense possessions in India. If there is much that is wonderful, much that is bold and daring, much political genius in the idea, it must be admitted that the honour of having inaugurated it belongs to Dupleix; and that England, which in the present day reaps from it the profit and the glory, has had but to follow the path which the Genius of France opened to her.

So was Dupleix a man of his time, but before his time? What actually did he do that Clive did not subsequently do?

During Dupleix's governorship, the French and English companies in Paris and London were in contact with each other, not always consistently, nor, necessarily, always with the knowledge of their governments. They were both traders, and commerce with dividends to their shareholders was their aim. They, therefore, generally agreed on policy, but the English found the large acquisitions of territory by the French difficult to rationalise when things were meant to be on an equal basis of competition. The fighting, which the English viewed as a French initiative, could not be ignored and had to be resisted in order to protect their trade.

The raising of 2,000 men to accompany Godeheu, despite the specific and openly declared intention of making peace and removing Dupleix, not unnaturally roused English suspicions. Ministers in London took notice and the French ambassador was summoned to be told that His Majesty's Government fully intended to support the rights and privileges granted to the East India Company by Royal Charter and, what is more, the 39th Regiment of Foot (later the Dorset Regiment whose motto is 'Primus in Indis') was mobilised for service in India. Additionally, eight ships of the line and five frigates were being prepared to sail. The ambassador was instructed by his ministers to conclude a treaty between the two companies, conceding all the points on which the Company insisted, knowing they were backed by their government. Before this, Godeheu was on his way to India.

All this calls into question the supposition that had the Compagnie fully backed Dupleix then the English would have acquiesced to the domination of the Carnatic by France. There can be little doubt that the English could not possibly accept this because it would effectively mean their complete loss of a trading empire. There was simply no deal.

Dupleix, somewhat to his own surprise, was well received on arrival in France and there were even people who though he might return to Pondicherry – after all, Godeheu was not there as his successor but merely an emissary of the Compagnie. He was promised a swift resolution of the financial claims he was making against the Compagnie for all the money he had allegedly used from his own purse for the furtherance of its interests in India. However, letters from Godeheu revealing uncomfortable questions about the accounts and the peace with the English on the spot, hardened the resolve of his detractors. Not only did he receive no redress but those whose fortunes he had made quickly dropped him when they saw which way the wind was blowing. Three days before he died, he wrote this bitter letter:

> I have sacrificed my youth, my fortune, my life, to enrich my nation in Asia. Unfortunate friends, too weak relations, devoted all their property to the success of my projects. They are now in misery and want. I have complied with all the judiciary forms: I have demanded, as the last of the creditors, that which is due to me. My services are treated as fables, my demand is denounced as ridiculous, I am treated as the vilest of mankind. I am in the most deplorable indigence. The little property that remained to me has been seized. I am compelled to ask for decrees for delay in order not to be dragged to prison.

He died on 10 November 1764.

Dupleix was an administrator and organiser but no soldier or politician. While promoting the trade of his own or the Compagnie's he was a master but he lacked the soldier's feel and the instinct of a Clive or Lawrence. He was a bad selector of subordinates and lacked the ability to appreciate a military situation; he only briefly left Pondicherry once between January 1742 and October 1754, so could he really see what was going on at the front? Politically, he could not grasp how the permanent acquisition of territory was upsetting the delicate neutral balance between him and the British. Cleverly, he manipulated the Indian princes but was consistently let down by their bad faith, which he should have anticipated.

Later overshadowed by Clive, Dupleix, nevertheless, remains an important and remarkable figure in eighteenth-century Indian history. With daring and early success he showed how there could be a European domination of India. Clive's policy after the Battle of Plassey was founded on the example set by him. Dupleix seized opportunities but failed, sometimes, to see where they were leading. It is difficult to see where his aim really lay since it changed as situations evolved. To be fair, it was surely for the glory of France, and his own, but on his terms.

It can be argued that if it had not been for Dupleix, there would have been no British Empire in India. He taught the English in the Coromandel to rely on their own strength and not to expect the Crown to do their fighting for them. In the four years' warfare they undertook, they found leaders such as Clive and Lawrence who, but for Dupleix, might never have surfaced. Without him, there would have been no British fleet stationed in Indian waters and no English professional regiment on hand when trade was extinguished in Bengal in 1756. However, even if fully supported, Dupleix would never have founded the French Empire in India. All French efforts at colonisation in the eighteenth century were paralysed by quarrels among local officials, widespread corruption and acquisition of private gain.

The final question is, was Dupleix a scapegoat? He certainly thought so himself and that he shouldered all the blame for the Compagnie and the government, which failed to support him when he needed it. It is difficult to argue that his dismissal benefited the Compagnie. It was, and had been for some time, in dire financial straits and its activities in the Carnatic had been doomed for a number of years, whoever was the governor. Dupleix had become an embarrassment to the Compagnie and the only way it was going to achieve any kind of peace with the English was to remove him and his intransigence. However, the blame could not be entirely levied at Dupleix; indeed, the Compagnie were flattered by his early successes and he wasn't made a marquis for nothing. While his star was in the ascendant, the directors were happy to forget his peccadilloes. Easy with hindsight, but if the Compagnie had sent an emissary of Godeheu's quality much earlier to control Dupleix and lay down quite clearly the parameters within which he was to operate, the scene might have been very different.

Another man who took the blame for his government 200 years later was David 'Dado' Elazar, the chief of staff of the Israeli Defence Forces in the Yom Kippur War. Was it his fault the Israelis were caught napping by the Egyptians and Syrians? Or did it go much deeper than that and was it convenient for the government to find a scapegoat quickly after the war?

TWELVE

Lieutenant General David 'Dado' Elazar

Atonement

October 1973

On 2 April 1974, Lieutenant General David 'Dado' Elazar, chief of staff of the Israeli Defence Forces (IDF) stood on the tarmac of Tel Aviv's airport with the editors of Israel's leading newspapers, preparing to leave on a tour of the Golan Heights. Despite the ceasefire following the Yom Kippur War the year before, the border area remained tense and subject to sporadic Syrian fire. Elazar wanted to gain as much support as he could through the worldwide media for what Israel had achieved and what it was doing. The aim was to establish a more permanent ceasefire, politically and diplomatically, rather than by force. His aide-de-camp, Avner Shalev, approached and told him he was wanted immediately by Prime Minister Golda Meir in Jerusalem. He knew only too well what it was about: the findings of the Agranat Commission.

The Agranat Commission of Inquiry was established by the government a month after the ceasefire in October 1973 to identify the reasons why Israel failed to detect the surprise attack by Egypt and Syria, and to assess the adequacy of the initial IDF response to those attacks. It was no surprise to Elazar that as chief of staff he, with others, was in the line of fire. However, while he accepted that he was not blameless for underestimating Arab intentions, he hoped that his outstanding performance during the war would outweigh it.

The Prime Minister handed him a copy of the report. Quickly skimming it, he reached the paragraphs that specifically applied to him. The committee recommended that he end his service. Understandably shocked, he immediately tendered his resignation, which was, regretfully, accepted. Bitterly upset, he immediately drafted a letter to the Prime Minister. However within nine days, Golda Meir's government fell, taking Moshe Dayan with it, so Elazar wrote a more formal one to the new prime minister, Yitzhak Rabin.

Two years later, on the first day of Passover, Elazar, aged 50, died of a broken heart, the scapegoat of Yom Kippur.

The origins of the Yom Kippur War lay in the Six Day War of 1967. Arab armies had massed on Israel's borders: Egyptians poured into the Sinai, Jordanians and Syrians closed up to the frontier and Kuwaiti and Iraqi forces were put on a war footing. President Nasser of Egypt expelled the United Nations Emergency Force. Arab media hysteria vowed to wipe Israel off the face of the earth. A stunned world looked on with impotence as cynical Soviets manipulated the United Nations Security Council.

On 6 June, however, Israel struck first and within six days had destroyed much of the opposition. They occupied the Sinai Peninsula, Gaza Strip, the West Bank of the Jordan and the Golan Heights. This outstanding victory had a profound effect on both sides. Israel was no longer the diminutive oppressed nation, overshadowed by powerful neighbours; it had beaten them into positions where they had to rethink their political and strategic options. The Egyptians, in particular, re-evaluated their military doctrines with Soviet assistance. They reorganised their forces in the light of the lessons they had learned the hard way while the euphoric Israelis brushed aside any of their own shortcomings and basked in the glory of total humiliation of their enemies. The next war, when it came, would merely be more of the same. Or so they thought.

Before the Six Day War, Israel had been tightly surrounded with close-in borders as a result of the 1949 armistice line. There was no depth for any strategic deployment as the Gaza Strip was occupied by Egyptians, Jerusalem was divided and occupied by Jordanians and, from the Golan Heights, the Syrians could look down on Israeli villages in the Jordan Valley. The Israeli General Staff's assessment was it could not allow an Arab attack that would sever Israel's main arteries, quickly reach its centres of power and overrun much of the country. The conclusion was that the only way Israel could deal with this threat was by a pre-emptive strike.

The territory won in the Six Day War, therefore, gave Israel the much needed room for strategic deployment and a buffer against its enemies. The Sinai Desert was a classic example, the occupation of which immediately separated Israel 150 miles from the Suez Canal, producing an effective defence of desert and the waterway as well as bringing the Egyptian cities of Port Said, Ismailia and Suez within range of Israeli attack. Jerusalem was now united and out of range of Jordanian artillery, and the Golan Heights were no longer in Syrian hands. However, importantly for political reasons, it made an Israeli pre-emptive strike now unnecessary; the Israelis could weather a first strike by the enemy with all the international condemnation that would ensue. The Israelis now had the Sinai Desert in which to deploy and from there could launch counter-attacks against enemy incursions in addition to maintaining a forward line of defence on the Suez Canal. Nevertheless, warning time for an attack was still short and the Israeli concept of operations was to maintain deployed forces sufficient to withstand initial attacks while they mobilised reserves. This was estimated at seventy-two hours.

In the Sinai Desert, the Israeli commanders faced the standard problem of defence in depth versus forward security on the canal line. The latter gave observation over any enemy build-up and an ability to deal with any immediate incursion, while the former gave space to concentrate, identify enemy main thrusts and deploy counter-attacks. The Israelis therefore constructed lightly manned fortifications on the Suez Canal which were, in effect, observation points, between which armour could patrol and deal with any immediate incursion. Although supported by artillery fire, they were not designed to prevent an all-out crossing by the Egyptians but merely to impose delay. The canal was not, in itself, a significant obstacle unless the Israelis had strong defence for its entire length and could cover any crossing with a major amount of fire, armour and air support.

The Israelis therefore constructed a sophisticated line of fortifications on the canal but with a view to defeating the enemy in depth. The Bar-Lev Line, as the whole system, including the rear manoeuvre forces, came to be called, was severely put to the test in March 1969 when

Nasser launched his War of Attrition. Nasser's aim was to cross the canal in strength and reoccupy the Sinai Peninsula. There was a considerable amount of fighting and the conflict only reached a conclusion with Israeli air attacks destroying Egyptian surface-to-air missiles on the canal and into the Gulf of Suez. In July 1970, Nasser accepted a ceasefire. Under cover of the ceasefire, the Egyptians were resupplied with updated missile systems by the Russians and moved the anti-aircraft assets to the line of the canal, covering well into Israeli-occupied Sinai. Before Nasser could start his next phase, which was to cross the Suez Canal under this new air-cover, he died, resulting in internal political and leadership problems in Egypt. In the meantime, the Israelis repaired and strengthened the Bar-Lev Line.

In 1971, Nasser's successor Anwar Sadat, in response to an initiative by UN intermediary Gunnar Jarring, declared that if Israel committed itself to withdrawal of its armed forces from Sinai and the Gaza Strip and implemented other provisions of UN Security Council Resolution 242, Egypt would then be ready to enter into a peace agreement with Israel. Israel responded that it would not withdraw to the pre-June 1967 lines. Sadat, however, had important domestic concerns in wanting war. He badly wanted to introduce economic reforms but hesitated to do so without reversing the humiliation of defeat in the Six Day War. Without this, he did not think that the Egyptian people would tolerate economic change.

Sadat hoped that by inflicting even a limited defeat on the Israelis, the status quo could be altered. Hafez al-Assad, president of Syria, had a different view. He had little interest in negotiation and felt the retaking of the Golan Heights would be a purely military option. Since the Six Day War, Assad had launched a massive military build-up and hoped to make Syria the dominant military power of the Arab states. With the aid of Egypt, Assad felt he could win convincingly against the Israelis and thus secure Syria's role in the region. Assad only saw negotiations beginning once the Golan Heights had been retaken by force, which would induce Israel to give up the West Bank and Gaza, and make other concessions.

Other Arab states showed more reluctance to commit themselves to a new war. King Hussein of Jordan feared another major loss of territory as had occurred in the Six Day War, during which Jordan was halved in population. However, he still saw the West Bank as part of

Jordan and wanted it restored to his kingdom. Moreover, during the Black September crisis of 1970 a near civil war had broken out between the Palestinians and the Jordanian Government. In that war, Syria had intervened militarily on the side of the Palestine Liberation Organization (PLO), leaving Assad and Hussein at loggerheads.

Iraq and Syria also had strained relations, with the former refusing to join the initial offensive. Lebanon, which shared a border with Israel, was not expected to join the Arab war effort due to its small army and already evident instability. In the months before the war, Sadat made a major diplomatic effort to try to win support for the war. He backed the claim of the PLO to the territories of the West Bank and Gaza and, in the event of a victory, promised Yasser Arafat that he would give him control of them. By the autumn of 1973 he claimed the support of more than a hundred states. These were most of the countries of the Arab League, the Non-Aligned Movement and the Organization of African Unity. He had also worked hard to curry favour in Europe and had some success before the war. Britain and France had for the first time sided with the Arab powers against Israel in the United Nations Security Council.

Important, at the time, to Israeli strategic thinking was the very overt support of the Americans. This consisted of not only significant arms supply but also political backing in the unequivocal reaction to Syria's invasion of Jordan during the civil war when King Hussein successfully eliminated the Palestinian uprising. What this did was to convince the Israeli leadership that the Arab world would hardly unite against the country at the risk of taking on the Americans.

In January 1972, Elazar was appointed chief of staff and this coincided with a distinct lack of enemy activity along the Suez Canal. Thus strongpoints started to be closed (thirteen by the spring of 1973) and force levels reduced, and the population began to query the large amount of seemingly unnecessary military expenditure. The aim, therefore, of the Bar-Lev Line – was it a warning tripwire or main defensive line? – started to become opaque.

There then followed protracted political activity between the Egyptians and Russians, who were uneasy bedfellows (Sadat had sacked their military advisers in the summer of 1972). The Americans engaged with not only Israel but also Saudi Arabia and Kuwait. The latter diplomatic exchanges thoroughly alarmed the Soviets who consequently increased their arms supply to Egypt. This included, in March 1973, the provision of Scud surface-to-surface missiles, which put Israeli towns within range of warheads fired from Egyptian territory.

Sadat made it abundantly clear that his aim was to resume the war with Israel. While the Israelis, of course, noted his remarks, they were put down to merely bluff and sabre rattling. They guessed that Sadat was incapable of carrying out his threats until he had received the long-range bombers he needed from Russia. Elazar was quoted as saying, 'How many times can a politician repeat the same threat? In 1971 he said that it was the year of decision; then he said that 1972 would be the year of decision; he promised that the territories would be liberated before Mohammed's birthday; he promised there would be a clash this year ...' Despite a certain amount of disdain and derision from his own people, Sadat, nevertheless, maintained excellent relations with his fellow Arab leaders, cosying up to the Saudi Arabians and, sensibly, keeping the madman Gadaffi at arm's length. A significant backdrop to all this was a developing oil warfare strategy, Sadat persuading the Saudis that the oil weapon could only be deployed in the wake of war with Israel, which would cement the Arab cause.

To Egyptian strategists, Israel had the advantage of air superiority, technological expertise, a well-trained army and guaranteed American support. However, they now had long lines of communication to different defensive areas, an inability to sustain heavy casualties due to the small population and, because of a fragile economy, a reluctance to engage in a long war. Added to this, with the success of the 1967 war, they had an exaggerated view of their own superiority and a complacent self-confidence. A former head of Mossad said later, 'We all constructed a position for ourselves, an attitude of exaggerated self-confidence, a sense of power, [a feeling] of "There's no one like me!" This feeling rested on two foundations: our great strength and the enemy's pitiful ability. It lulled us into a mood of over-confidence which may be summed up in that unfortunate sentence: "It simply can't happen!"' To deal with this, the Egyptian generals realised they needed to strike first, with surprise, and attack on several fronts at the same time, having acquired from Moscow all that they needed for a sustained campaign before they started. Close coordination with the Syrians was essential, holding the Jordanians in reserve. A simultaneous attack along the 110-mile length of the Suez Canal would ensure the Israelis had no indications which were to be the main thrusts.

A number of meetings between Syrian and Egyptian defence officials took place with the result that firm plans for the attack were completed by June and ratified by Presidents Assad and Sadat. Jordan was reluctantly brought into the fold. Sadat's clandestine meeting with Yasser Arafat to persuade the PLO to come alongside was predictably leaked but no one, least of all the Israelis, took it seriously. During that summer, further missile systems were supplied to both the Syrians and Egyptians by Russia. It is important to realise what Sadat's aim actually was. Unlike the 1967 war in which the Arab mission was to eliminate the Jewish nation, Sadat's aim was more restrictive: to recover the territories lost in the earlier war by an initial devastating assault, which would lead quickly to a diplomatic ceasefire and a favourable international agreement. The Arab plans this time, therefore, were only prepared for the initial phases with limited military goals. Sadat and his allies were now ready to go.

The IDF's Directorate of Military Intelligence's Research Department (AMAN) was responsible for formulating the nation's intelligence estimate. Its assessments of the likelihood of war were based on several hypotheses. First, it was assumed correctly that Syria would not go to war with Israel unless Egypt did so. Second, it learned from various sources that Egypt wanted to regain all of the Sinai. However, Egypt would not go to war until the Soviets had supplied enough fighter-bombers to neutralise the Israeli Air Force and Scud missiles to be used against Israeli cities as a deterrent against Israeli attacks on Egyptian infrastructure. Since the Soviets had not yet supplied the fighter-bombers and the Scud missiles had only arrived in Egypt in March and it would take at least four months to train the Egyptian operators, AMAN concluded war with Egypt was not imminent. This assumption about Egypt's strategic plans, known as 'the concept', strongly prejudiced AMAN's thinking and led it to dismiss other warnings.

The Egyptians did much to further this misconception. Both the Israelis and the Americans felt that the expulsion of the Soviet military observers had severely reduced the effectiveness of the Egyptian Army.

The Egyptians ensured that there was a continual stream of false information on maintenance problems, lack of spare parts and a lack of personnel to operate the most advanced equipment.

During the week leading up to Yom Kippur, the Egyptians staged a week-long exercise adjacent to the Suez Canal. Israeli intelligence, detecting large troop movements towards the canal, dismissed it as mere training. Movements of Syrian troops towards the border were puzzling, but not a threat because, AMAN believed, they would not attack without Egypt and Egypt would not attack until the Soviet bombers arrived.

King Hussein of Jordan declined to join Egypt and Syria. On the night of 25 September, he secretly flew to Tel Aviv to warn Israeli Prime Minister Golda Meir of an impending Syrian attack. Believing her own intelligence community, Meir ignored the warning.

If a plan was being made to attack another country, it would not be difficult to select a day when its population would be on holiday, observing a religious festival or recovering from some major event. Offices would be closed, headquarters would be on minimum manning and important leaders and staff out of touch. To attack a Christian country, Christmas or Easter would be ideal; a Muslim one, Eid al-Fitr; for Israel, it could not be better than Yom Kippur.

Yom Kippur, also known as the Day of Atonement, is the holiest and most solemn day of the year for Jews. Its central themes are atonement and repentance. Jews traditionally observe this holy day with a twenty-five-hour period of fasting and intensive prayer, often spending most of the day in synagogue services. Not only the observant but also most secular Jews fast, abstain from any use of fire, electricity, engines and communications, and all road traffic comes to a standstill. Many soldiers leave their military establishments for home during the holiday and Israel is at its most vulnerable.

One such day was Friday, 5 October 1973.

To soldiers of any standard or nationality, Moshe Dayan, Israeli minister of defence, was a leader. He had the charisma, common touch and personal courage that made people instinctively trust and follow him. He had the bravado and self-confidence to overcome obstacles and encourage lesser men to do things of which they never thought themselves capable. But, like many men of his quality and stature, there were flaws.

In 1941 a French soldier shot at him, the round hitting his binoculars and destroying his left eye. Far from allowing this to be a disability, his black eyepatch became his trademark, instantly making him recognisable to friend and foe alike. He became the symbol of Israel's warrior class. Born on a kibbutz, he became an emblem of what it was to be a Jew of the new nation, standing on his own feet and willing to take on opponents on their own terms.

He became a vital contributor to Israel's freedom and the building of the nation. He was heavily involved in three of its wars and, later, one of the architects of the country's first treaty with an Arab state. He was a natural soldier with an intuitive grasp for the indirect approach and the unorthodox. He was imaginative and unconventional, which endeared him to his soldiers but not always to his fellow officers and politicians. Never deflected from his aim, he cared little for the superficial trappings of traditional military life; the important thing was how to fight well and win in battle. Original thought and surprise were key factors in the way he approached any analysis of a situation.

A fighter, not a negotiator, he worried that after the wars of 1948 and 1956, Israel's withdrawal into small nationhood rendered it vulnerable to Arab dominance and ultimate destruction. With the success of the Six Day War in 1967, therefore, retention of large amounts of Arab territory was essential, he believed, to defence in depth and the establishment of protection zones around the country. Dayan was intimately involved in this policy and was wholly supported by the population and politicians, making Israel a bully and an oppressor in many people's eyes. He set the strategy of long-term occupation of East Jerusalem, the West Bank, the Gaza Strip, Sinai and the Golan Heights. While trying to persuade the Arabs that this was a benign policy, he ignored their desire to see the restoration of their lands even in the long term. Compromise was not a word in his dictionary.

After the Six Day War, Dayan acquired the stature of a demi-god; he could do no wrong, he was the saviour of the nation. He believed in his own myth; he was above the law, other men's rules did not apply to him. He was a notorious philanderer who believed his private life had no bearing on his official one. He was a pilferer of national archaeological treasures, an activity that would land others in jail. His lifestyle took its toll on his family; he was divorced and his son, Assi, and he were estranged for years.

He was a man of exceptional ability but preferred to concentrate on matters that interested him and ignore those that did not. Curiously, for a dynamic and authoritarian leader of his quality, he preferred to share responsibility with others. At meetings, he was invariably accompanied by his chief of staff and head of intelligence. With most senior commanders this is not abnormal but, in Dayan's case, he used their presence to shift responsibility and, if it came to it, blame. 'They said it, not me', would follow. He enjoyed visiting soldiers at the front and was a tonic when things were going well. He was not interested in administration or the day-to-day housekeeping of a large army which, with a sizable reservist element, required a great deal of detailed management to make it work under stress. With some leaders this can be forgiven if they surround themselves with people who can handle the boring aspects of military life; Dayan did not. Additionally, he failed to see that in a democracy, as a minister, parliamentary responsibility fell heavily on him. The fall came at Yom Kippur, 1973.

But what of David Elazar, the man who did take the responsibility, salvaged victory from disaster and then had blame heaped upon him? Born in Sarajevo, Elazar emigrated to Palestine in 1940 and settled in a kibbutz. He fought in a number of major battles during Israel's War of Independence and eventually commanded the famous HaPortzim Battalion. He remained in the army after the war, transferring to the armoured corps following the 1956 Sinai campaign. He commanded the corps from 1961 to 1964, when he was appointed GOC Northern Command. He held this post during the Six Day War of 1967 and directed Israel's capture of the Golan Heights in just two days. After the war, Elazar was chief operations officer on the General Staff and, in January 1972, was appointed chief of staff.

His first few months were plagued with terrorism. On 30 May, the Japanese Red Army killed 25 civilians and wounded 71 at Lod Airport. Then on 5 September of that year, the massacre of the summer Olympics took place in Munich. In response to these attacks, Elazar ordered a major strike against Palestinian bases in Syria and Lebanon. Three Syrian jets were shot down and dozens of militia were killed in heavy artillery fire. In April 1973, a number of Palestinians, including several key leaders, were assassinated in Beirut by the IDF. One of his more difficult decisions was to deal with a Libyan jet that strayed into Israeli airspace, possibly on a terrorist mission. When it did not respond, it was shot down by the Israeli Air Force over the Sinai Peninsula on Elazar's direct order, killing over a hundred. Only later did it transpire that it was a civilian aircraft that had made a navigational error.

Golda Meir, Moshe Dayan and David Elazar met at 8 a.m. on 3 October 1973. The day before, Dayan had asked Elazar to conduct his own written appreciation of the current situation. He queried whether the known build-up of Egyptian forces was a confidence trick? Elazar doubted it and thought it was merely an exercise. Dayan began the meeting by suggesting that war was not imminent. Egypt would not attack by itself and there would be no joint Egyptian-Syrian attack. While he accepted that the manoeuvres were unusual, he did not draw any adverse deductions. A 'Crisis? What crisis?' atmosphere prevailed.

The reality was that both Dayan and Elazar assumed that the head of intelligence, Major General Eliyahu Zeira, had exploited the 'additional means' and kept them up to date on what emerged. In Hebrew, the phrase *'emtsayim me'yukhadim'*, meaning 'additional means', can also be translated as 'special devices' – in other words, highly delicate and secret sources of intelligence. Later, the Agranat Commission was to criticise Zeira that, because of his faith in his personal analysis, he 'was overcautious and did not take advantage of the additional means at his disposal that might have revealed important supplementary operational information'. The report went on to say 'his superiors were misled into thinking that [he was keeping them informed]'. It further states that Dayan's confidence 'rose when the chief of intelligence told him on October 5th [sic], that he was exploiting every possible source of information and advance warning'. Until well into the war, both Dayan and Elazar were convinced that the 'additional means' was being developed. It is now known that vital intelligence from the head of Mossad reached

Zeira on the eve of Yom Kippur. It went no further and was not passed on to Dayan or Elazar at the time. Had it done so, the Reserve Division, the main force of the IDF, would undoubtedly have been called up.

For a number of years before the Yom Kippur War, Mossad had a source deep inside the Egyptian decision-making circle. He was Ashraf Marwan, the son-in-law of President Nasser – the 'additional means'. He provided first-class intelligence, including Sadat's 1972 war plans and the 1973 revision. On 18 April 1973, Marwan sent a flash message that war was imminent. Major General Zvi Zamir, head of Mossad, personally interviewed him and Marwan revealed that on 15 May, Egypt and Syria would launch a surprise attack.

Golda Meir called an emergency meeting attended by her major advisers and, as a result, Israel called up tens of thousands of reservists and deployed additional brigades and support equipment in the Sinai and the Golan Heights. The stand-to lasted for three months and cost $35 million. In fact, Sadat had postponed the operation in the light of a Soviet/American meeting in Washington. Marwan was not wrong but there were then those who accused the Israeli leadership of 'crying wolf' and this inevitably made them nervous of an expensive mobilisation that could turn out to be a false alarm. Elazar was criticised for this 'unneces-sary' expenditure.

Late on the night of 4/5 October 1973, Mossad received a call that Marwan wanted to see Zamir immediately. Zamir was woken with the message at 2.30 a.m. on 5 October and flew as soon as possible to the safe house in London to meet Marwan. Before he left, Zeira had telephoned to tell him of the rushed evacuation of Soviet families from Egypt and Syria. Zamir alerted Zeira that he was meeting his source in an emergency and to let the Prime Minister's office know what was happening. Zamir did not meet Marwan until 10 p.m. that night when he was told that Egypt and Syria were to attack 'tomorrow' (6 October). The agent was unsure of the actual time but it became 'sunset' or 'dusk' in the minds of his interrogators. Zamir wired this to Tel Aviv at 2.30 a.m. on the 6th.

Zeira's view was unchanged; this news did not fit the 'concept' and, in the light of the false alarm in April, it was likely Marwan was a double agent. He still believed the possibility of war was 'lower than low'. Zamir did not agree but was reassured by what he thought were Elazar's alert measures. Zeira failed to brief Dayan and Elazar as to the full implications of Zamir's meeting with Marwan and what he had said, preferring his own analysis rather than letting his chiefs make the decision.

As a postscript, on 2 June 2007, Marwan's dead body was found on the pavement in London in suspicious circumstances. He was given a hero's funeral in Egypt thus promoting the theory that he was a double agent.

Dayan was privately worried that if the Americans saw Israel mobilising reserves, they would panic and impose a settlement forcing Israel to withdraw prematurely from some of the occupied territories. In addition, the Israelis had become used to peace and were ambivalent about a call-up, which had happened twice before without, as they saw it, any reason. Despite his reputation, Dayan did not wish to be seen as a warrior chief just prior to the elections. Elazar, however, presented his analysis in which he recommended a pre-emptive strike against Syria. Israeli warplanes, he said, could attack their airfields at noon, missile sites at 3 p.m. and ground forces at 5 p.m. His suggestion was refused.

European nations, under threat of an Arab oil embargo and trade boycott, had stopped supplying Israel with arms. As a result, Israel was totally dependent on the United States for resupply, and was particularly sensitive to anything that might endanger that relationship. Later commentators argued that the decision not to use a pre-emptive strike was a wise one. While the American airlift of supplies, which began on 13 October, did not immediately replace Israel's losses, it did allow Israel to use up its current stocks without restraint, knowing they would be replaced. Had they struck first, according to Henry Kissinger, they would not have received 'so much as a nail'.

The evacuation of Soviet families from both Syria and Egypt was a worry. Was this because the Russians knew war was imminent or did they expect an Israeli attack and were protecting their people? Either way, it did not fit the 'no war' scenario as put forward by the Israeli intelligence chief who, now with genuine doubts as to his appreciation, fell in with every alert measure proposed by Elazar. On Friday, 5 October, the first day of Yom Kippur, Elazar issued a category 'C' alert – the first since the Six Day War. This was the highest mobilisation order short of calling up reserves. With the majority of the air force on full alert, he was confident that he could deal with any aggression by either Egypt or Syria.

Dayan's mood was still influenced by the thought of the forthcoming elections. For weeks the population had been told that no war was expected for the next few years. If he now initiated excessive alert measures on Yom Kippur – of all days – and they turned out to be a false alarm, then confidence in the country's leadership would evaporate. The general public were thus oblivious; newspaper editors had been asked not to exaggerate the significance of the Arab movements, reports from the border correspondents had been censored and military PR had played down any concerns. Additionally, if the Israelis were seen to be mobilising, this could frighten the Arabs into a war that they may have only half intended.

The Prime Minister met her military staff at 10 a.m. and Elazar explained the precautionary measures he had taken. He said that while he did not expect an attack, he had no positive proof that one was *not* forthcoming. Dayan agreed but recommended a Cabinet meeting of such ministers that were available. Elazar outlined his view, again, that they would receive several days' warning before an attack. He fully expected critical intelligence sources to give him this early indication. Although his private instinct was that war was likely, he feared being labelled an alarmist. He finished his staff conference with the words,

> We shall be ready for any contingency. As you know, we have no interest in a war, and I certainly would not want it to come upon us as a complete surprise. It cannot be a *complete* surprise. However, if it breaks out today, it will be an almost complete surprise – not that I have doubts about the final outcome, but this is not the kind of opening we would prefer. Yet if we receive warning that it will happen in twenty-four hours, and we have enough time to organise, I'm sure that we will do the job very well, and I hope we will be able to implement the contingency plans now in the drawers. *Hatima Tova!* [the traditional Yom Kippur greeting for a good year to come]

By now, Syria had 45,000 troops and 900 tanks on its border, faced by 5,000 Israelis with 177 tanks. On the west bank of the Suez Canal, Egypt positioned 120,000 men and 1,200 tanks against the Israelis' 8,500 soldiers and 276 tanks.

At 4.30 a.m. on Saturday the 6th, Elazar was woken with the Mossad message that the attack was to begin at 6 p.m. (this had been 'translated' from the original 'sunset' or 'dusk') that day. If this was to be believed, and Mossad was usually uncomfortably correct, the IDF had a mere fourteen hours to mobilise rather than the minimum forty-eight and ideal seventy-two hours. Near panic ensued among the Cabinet ministers. Elazar immediately stood the air force to and asked how soon it could put in a pre-emptive strike. At 11 a.m. it could attack the Syrian missile sites, was the reply. At 6 a.m., Elazar warned the air force for an immediate strike, but, because cloud was obscuring the missile sites, the target was switched to the airfields for a 1200 hours mission. However, when he heard this, Dayan vetoed it. He still maintained that the Arabs had to be seen to start the war and he hoped it could be averted. Elazar strongly disagreed, believing fighting was inevitable. He pushed for four divisions to be mobilised together with the rest of the air force at once. Dayan demurred: fine for two divisions, one north and one south, and the air force, but no general mobilisation. They took their unresolved argument to the Prime Minister. Dayan, uncharacteristically, weakened and Meir then sanctioned a partial call-up of 100,000 men, well short of general mobilisation, but no pre-emptive strike. The order did not go out until 10 a.m.

Elazar then suggested that even if the Syrians attacked that evening, he could still counter-attack and destroy them but he would need three divisions. Dayan's dismissive response was that the chief of staff wanted to counter-attack in a war that had not yet begun. The Cabinet met at noon, approved the limited call-up and vetoed the pre-emptive strike. Mossad was not quite correct; the Egyptians and Syrians attacked that afternoon.

The Egyptian Army put great effort into finding a quick and effective way of breaching the Israeli defences. The latter consisted of large barricades made primarily from sand. Egyptian engineers initially employed explosive charges to clear the obstacles but then found that high pressure water cannon with water from the canal were extremely effective. Troops then crossed the canal in small boats and inflatable rafts, capturing or destroying all but one of the Bar-Lev forts. In a meticulously rehearsed operation, the Egyptian forces advanced approximately 10 miles into the Sinai Desert with the combined forces of two army corps. The Israeli battalion garrisoning the Bar-Lev forts was vastly outnumbered and quickly overwhelmed.

Anticipating a swift Israeli armoured counter-attack, the Egyptians had armed their first wave with unprecedented numbers of man-portable anti-tank weapons, rocket-propelled grenades and the more devastating Sagger missiles. One in every three Egyptian soldiers had an anti-tank weapon. In addition, the ramp on the Egyptian side of the canal had been increased to twice the height of the Israelis', giving them an excellent vantage point from which to fire down on the enemy, as well as engaging approaching tanks.

The Egyptian units would not advance beyond a relatively shallow strip for fear of losing the cover of their surface-to-air missile (SAM) batteries. In the Six Day War, the Israeli Air Force had quickly destroyed the defenceless Arab armies, which were without this protection, and they had learned their lesson. This time, Egypt and Syria had heavily fortified their side of the ceasefire lines with SAM batteries, against which the Israeli Air Force had no effective countermeasures. Israel, which had invested much of its defence budget building the region's strongest air force, saw it rendered almost useless by these batteries. The Egyptians believed the crossing would lose them 10,000 men. In the event, they only lost 208.

In the Golan Heights, the Syrians attacked two Israeli brigades and eleven artillery batteries with five divisions and 188 batteries. At the onset of the battle, the 177 Israeli tanks were confronted by 1,400 Syrian tanks. Every Israeli tank deployed on the Golan Heights was engaged during the initial attacks. Syrian commandos, dropped by helicopter, took the most important Israeli stronghold on Mount Hermon, which was full of surveillance equipment.

Fighting in the Golan Heights was given priority by the Israeli high command. The battle in the Sinai was sufficiently far away that Israel was not immediately threatened; however, should the Golan Heights fall, the Syrians could easily advance into Israel proper. Reservists were directed to the Golan as quickly as possible. They were allocated to tanks and sent to the front as soon as they arrived at their depots, without waiting for the crews they trained with to arrive, without waiting for machine guns to be installed in their tanks and without taking the time to calibrate their main armament.

As the Egyptians had done in the Sinai, the Syrians on the Golan Heights took care to stay under cover of their SAM batteries and made full use of their Soviet-made anti-tank weapons.

In Tel Aviv, shock and despondency was setting in. This was not the way it was meant to happen. Fragmented reports were coming in of overwhelming enemy forces thrashing weak and unprepared Israeli troops. Dayan was stunned and disorientated. The hero of all previous wars was reduced to a near wreck. He now feared giving orders and radiated desperation and guilt. Was the Bar-Lev Line intact? No one knew. Highly unlikely, so concentration, correctly, must be put on the northern sector. Attack from the Golan Heights was the most dangerous, poised as the Syrians were to strike directly into the heart of Israel.

Both Meir and Dayan addressed the public on television that night, assuring the population that all was well and troops were properly deployed to meet the aggressors. The misleading broadcasts had the uncomfortable veneer of those put out by dictators about to meet their end. Even by the standards of the lowest spin doctor, Dayan's words were a travesty of the truth. The reality, at that point, was that Israel, totally unprepared, had its back to the wall, and unless it galvanised its forces immediately, it would face unimaginable losses of men and territory.

The following day, a shaken Dayan visited the Golan area of operations. Whereas previously any visit of his boosted morale and cheered the soldiery, not now. He exuded an air of despondency and defeat. He involved himself in unnecessary minutiae, then gave orders (for wiring the Jordan bridges for demolition for example, which Elazar countermanded) that had no semblance of sense. The orders that, beforehand, would have been carried out without question were now either queried or quietly ignored. An air of cognitive dissonance was all too obvious. Elazar's presence, on the other hand, gave encouragement to men who desperately needed it. One senior commander, quoted in Hanoch Bartov's *Dado*, recorded, 'When you're faced with the kind of situation we were, and you sense someone else's confidence, that help is available and not just in words, but in terms of the kind of decisions that make a difference to the outcome of the battle, naturally it has an impact on you.'

Having been arguing the day before about the question of mobilisation, Dayan and Elazar were now contemplating withdrawal from the

Sinai front, though in Cabinet, Elazar was giving off a very confident air and talked of a counter-attack in the south. Sensing how much he was losing face with his Cabinet colleagues, Dayan passed the responsibility to Elazar. If, he said, Elazar, looking south, was confident of making a counter-attack work, then he had his support. Dayan had lost control. He had failed to realise the Arabs could, and would, attack on Yom Kippur and failed to see the mass of powerful weapons that Sadat had concentrated on the Suez Canal. For Meir, an old woman of 75, to have lost her rock, Dayan, was as much as she could bear. How could she prosecute the war without his support?

Dayan had given up and was talking of 'the fall of the Third Commonwealth' and the 'Day of Judgement'. Another Masada in his mind? Elazar now effectively emerged as the decisive authority on the conduct of the war and, on Sunday the 7th, produced a plan to counter-attack the Egyptians in the south. 'Nerves of Steel' Chaim Bar-Lev was brought out of retirement and sent to boost the command in the Golan Heights.

The Egyptian forces had, by now, consolidated their initial positions. On Monday the 8th, Major General Shmuel Gonen, commander of the Israeli southern front, who had only taken up his post three months before on the retirement of Major General Arik Sharon, ordered a counter-attack by an armoured brigade against entrenched Egyptian forces. Despite the brigade commander's reluctance, the attack proceeded and the result was a predictable disaster for the Israelis. However, Sharon, who had been reinstated as a divisional commander at the outset of the war, towards nightfall stopped an Egyptian counter-attack with his division. On 9 October, Elazar replaced Gonen with Bar-Lev as GOC Southern Command.

Meanwhile, on the northern front, the Syrians, who at the start outnumbered the Israelis in the Golan 9:1, by the end of the first day of battle had achieved moderate success. They had expected it would take at least twenty-four hours for Israeli reserves to reach the front line. In fact, they began reaching forward positions only fifteen hours after the war began. However, by nightfall, a Syrian tank brigade passing through a gap, turned north-west up a little-used route that cut diagonally across the Golan. This would prove one of the main strategic hinges of the battle. It led straight from the main Syrian incursions to not only the location of the Israeli divisional headquarters but also the most important crossroads on the Golan Heights.

Over four days of fighting, the Israeli 7th Armoured Brigade managed to hold the rocky hill line defending the northern flank. In the south of the Golan Heights, however, an Israeli armoured brigade, without suitable ground to use tactically, began to take heavy casualties. The brigade commander, his second in command and operations officer were all killed and at this point, the brigade stopped functioning as a cohesive force. There was now a real danger that the Syrians could advance to the edge of the plateau of the Golan Heights and command the Jordan Valley. From there they could dominate all the roads leading up to the Golan and prevent Israeli reinforcements using those routes. Elazar proposed driving deep into Syria to get within artillery range of Damascus thus demonstrating to all Arabs that this was the penalty for starting a war with Israel. Meir agreed and a plan was made.

On the southern front more Egyptian forces were crossing into the Sinai but Egypt still had considerable forces west of the canal. The argument within the Israeli Cabinet was whether to take on the enemy in the Sinai or cross the Suez Canal and attack the forces waiting to cross from the flank. Bar-Lev and Elazar favoured a crossing, Dayan lapsed into ambivalence. Sharon was dying to cross with his division; he could see that this was the only way to hit the Egyptians rather than sitting waiting to be attacked. It was a dynamic and imaginative move that would have been heavily endorsed by Dayan in his old days. Dayan sloped his shoulders and referred Sharon to 'command headquarters'. The plan was rejected. However, on 14 October, the Egyptians crossed over the canal with 1,000 tanks, 280 of which were destroyed by the Israelis. The crossing plan was resurrected. The following night, the Israelis launched their attack to cross the canal. Previously they had been highly vulnerable to the Egyptian SAM and anti-tank batteries, so, with a change in tactics, they used paratroops and infantry to infiltrate enemy positions with considerable success.

Sharon's division attacked the Egyptians just north of Bitter Lake. The Israelis struck at a weak point in the Egyptian line, the junction between the Second Army in the north and the Third Army in the south.

In some of the most brutal fighting of the war, the Israelis punched a hole in the Egyptian defences and reached the Suez Canal. A small force crossed the canal and created a bridgehead on the other side. For over twenty-four hours, troops were ferried across the canal in light inflatable boats, with no armour support. They were well supplied with anti-tank rockets, efficiently taking on Egyptian tanks. Once the anti-aircraft and anti-tank defences of the Egyptians had been neutralised, the infantry once again were able to rely on overwhelming tank and air support. The tide was starting to turn. The Israelis were within 63 miles of Cairo.

Things were also starting to go Israel's way in the Golan Heights, as the arriving Israeli reserve forces were able to contain and start to push back the Syrian offensive. The Golan Heights were too small to act as an effective territorial buffer, unlike the Sinai Peninsula in the south, but were a strategic geographical stronghold and a crucial key to preventing the Syrian Army from bombarding the cities below. By 10 October, the last Syrian unit in the central sector had been pushed back across the pre-war border.

A decision now had to be made by the Israeli Cabinet whether to stop at the 1967 border or to continue into Syrian territory. Some favoured disengagement, which would allow redeployment into the Sinai to reinforce the crossing troops, others pressed for continuing the thrust into Syria, towards Damascus, which would neutralise Syria and give Israel a valuable position of strength from which to negotiate once the war ended. The counterargument to this was that Syria still had strong defence in depth and it would be better to fight from defensive positions in the Golan Heights rather than on the flat Syrian plains. Nevertheless, between 11 and 14 October, Israeli forces pushed into Syria, reaching a position from which they were able to shell the outskirts of Damascus, only 25 miles away. However, fighting was still happening in the Golan with counter-attacks being launched by Iraqi and Jordanian forces with the Syrians, preventing any further substantial Israeli gains.

By the end of the third week of conflict, America and Russia achieved a United Nations Resolution calling for a ceasefire on 22 October. After another thirty-six hours of hostilities, the ceasefire was established.

Considering the way in which the Israelis had been so badly caught out at the beginning, the achievements were formidable. They had destroyed 2,500 Arab tanks and 400 planes; the Suez Canal had been crossed and they had been within 25 miles of Damascus. But at what a cost: the toll was 2,552 Israelis killed and another 3,000 wounded, and 107 planes and 840 tanks lost.

Then the recriminations began.

President Sadat of Egypt suffered a military defeat but, in the end, achieved, with American help, a significant diplomatic triumph by ultimately regaining much of the territory lost in the 1967 war through a substantial peace agreement. While Israel gained an impressive victory, it did so with great loss of life and enormous public dissatisfaction with the political and military leadership. Its self-confidence and morale was reduced to a low ebb.

The deterrence of American support for Israel and Israel's strategic policy of early warning, air supremacy, ability to deploy reserves quickly and rapidly counter-attack into enemy territory were seen to fail. The early warning fell short due to the inadequacy of the intelligence system. The Israeli intelligence experts claimed to have briefed their chiefs on the *capabilities* of the Arabs – their preparations, their deployments, their planning conferences, their weapon holdings and their readiness. What they failed to do, however, was to identify their *intentions* – the most difficult aspect of any intelligence assessment. The Israelis simply had no idea of when the Arabs intended to attack, where and with what.

When the Israelis realised what was afoot, they agonised over initiating a pre-emptive strike. Elazar, as we have seen, recommended a pre-emptive strike against Syria, which was rejected on the basis that Israel would be accused of being the aggressor thereby losing American backing. Even with hindsight, this is difficult to assess. Was Elazar right or wrong?

The Bar-Lev Line was neither one thing nor another. It was over-manned for a mere tripwire early-warning observation line but not strong enough to resist a full-scale attack along the whole of the Suez Canal. The Israeli strategists had not followed the problem through. The static line of defence at the expense of a mobile reaction force was a mistake.

The Israeli Air Force faced an enormous problem. On the one hand it needed to acquire air superiority against enemy aircraft and missile defence as soon as possible, on the other, it needed to support ground forces that were desperate without it. The Arabs knew they would lose against Israeli pilots in air-to-air combat, therefore relied on surface-to-surface and surface-to-air sophisticated missile systems supplied by the Russians. Israeli intelligence officers assumed that, given the generally accepted Arab aim of eliminating the Jewish homeland, the Egyptians would wait until they received the long-range bombers before attacking.

Initially, after the end of the war, public opinion was fairly muted. Many reservists were still deployed and sporadic shooting was still taking place on the borders. Slowly, as the losses began to be realised, wrath was turned on the government and leadership, particularly Dayan. He ignored it and remained defensive of his behaviour. He had the full support of Golda Meir and the Cabinet. No doubt, they realised that if he went, so would they. It was a self-protection operation.

There were increasing calls for an investigation into what had happened. Dayan, predictably, was against it on the grounds that no civilian judge could fairly assess what went on in a battle where commanders were under extreme pressure. On the other hand, he realised that if he protested too strongly, he would be suspected of having something to hide.

On 21 November, the Agranat Commission was appointed. The committee sat for 140 sessions, during which they listened to the testimony of fifty-eight witnesses. Its remit was to investigate:

1. The intelligence information for the days preceding the Yom Kippur War on the enemy's moves and intentions to launch the war, the evaluation of this information, and the decisions taken by the responsible military and civil authorities in response thereto.
2. The general deployment of the IDF in case of war, its state of readiness during the days preceding the Yom Kippur War, and its operations up to the containment of the enemy.

It did not examine the later stages of the war when the IDF went on the offensive.

The Commission's deliberations were delayed by the elections that were held in December. Meir's party won by the narrowest of margins; the population was critical of the way in which the war had been run but not so strongly as to eject her party. However, discontent was seething below the surface, stoked by soldiers returning home having witnessed, at first hand, some of the ineptitude and inadequacies of their commanders and political masters. Dayan had lost his charisma and his men were now calling for his dismissal. Protest mounted but with minimum agenda, no political grouping and little aim except to get rid of the government. Meir and Dayan vacillated about his continuing in office; he resigned in March 1974 and Yitzhak Rabin was appointed minister of defence, but was it was never ratified and Dayan remained in office.

On 1 April, the Agranat Commission's interim report was published. Meir and Dayan were exonerated on the basis that their responsibilities were beyond the Commission's remit. 'We do not feel called upon to give our views on what can be considered the Ministers' parliamentary responsibility,' it said. The blame was firmly placed on Elazar, with the recommendation that he be removed from the office of chief of staff. Gonen, the southern front commander was suspended pending further enquiries and four intelligence officers were removed, including Zeira, head of AMAN. It was critical of what it called the 'concept' in military intelligence thinking. This was based on the assumption that Egypt would only attack if it had the air power to take on the Israeli Air Force. It held that neither Egypt nor Syria would go to war without the means to neutralise the Israeli Air Force by destruction of its airfields. The only suitable means, the Israelis reasoned, were long-range aircraft and missiles, which Egypt and Syria did not possess in significant numbers. It was also thought that Syria would only attack if Egypt did. In the absence of any upgrading of Egypt's air force it was concluded there was no threat of imminent war. Zeira was one of the proponents of this scenario. In essence, the concept laid down first that the Arabs were not ready for an all-out war with Israel. Though they had the ability to launch a limited war, they knew perfectly well that Israel would not accept that and would quickly escalate it. Secondly, Zeira's view was that, if there was to be a war, it would be a short one. The third assumption was that in an overall war, the Arabs would be quickly defeated. This led to complacency and evidence being ignored, the Commission said.

The report astounded some members of the Cabinet. One minister was quoted as saying that it was a grave and inexcusable injustice that the men in uniform alone should have been singled out for all the blame. Elazar maintained he had been unjustly treated and the Minster of Defence (Dayan) should also take the blame. The Commission said, 'We … reached the conclusion that by the standards of reasonable behaviour required by one holding the post of defence minister, the minister was not required to issue orders additional to or different from those proposed to him by the General Staff in accordance with joint assessment and consultation between the chief of staff and chief of intelligence.'

One might have expected this sort of judgement to apply to an inexperienced civilian politician but Dayan was not only a battle-hardened soldier of enormous military skill but had held the office of chief of staff himself, so knew exactly what he was doing. It made him out to be an outside onlooker and bureaucrat who was misled by his military experts.

The public simply would not accept this. The report was ridiculed and there were shouts for Dayan's resignation, particularly from demobilised soldiers. It ripped Meir's party apart and, failing to put together a strong government, on 10 April she and the entire government, including Dayan, resigned.

In a sense, the key player at the decision-making level in the Yom Kippur War was not Golda Meir, Moshe Dayan or even the outstanding divisional and brigade commanders, but David Elazar. Yet, unbelievably, he was held to blame and made the scapegoat for the way in which the Israelis were caught by surprise.

In action, Elazar had a stability and strength of character where Dayan dismally failed. He never lost his composure and exuded confidence and authority throughout the armed forces. He handled operations so well that, in the end, Israel was in a far better position to negotiate peace than could possibly have been envisaged at the start. His crucial decision on 7 October to reinforce the northern front and to counter-attack undoubtedly saved that situation. It was his decision, having taken the Egyptian incursions into the Sinai head-on, then to allow Sharon to cross the Suez Canal and take out the enemy with infantry infiltrating from the flank, which was the winning blow. His ability to think ahead, when those around him were vacillating and reacting to immediate problems, was critical to Israel's eventual success.

On 2 April, the day after the publication of the Agranat interim report, Elazar wrote to Golda Meir. A further, more detailed letter was written later to the new prime minister, Yitzhak Rabin. A Hebrew language copy of the letters is in the possession of his son, Yair, and has been made available to the author. It is factual and unemotional but firmly underlines the wrong done to him.

Elazar undoubtedly bears some responsibility for the faulty evaluation of the intelligence input, although, unlike Dayan, not all of it was available to him on a timely basis. He was certainly misled by the intelligence he was being given on Friday, 5 October. Just because others in the General Staff believed the force levels on the frontiers were adequate, that does not absolve him from questioning their assumptions. However, once it was clear war had broken out he acted with speed and decisiveness, calling for an immediate call-up. The fact that this was delayed because of his argument with Dayan is not his fault. There were faults in the General Staff in that supervision of administrative details was slack and the state of training was less than adequate. It was easy, therefore, after the war to point the finger at Elazar as the head of the General Staff and blame him, but there were others who were considerably at fault.

Golda Meir publicly announced, 'If there was a hero in the Yom Kippur War, it was Dado.' Yet, weakly, she allowed him to be the scapegoat for it.

Elazar, a highly professional soldier, would have recognised the qualities of Roméo Dallaire and would most certainly have had him in his team if he could. A Canadian, Dallaire was given an impossible task in the carnage of Rwanda in 1994. Under-resourced, with too few troops and a weak mandate from the United Nations, nevertheless he did the most remarkable job and many Rwandans owe him their lives. In this final chapter, he is no scapegoat but an example of how an organisation, whether it is a government or, as in this case, an international establishment, can hang a man out to dry.

THIRTEEN

Lieutenant General Roméo Dallaire OC CMM GOQ MSC CD

Massacre in Rwanda

April 1994

The hospital ward was overflowing with screaming and moaning wounded, lying alongside the dead; puddles of blood covered the floor and splashed on the walls. A lone doctor, his filthy white coat drenched with blood, moved among them. A rear door opened onto a large court-yard in front of the morgue. The stench and flies were overwhelming. At the entrance to the morgue was what seemed to be a pile of sacks of potatoes. On closer inspection it turned out to be a heap of mangled and bloodied white flesh in tattered Belgian para-commando uniforms. Ten in all, the corpses of these United Nations soldiers had had their boots removed, some still had armoured jackets on but these were open to reveal bullet wounds to their chests. Some had been shot in the head and many showed deep gashes from *pangas* (machetes), signs of a basic and rudimentary torture.

It was 7 April 1994. Welcome to Rwanda.

'Rwanda, that's somewhere in Africa, isn't it?' queried Major General Roméo Dallaire on being told he was to head a UN mission to that country. He was right. Rwanda is a small, land-locked country, about the size of Wales, in the middle of sub-Saharan Africa. With the Democratic Republic of the Congo to the west, Uganda to the north, Tanzania to the east and Burundi to the south, it has no importance to the rest of the world. It has no strategic value; any colonial pickings, if there ever had been any, have long gone; there is no oil, no diamonds, no gold, no bauxite and too many people barely making a living from subsistence agriculture.

In this land, and in Burundi, live the Hutus and the Tutsis. They have a complex relationship that is difficult for outsiders to understand; it is not one of simple tribe, race, caste or ethnic background. Anthropologists claim the pygmy hunter-gatherers were first to arrive in this part of Africa, followed by small, round Hutus, who farmed. The taller Tutsis – wanderers and cattle drovers – appeared from the north-east and, allegedly, because they drank milk and ate meat, became intellectually superior to the Hutus. They acquired airs and graces and tended to dominate the Hutus and rule over them. This suited the German colonialists in the 1890s, who firmly supported the system. After the First World War, the Belgians took over and further consolidated the position by making the Tutsis the educated 'middle class' of low-level government administrators, teachers and local gendarmerie.

The stereotype exists of the tall, elegant Tutsi and the short, round Hutu, and while the distinction is impenetrable to an outsider, a local will maintain he can tell the difference. Like many stereotypes, this is not foolproof since, as was shown later, during the worst of the atrocities identity cards were imposed on the population to make certain who was to be killed and who wasn't. The Hutus and Tsutis, however, are not separate tribes. They speak the same language, worship the same way and belong to the same overall society; there is inter-marriage and social mobility. Before Europeans arrived, they had a reasonably harmonious relationship, with responsibilities fairly split and the occasional bloody dispute.

The Belgian policy of divide and rule, of course, polarised and hardened the differences and, with independence in sight, power struggles arose for the leadership of the country. The Hutu manifesto in 1957 called for majority rule and, with Belgian help, many Tutsis were ousted from their jobs and replaced by Hutus. They argued that the problem with Rwanda was the Tutsis. Tutsis, who believed the opposite and that they were superior, demanded early independence. In 1959, a series of violent atrocities led to the death of approximately 2,000 Tutsis. A UN commission blamed the Belgians and the government, and reported that the outlook for Rwanda looked bleak. Indeed it was.

With independence in July 1962 came a Belgian-backed Hutu president who surrounded himself with Hutu acolytes. Livelihoods were extinguished for the thousands of oppressed and victimised Tutsis, who now fled to southern Uganda and other neighbouring territories. Desperate returnees were easily put down and gave the Hutu government the excuse to start a systematic planned campaign to eradicate the Tutsis. Coordinated killing sprees were widespread and included rape, mutilation, burning and dismemberment. Peasants were brutally hacked to death with hoes, shovels and the ubiquitous African *panga* (a long, heavy-bladed knife that is used for almost everything in the rural communities). A few reports of these atrocities got out but were dismissed as mere tribal warfare, endemic in the 'Dark Continent'.

In 1972, the reverse happened in Burundi, where the Tutsi government cracked down on the Hutus, massacring an estimated 200,000. For the first time the word 'genocide' was murmured in international corridors but world reaction was silent; the usual report was drafted, reviewed, circulated, collated, sent on and quietly forgotten. This was, of course, just what the Rwanda Hutus wanted; they now had further excuses to intimidate and kill on an organised basis. Juvénal Habyarimana, a name that was later to rattle round the world, seized power in Rwanda. A ruthless and brutal military leader, he created a one-party state the Gestapo would have been proud of, with spies and eavesdroppers ready to sell their grandmothers. His predecessor and his wife were secretly starved to death.

Habyarimana allied himself closely with the French, who still saw themselves as having some authority in Africa and had a pathological fear of Anglo-Saxon influence. From the Fashoda humiliation of 1898, to the debacle of Indo-China and Algeria, to the push and shove of the Americans and the world language of English, the French finally drew their line in the sand in the francophone area of Central Africa (Mali, Niger, Senegal and Cameroon). Mitterrand saw his world statesmanship dissolving. Rwanda was the final resting place; no surrender from here.

Stateless Tutsis in the Ugandan refugee camps, with nothing to lose, joined Yoweri Museveni in his rebellion against President Milton Obote in the early 1980s. His National Resistance Army was officered by a number of Rwandans. Winning the war for him, some were rewarded with reasonable jobs in his emerging government but were, generally, distrusted by the Ugandans. When, however, they were refused land and citizenship, they vowed to return to their own country and regain their rights.

The Rwandan Patriotic Front (RPF) was formed from these Tutsi refugees in 1987, and on 1 October 1990, its enthusiastic volunteers invaded their former homeland. They tended to be second generation Tutsis with combat experience in Museveni's campaign. Looking a bit ragtag in their gumboots, they were, nevertheless, a tough, reasonably disciplined force by existing standards. The invasion, though, petered out in the north of the country after Habyarimana appealed to the French for military help. Ostensibly, French troops were sent to 'protect their own nationals' and provide a lifeline if events deteriorated. In practice, 'advisers' to the wholly inadequate Rwandan Army and helicopters pushed the invaders into operating in guerrilla bands. Substantial arms shipments were made by France to the Hutus, carefully transported through Egypt to circumvent EU directives banning arms sales to states in civil unrest. (Interestingly, Boutros Boutros-Ghali, later to become the UN Secretary-General, was a foreign office official in Cairo at the time.) A second invasion by the Tutsis was again put down but not before they had freed prisoners from a notorious jail and inflicted casualties on their enemy. This resulted in heavy reprisal massacres by the Hutu government. Clandestine plans were now initiated to rid the country of the Tutsis for ever.

The Hutus began to arm local villagers into a civil defence force, ostensibly to resist any outside attack from neighbouring states but, in reality, to start up cells for the ultimate destruction of the Tutsis. At the same time, the army was increased and trained by French advisers. A name to send a chill down any Tutsi backbone came to the fore: Colonel Théoneste Bagosora. Violence became widespread and went unpunished. The law could not be upheld and the courts were totally overwhelmed and inadequate. An armed youth group now emerged: the Interahamwe. Its members were given military training, taught how to use weapons and how to kill quickly. Radio Rwanda broadcast blood-curdling propaganda against the Tutsis and the killing flowed from that.

In July 1992, peace negotiations between the Hutu government and the RPF started in Arusha, Tanzania. These were sponsored by the Organization of African Unity (OAU), with Belgian, French and American observers. Encouraging signs emerged but were overshadowed by vitriolic invective from hard-line Hutus in Rwanda. Plans to eliminate Tutsis were secretly continuing. The dark hand of the French was ever present.

In February 1993, the RPF carried out a significant attack from the north. If it had not been for French troops opposing them, they would have reached Kigali. The RPF had proved to be a formidable force and worried Mitterrand enough to send reinforcements to Rwanda. Masses of people were displaced and huge refugee camps had to be established. It drove the belligerents back to the negotiating table in Arusha. The aim for both sides seemed to be an achievement of a settlement but with little desire to implement it. The 'agreement' became known as the Arusha Accords. Hardmen, like Bagosora, cynically regarded the whole thing as a complete waste of time. Habyarimana, the president, did not even bother to attend.

Throughout 1993, violence increased and, in Kigali for example, four or five people a day were being killed by soldiers. With recurring riots by the unpaid civil servants and teachers, assassinations of a few prominent political leaders on all sides and sporadic small arms and grenade incidents at night, the security situation in the capital continued to deteriorate to the point where redeployment of UN forces, already under strength in the demilitarised zone, to Kigali was absolutely essential. Two massacres involving about forty victims in the Hutu heartland to the north exacerbated the frictions and political impasse.

Unbelievably, in the same year, Rwanda imported huge numbers of machetes (*pangas*) and agricultural tools to the tune of US$4.6 million – far in excess of what could be actually used in its collapsing agriculture. Rwanda, one of the poorest countries in the world, became the third largest importer of weapons in Africa. The money came from international organisations that were under the impression that they were alleviating famine and the refugee problem. When questioned as to where all this money was going, Habyarimana blandly replied that he needed it to defend the country against the RPF and Ugandan aggression. Amazingly, this appeared to satisfy the auditors. France and Egypt were the main suppliers, to the tune of many millions of US dollars-worth of grenades, small arms, rockets, mortar bombs and ammunition.

The formal signing of the Arusha Accords on 4 August 1993 made little difference. The provisions of the agreement made much sense and, indeed, went far to reach a settlement, but this assumed that the signatories had the intention of accepting the clauses. Neither side, of course, did. Outsiders naively welcomed it as a diplomatic success while the hardliners of both the Hutu regime and the RPF merely saw the Arusha Accords as a pause to take breath before their next assault. The abuse of human rights, although properly reported by UN representatives, disappeared from the world scene. Leaders wanted the Accords to work and weakly ignored the realities. Reports were quietly shelved.

Into this steaming cesspit stepped Roméo Dallaire, a Canadian general. To many Rwandans he was their saviour; to the Belgians he was a convenient scapegoat for the deaths of their soldiers; to most of the world he was the unlucky victim of UN incompetence and the arrogance and perfidy of its Security Council. He tells a story of betrayal, failure, naivety, indifference, hatred, genocide, war, inhumanity and evil. He brushes over, with characteristic self-deprecation, his own outstanding personal courage in the face of countless life-threatening situations where he could have been killed without a moment's thought.

Dallaire was born in 1946 to a French Canadian staff sergeant and a Dutch war bride. In the early 1960s, when he went to the Royal Military College, Canada was still very much divided into English-speaking and French-speaking communities. Coming from Montreal, Dallaire was one of the latter. Tolerance in the Canadian military was mixed, but Dallaire's strength of character saw him through any difficulties and prejudices. On commissioning in 1969, he joined a French-speaking artillery regiment. This was one of the first French language units to be created to encourage the career prospects of francophones. The previous year, the army had been integrated with the navy and air force under the policy of 'unification'. The newly formed Canadian Forces was the first combined command military force in the modern world. The army became known as Force Mobile Command. The experiment was not popular and resulted in anomalies such as army officers wearing rings of rank on their lower sleeves like the navy. People had no idea whether they were speaking to a sailor or a soldier, as they were dressed the same.

After Korea, the Canadian Army was seeking a role and concentrated on its support for NATO in north-west Europe together with NATO allies. It was also an ideal force for UN peacekeeping operations – it lacked the tarnish of a former colonial power and, together with the Irish, was seen as non-political. It was efficient, disciplined, properly trained and equipped to handle situations in countries that would not accept Western-orientated troops.

Dallaire's first taste of non-combat operations was the experience of riot control and vital point protection in the light of the Front de Libération du Québec (FLQ) terrorist activities in 1969. Keeping the peace on the streets of Montreal when the police went on strike was to give him a small taste of what life was going to be like a few years later. With the kidnap and murder of the Quebec cabinet minister, Pierre Laporte, the situation became worse and Dallaire and his men, now on the streets of Quebec City, had clear orders for opening fire. Leadership in a French-speaking unit at the time was severely tried and, to his great credit, Dallaire survived that test.

In 1973, a posting to Germany followed some training appointments. He married in 1976 and returned to a staff job in Canada. In 1982, he was promoted to lieutenant colonel and, to his delight, was given command of the regiment into which he had been commissioned. After further staff appointments he was promoted to brigadier general (brigadier in the British Army) and became the commandant of the Royal Military College. During this time, he attended the Higher Command and Staff Course in England where he made a number of British friends. On return from the course, he was made commander of the 5th Mechanised Brigade Group. While in command, many of his troops were sent on peacekeeping missions across the world, from Cambodia to the Balkans to Kuwait. Dallaire, not unnaturally, became expert in the UN doctrine of lightly armed, multinational, blue-helmeted, impartial and neutral peacekeepers. With their consent, they were put between two warring factions, such as in the Sinai from 1956 to 1967, or to assist in implementing a peace agreement, as in Cambodia. This worked well when the participants knew the rules and played the game. The rules, however, were, at best, changing or were simply not understood and ignored. Casualties among peacekeeping troops started to mount.

Dallaire clearly had had his card marked, for, on 27 June 1993, he received a call that the UN was considering a mission to Rwanda and he was to lead it.

The trouble with soldiers is that they tend to be people who look at problems as things that are there to be solved. There is no such thing as shelving or 'putting on the back burner'. On commissioning, they are indicated the objective by their platoon sergeant and told, 'There it is, go and tackle it – preferably now.' Glasses are always half full, never half empty. Dallaire was no exception. He had been highly selected from an international forum, to his great pleasure, to head a mission into a country about which he knew nothing, where he had little idea of what was going on, with a non-existent team, unbriefed and with an aim that was opaque to say the least. It did not occur to him to examine the situation with a view to assessing whether what he was being told to do was, in fact, feasible, and, if it wasn't, to refuse the offer or make conditions on which he could accept it. It did not work like that. Anyway, there wasn't time. There never is. He was a senior officer, well versed in the UN peacekeeping concept, although without any practical experience in the field, and he was a man who did what he was told. There is an understandable assumption of people of his seniority that the people doing the telling know what they are doing. More experience of the UN headquarters would have told him that this was very far from reality.

He was briefed that in response to a request from the president of Uganda the UN was to send a small monitoring team, while peace talks were continuing in Arusha, to ensure that weapons and soldiers were not crossing from Uganda into Rwanda to reinforce the RPF. A classic confidence-building measure, its scope was to encourage the warring factions to seek a proper peaceful outcome. There would be a total of eighty-one unarmed UN observers on the Ugandan side of the border. On the face of it, there was nothing very difficult about it; this sort of thing had been successfully done a number of times across the world.

Managing to acquire a Canadian major as his military assistant, Dallaire flitted between Ottawa (the Canadian Defence Ministry) and the UN in New York. Neither establishment filled him with great confidence; the desk officer in New York was an Argentinian who also ran the missions in Angola, Mozambique, Central America and Liberia. His number two was an ex-Cuban freedom fighter who was the political officer for Central Africa. Anyway, the four of them got on with it as best they could. Behind and above them was the Department for Peacekeeping Operations (DPKO) running 80,000 people with sixty contributing nations. Well-known eminences such as Kofi Annan and Iqbal Riza presided from afar.

There was a suspicion that there might need to be a bigger mission inside Rwanda itself in due course but this was quickly scotched on the grounds of expense. There was no political will to become involved, apart from a minimum effort from Belgium and France, and certainly no one else was in the least interested. All effort was directed to the Balkans and the United States had no intention of having a rerun of its Somalia disaster.

Dallaire's small team kicked their heels, waiting for the Ugandans to sign the mission agreement for them to deploy. On 8 August, Dallaire was told the Rwandans had signed the Arusha Accords and an international peacekeeping force was urgently required to ensure the agreement was upheld. The DPKO decided to send a reconnaissance team, led by default by Dallaire as the political head of the team fell suddenly sick the day before leaving New York. The reconnaissance team was sent as soon as possible with a view to establishing the main force by 10 September. He was warned not to come back with some grand idea of needing a brigade. The requirement was 'something small and inexpensive, otherwise it will not get approved by the Security Council'. How often have soldiers been given that political direction?

Dallaire and his team landed at Kigali on 19 August 1993, highly conscious that they only had a few days to come up with an acceptable plan. As with many reconnaissances into impoverished, war-torn developing countries, there was little in the way of office set-up, stable electricity, clean water or reliable transport. However, Dallaire handed out responsibilities for the administrative aspects of the potential operation to his colleagues and kept himself for meeting what in Paris would be called the '*grand gratinées*': the big cheeses. Without a civilian UN representative, he had to do the whole thing himself. He went about his task with enthusiasm and optimism, which perhaps sometimes blinded him to the deep venality of some of the hardliners he met.

He saw both the RPF and the Rwandan Army, contrasting them both with his experienced military eye. The former were clearly a force to be reckoned with under the charismatic Paul Kagame. The low-level soldiers of the Rwandan Army were in stark contrast: poor leadership and morale, lack of weapons and medical supplies, living for their two beers a day. The elite, French-trained Presidential Guard were very different; aggressive and self-assured, they treated Dallaire with arrogance and disdain to the point of deliberate rudeness. He could see they were going to be trouble. He also had his first taste of the desperation and filth of a 600,000-person refugee camp with its stench of vomit, urine, faeces and death, and the 300,000 new refugees in the south generated by the Burundi Tutsi-led *coup d'état*.

Until now, Habyarimana had refused to see Dallaire and only at his insistence did the President receive him on his last day in the country. The meeting did not boost Dallaire's optimism, but rather increased his already acute sense of urgency to get the mission deployed and effective as soon as possible.

He left for New York, via Dar es Salaam and Addis Ababa, with a good deal of satisfaction. He reckoned he and his team had worked out a plan covering all the major political, military and humanitarian problems, which would satisfy a classic Chapter VI UN mandate. That is to say, 'Pacific Settlement of Disputes stipulates that parties to a dispute should use peaceful methods of resolving disputes, such as negotiation and mediation. It authorizes the Security Council to issue recommendations, but they are generally considered advisory and not binding.' Little did he realise that many of those he met were to become the 'genocidaires'. They were the ones doing the assessing, not him. They had already concluded that the UN and OAU did not have the will or resources to establish the sort of force that would stop them carrying out whatever they wanted. They guessed that even a token force, once it started taking casualties, would quickly fold.

Dallaire's strength was that he really believed in what he was doing. This gave him the determination to overcome the many obstacles in his way. First of all, he had to draft a technical mission report. This formed the basis for a formal report to the Secretary-General. It then went to the Security Council as a report and recommendation, and hopefully, this would result in a Security Council resolution mandating the mission. The bureaucrats must have loved it, but how intensely frustrating for Dallaire and his team. There was no question of meeting the 10 September deadline.

He knew that he needed between 5,500 and 8,000 troops for the task but, aware this was totally unachievable, reached what he considered the minimum below which he could not go – 2,600. Giving up the proper requirement for armed monitoring teams, he would be forced to rely on isolated unarmed observers who could call in a rapid reaction force when needed. The latter, of course, required armoured personnel carriers and helicopters to accomplish this. In all this bargaining and counter-argument, what was being missed was what was needed absolutely immediately: a force to protect the civilians at risk, forget everything else for the time being.

As bad luck would have it, the Rwanda mission statement was before the Security Council two days after the deaths of the US soldiers in Mogadishu. Without the Americans, it was highly likely the Rwanda operation would simply be swept away. However, a compromise was reached. A mission was established – the UN Assistance Mission for Rwanda (UNAMIR) – with the weakest possible mandate and minimum funding. It relied on the fact that there was a ceasefire and a peace agreement.

Dallaire landed at Kigali on 22 October with the three staff officers who had been with him in the Uganda mission to find that in a Tutsi coup in Burundi, the president and a number of ministers had been assassinated. There was hysteria in Kigali. Rumour and counter-rumour abounded, all, of course, to the satisfaction of the Hutu hardmen who rubbed their hands with glee. A head of mission – Dallaire's superior as the Special Representative of the Secretary-General – was appointed. He was Jacques-Roger Booh-Booh, an old crony of Boutros Boutros-Ghali's. In his 2003 memoir, *Shake Hands with the Devil*, Dallaire makes a number of criticisms about Booh-Booh's actions and management style, such as that he kept to diplomatic hours and did not take the lead on international political efforts (allegations that were subsequently refuted by the latter in his own memoir of 2005, *Le Patron de Dallaire PARLE*).

For those who have never worked under the UN system – and Dallaire, although having posted many of his soldiers to do so, had not – administration was a nightmare. For example, soldiers have to eat and drink. Normally, food and water is therefore automatically provided for the number on the posted strength of the unit. Not so with the UN; it had to be separately requisitioned. If torches were demanded, you had to remember to request batteries and bulbs. Sink this sort of bureaucracy into a country that could barely look after itself, then life became unnecessarily difficult. At a higher level, twenty-two armoured personnel carriers (APCs) and eight helicopters were to be provided from UN resources. No helicopters arrived and only eight APCs of which a mere five were serviceable and even they did not arrive until March 1994, in bad order from Mozambique, with no spares, tools or manuals. In *Shake Hands with the Devil*, Dallaire describes how operations were hampered by one ageing and obstructive UN administrative officer who did things by the (UN) book, which meant too little arrived, too late.

That November the massacres started or, rather, recommenced from where they had left off. This was the first, probably deliberate challenge to UNAMIR. Hands were cut off, eyes gouged out, skulls crushed and pregnant women cut open. For the first months, hatred was subtly diffused by the very popular RTLM broadcasting station, which poured verbal vitriol personally onto Dallaire, and accused the peacekeepers of failing to apprehend the culprits.

About seventy-five Belgian paratroops then arrived, whose attitude Dallaire found unimpressive. They had been involved in a rather different operation in Somalia and had to be talked through the more restrained rules of engagement in Rwanda. They refused to live in tents under some 'agreement' they had with the UN and therefore had to be housed in buildings around Kigali. Dallaire wanted them, understandably, at the airport, the lifeline in and out of the country, but hard-standing accommodation was limited at best and the UN administrative staff refused to authorise renting or constructing suitable accommodation for the whole Belgian contingent.

Next, the Bangladeshi battalion arrived. Normal battalions are commanded by a lieutenant colonel with a brace of majors. This unit appeared commanded by a full colonel with six lieutenant colonels, countless majors and innumerable other officers. They came in virtually what they stood up in and expected the UN to provide everything. For developing world armies, the UN was a gravy train, saving their governments from having to pay or administer them. Having said that, the Tunisian and Ghanaian contingents did extremely well.

In December, the RPF battalion moved into Kigali in accordance with the agreement. They were securely housed in the city but were extremely provocative cuckoos in the Hutu nest. By the end of the year, though, Dallaire was as confident as he could be. He had met the initial military target. The ground was prepared for the interim government to step down and the transitional one to be sworn in. However, he desperately needed the troops and logistical supplies for the next phase. The UN dragged its feet yet again.

Now came a prime example of the difficulties and frustrations Dallaire had with the operational side of the UN. He and his closest staff were approached by a source deep inside the Presidential Guard. Codenamed 'Jean-Pierre', the informant had been the chief trainer of the Interahamwe thugs. He had become disgusted and horrified with the plans that were being made to create highly efficient death squads which, when turned on the population, could kill a thousand Tutsis in Kigali within twenty minutes of receiving the order. Until now, they had been armed only with *pangas* and clubs but a large shipment of small arms, ammunition and grenades had recently been received and located in four caches in Kigali. Apart from being against the 'rules' of Kigali as a weapons-secure zone, this represented a major escalation of the potential killing ability of the Hutu. Jean-Pierre also told them of plans to provoke the Belgian soldiers into opening fire. Had they done so, a number of peacekeepers would have been immediately killed with the object of persuading the Belgian Government to withdraw their troops, having no stomach for sustaining casualties.

Dallaire determined to raid the caches, which would send a powerful signal to the Hutu leadership that he knew what they were doing and was ahead of them. There was a snag. Under the mandate, Dallaire had to go through Booh-Booh. He was not allowed to approach the military people in the UN except on administrative details. He was, understandably, very worried about the security of Booh-Booh's office. To make matters worse, there was now a non-permanent Rwanda member on the Security Council (a Hutu, of course) so much classified material would be seen by him. He decided, therefore, to use the channels to New York, as he had done before Booh-Booh arrived as 'head of mission'. He sent a coded signal, explaining carefully that it could be a trap, but nevertheless that he wasn't seeking permission for the raid (he believed it was justified under the rules) but merely informing them what he was going to do.

To his astonishment, he received an immediate reply from Kofi Annan. It ordered him to abort the mission at once. He was reminded of the terms of the Chapter VI peacekeeping mandate – not only was he not allowed to conduct deterrent operations but also, in the interests of transparency, he was to give the source's information directly to President Habyarimana, as well as to General Kagame on the RPF side. He was appalled. With all the background of bloodletting and arming of the killers, the whole peace accord and the mission itself was now in extreme jeopardy. Call after call to New York merely gave Dallaire the impression that he was seen as a dangerously loose cannon. This failure to raid the caches came back to haunt him for years afterwards.

Before he disappeared and was never heard of again, Jean-Pierre managed to deliver more information that convinced Dallaire he was now dealing with a well-organised conspiracy inside the country to destroy the Arusha Accords. Accordingly, he took steps to reinforce the protection of his bases and requested further defence stores from New York. To no one's surprise, the demand fell on deaf ears. The mine threat was also on the increase and, again, there was no response from New York for funding or mine clearance experts to deal with it.

Dallaire's third formal report to New York at the end of January, in which he sought clarification of the tracking of weapon stores and neutralisation of armed gangs rules, in addition to setting up a radio station to combat the propaganda of the RTLM, was met with a further damp blanket from Annan reiterating the role of UNAMIR was to 'be limited to a monitoring function'. Dallaire was still convinced, though, that with the authority and resources, he could achieve his aim. Lesser men would have gone under at this point.

Lynchings, rioting, assassinations and multiple killings were on the increase. Hysteria and mob violence erupted on the streets of Kigali. Vehicles were ambushed and their occupants slaughtered. Ominously, the interim government that, by now, should have been replaced, began extensively checking identity cards indicating Hutu or Tutsi.

On 6 April, Dallaire received the Security Council's resolution that if the transitional government was not in place in six weeks' time, the mission would be 'reviewed' – in UN-speak, pulled out. New York asked for his evacuation plans for non-Rwandan nationals. He had no port, one airport, three roads to the border and no trains. He had no increased authority, no reinforcement and, to cap it all, was required to 'make savings'. At 8.20 p.m. that night, President Habyarimana was returning from Dar es Salaam when his plane was brought down by one, if not two, surface-to-air missiles over Kigali airport. There were no survivors. Real mayhem was about to begin.

The Presidential Guard and other Rwandan army troops ran wild at the airport and illegal roadblocks manned by panicky soldiers were being set up throughout Kigali. Shots and explosions were frequent. Dallaire's immediate reaction was to protect Prime Minister Madame Agathe Uwilingiyimana so that she could broadcast a calming message over the radio to the nation. Extra Belgian and Ghanaian UNAMIR troops were sent to her compound. In the meantime, Dallaire went to a 'crisis committee' set up by the sinister Colonel Bagosora. The blame for the shooting down of the plane was, naturally, laid at the door of the RPF but the extremist radio station RTLM was already putting it out that it was the Belgians. Dallaire had, though, strong suspicions that it was an extremist plot, initiated by Bagosora, who feared the President was going to accede to the Arusha Accords too readily.

Dallaire gave a brief report to New York, which merely repeated that his men were not to open fire unless fired upon. Booh-Booh was woken up but proved to be little help. There was little doubt in Dallaire's mind that this was a well-thought-out conspiracy by Bagosora and his cronies, with no intention of allowing a transitional government to be put in place, nor to fulfil the Accords. How right he turned out to be.

It is difficult to imagine the difficulties Dallaire was under. His 'command' radio net depended on insecure civilian Motorola radios – different contingents brought their own radios, which were incompatible with each other, and the Belgian, Bangladeshi and Ghanaian units talked on their own frequencies with a wide variety of languages, accents and technical skills. Of the 2,538 UNAMIR military in Rwanda, Dallaire had only one staff officer whose first tongue was English, the approved UN standard operating language. He and his small staff were being bombarded with calls from terrified individuals pleading for protection, on occasions being slaughtered while on the telephone. Some made it to the relative safety of the various UNAMIR bases. It was difficult to move around Kigali without the authority or firepower to force his way through the roadblocks. He could not use force without the risk of certain casualties, playing into the hardliners' hands. His only options were negotiation and bluff.

On 7 April, Dallaire learnt that Madame Agathe and her husband had been murdered by the Presidential Guard but her children had escaped. The fate of her Belgian and Ghanaian guards was unknown. To make matters worse, Kagame and his RPF were threatening to become involved. The only way to prevent full-scale civil war was now for Bagosora to talk to Kagame. Both refused.

Later in the day, Dallaire was told his Belgian soldiers were in the Kigali hospital. On arrival, he was taken to the pile of bodies where, because of the mutilation, he initially counted eleven. It turned out to be ten. He was numbed and waves of intense anger rolled over him, tempting him to extract immediate retribution. He managed, with immense self-control, to threaten the nearest Rwandan officers that the full force of the UN in New York would descend upon them if the perpetrators were not found and punished. For him, this was the turning point: either New York gave him the authority and forces to stop the apocalypse or, like Somalia, use the deaths as an excuse to get out. He was told not to risk UNAMIR troops, but to help with the security of UN personnel and expatriates and update the withdrawal plans. No other help was forthcoming. It was day one of a hundred-day civil war of untold carnage.

UNAMIR was now in chaos. Food and water was running low and fuel was virtually non-existent not only for vehicles but also for generators to charge radios. The contingent at the airport, the sole lifeline, was not in control of the terminal and increasing numbers of terrified Tutsis and moderate Hutus were seeking protection. Dallaire had one functioning satellite phone with a fax facility. The mission had virtually descended into self-protection mode. The reaction in New York was for national governments to look to their own survival plans for their expatriates stranded in Rwanda. Thoughts were turning to pulling out the UNAMIR rather than any attempt to stop the massacres, which were increasing ten-fold by the hour.

The one word no one in New York was using was 'genocide'. The reason is that it lays mandatory responsibility on nations to take appropriate action to prevent it occurring and, once it has, interfere to stop it. The UN convention on genocide bans

> acts committed with the intent to destroy, in whole or in part, a national, ethnic, racial or religious group. It declares genocide a crime under international law whether committed during war or peacetime, and binds all signatories of the convention to take measures to prevent and punish any acts of genocide committed within their jurisdiction. The act bans killing of members of any racial, ethnic, national or religious group because of their membership in that group, causing serious bodily or mental harm to members of the group, inflicting on members of the group conditions of life intended to destroy them, imposing measures intended to prevent births within the group, and taking group members' children away from them and giving them to members of another group.

It could not be plainer. The Americans and British thought the word 'genocide' inflammatory and unhelpful.

One such example of genocide occurred at the Polish Mission in Gikondo on 9 April when, in two hours, some 500 men, women and children were hacked to death in a Catholic church. It was a coordinated and planned operation between the Presidential Guard and the Interahamwe. The attackers made no attempt to conceal their identities in the sure knowledge that they would never be punished. Further horrific tales of massacres were rife. Embassies were being closed; the diplomats were retreating with their tails between their legs. The extremists now saw that they could continue their genocide without the prying eyes of the world. Dallaire was ordered to plan a withdrawal of his mission, along with expatriates who were now heading south by vehicle into Burundi. He refused, saying that a number of people needed his protection and, what is more, he required reinforcement to do so. He was adamant that he was equipped only for peacekeeping, not peace enforcement. If only the troops sent to assist the evacuation of nationals had been made available to Dallaire with an enforcement mandate, he could undoubtedly have stopped the killing.

With a so-called interim, and palpably illegitimate, government now sworn in, the RPF were even more determined to win the war and shelling could be heard from the north of Kigali. On 12 April, the Belgian Government unilaterally decided to evacuate its component of the UNAMIR and cravenly suggested that other contributory nations did the same. Dallaire utterly refused; the Rwandans needed protection, even if it was only a fig-leaf, now more than ever. The UN, with Boutros-Ghali out of touch somewhere in Europe, reluctantly agreed but supported this decision with further inaction. Dallaire continued to press for a cease-fire but the RPF refused to negotiate unless the killing stopped and the extremists would not agree unless a ceasefire happened first; the UN was not prepared to reinforce UNAMIR or give it any additional authority unless a ceasefire was in place. Result: paralysis.

Meanwhile, the massacres spread. In Kigali alone 10,000 were being killed a day. People were being slaughtered in churches, mission stations, markets and playing fields. Massacres of between 20,000 and 50,000 victims were common in the countryside. As Dallaire wrote in *Shake Hands with the Devil*, 'The odour of death in the hot sun; the flies, maggots, rats and dogs that swarmed to feast on the dead. At times it seemed the smell had entered the pores of my skin.' The radio station RTLM, run by a Belgian-Italian, not only lashed out its daily vitriol but was a conduit for instructions to the killing squads throughout the country. In a land where there was little form of communication, everyone tuned into its broadcasts. Long ago Dallaire had given up trying to persuade the UN to fund a jamming set-up or, indeed, produce its own radio station to counter the RTLM propaganda.

He was bombarded with differing plans from New York. Deadlines were issued for withdrawal of the mission if there was no ceasefire, and he was told to tell the belligerents. He could see these threats were utterly hollow; neither side had any intention of reaching a ceasefire and many would be quite happy to see Dallaire and his men go, which would then give them a clear run to their nefarious ends. Reducing his force down towards the 250 minimum, he was appalled to see a photograph flashed across the world of the Bangladeshi contingent running for their aircraft, jettisoning their kit as they went. What propaganda for his opponents; rats and sinking ships were words that came easily to mind. Dallaire desperately needed to have the press on his side but editors simply were not interested. Black tribes killing each other in Central Africa was not news; white nuns being raped might raise a flicker but not for long. There were exceptions, though, to this. People such as Mark Doyle of the BBC and Aidan Hartley did their best.

In early May, Dallaire proposed a further option. He stressed his demand for additional troops was not a Chapter VII mandate – in other words, an armed intervention operation – but an enhancement of Chapter VI to provide protection and humanitarian aid. He required four APC-borne battalions that would also be capable of taking on the militias and seizing arms caches under fire. Meanwhile, the UN was fiddling around with the idea of 'safe zones' in neighbouring countries. Dallaire realised this was a complete non-starter; endless negotiations would have to be handled and getting the refugees across war-torn Rwanda would be almost impossible.

Then, on 17 May, a glimmer of hope arrived. The Security Council approved a UN force of 5,500 to stabilise Rwanda. However, before anyone could be too overjoyed, it had to be established who was to contribute to the force, who was to pay for it and how and when it was to deploy. It was to be subject to further reconnaissance and fact-finding missions – as though no one knew what the situation was – and more papers to be circulated, addressed and tabled. Under Chapter VI it needed the consent of the belligerents. The RPF, alone, who were on the brink of winning the war, were certainly not going to agree to any intervention in their ruling the country. Meanwhile, thousands were dying by the day.

Dallaire was becoming more and more exasperated. The Americans offered fifty APCs, but these were to be lent, not given – the rent would be US$4 million and another US$6 million to transport them. They were eventually delivered to Entebbe, stripped of spares, radios and machine guns, and there were no vehicles capable of transporting them to Kigali. The British were not much better. They offered aged 3-ton trucks rusting in Germany for a sizeable sum up front, which was later withdrawn with embarrassment. In the end, the trucks promised by Lynda Chalker, Minister of State for Overseas Development at the British Foreign Office, arrived.

In Kigali, the extremists were revving up for a fight to the end. They had about 4,000 troops, many of whom were the Interahamwe, who were not about to give any mercy to the Tutsis. On the other side, the RPF were recruiting Tutsis from the refugee camps in Uganda and carrying out their own revenge killings of Hutus. The plan was to dominate the countryside and strangle Kigali until the extremists gave in or, ultimately, fight for the city. The war was on the turn with the demoralised Rwandan Army looting, murdering and deserting in droves.

Dallaire's men were in bad straits with water, medicine and food running low. Stress levels were extreme and the leadership severely tested. Unbelievably, UN requisition for water alone had to be subject to a call for proposals and then the three best bids analysed. RTLM broadcast their 'kill Dallaire' exhortation to their followers. The UN flag and white-painted vehicles were no longer any protection, if they ever had been.

At the end of May, Annan's chief of staff Iqbal Riza and the Secretary-General's military adviser, Major General Maurice Baril, visited Rwanda and wrote a hard-hitting report, in which they stressed that the killings had to stop with a ceasefire. The immediate problem was to relieve the suffering of the refugees and banish the fear of the civilians under threat. This could not be done without adequate security conditions for the humanitarian process to take place. While this was just what Dallaire needed – an authority to act – he did not have the troops to do it with.

Then came Operation Turquoise – the finale of French cynicism and duplicity. This was to establish a safe haven in the south-west of the country for displaced people. On the face of it, this was fine. It had all the trappings of an international humanitarian effort and the backing of Boutros-Ghali. Dallaire was excluded from initial discussions and, indeed, the Rwandan government forces knew about it before he did. The reality was that the French intended to split the country in two and the safe haven was to be a sanctuary for the Hutus and *genocidaires*. Through 'Turquoise' territory, they would be able to reach the Democratic Republic of the Congo. If the French had been so keen on the humanitarian process, Dallaire argued, why hadn't they reinforced UNAMIR? The extremists whooped for joy. Here were the French coming to rescue them and protect the western areas of the country from RPF attack. The killers were going to be safe.

On 4 July, the RPF took Kigali and 37,000 troops of the Rwandan Army fled the country.

Dallaire was now faced with a new problem – keeping the French and RPF from each other's throats. The RPF, with considerable justification, saw the French as supporters of the Hutus and, by extension therefore, the *genocidaires*. The French had far too much murky baggage of their pre-war dealings to be proud of and the RPF knew, literally and figuratively, where the bodies were buried. Dallaire was adamant that the French should go nowhere near Kigali and remain within the 'Turquoise' zone. If they had, he feared a major conflict in the city. He met the French commander and found him reasonably inclined but, of course, in reality, he answered to Paris rather than New York. Dallaire's Chapter VI mission was the separation force between the UN-sanctioned Chapter VII Turquoise force and the advancing RPF. The French would not disarm anyone in the Turquoise zone unless they posed a threat. So the *genocidaires* happily walked around with their weapons.

Dallaire's main aim now was to see in the reinforced mission, known as UNAMIR 2, and replace the French with it. The refugee problem both within Rwanda and in neighbouring countries was becoming overwhelming. World aid started to roll in. The people bringing it were outsiders. In a way, Dallaire resented it. They were not of his team, they had not weathered the appalling stress that he and his men had and they had not been there when they were needed. Dallaire's adrenalin was evaporating; the trauma that he had experienced and the emotions that he had been through were starting to tell.

On 4 August, physically and psychologically exhausted by almost four months of constant horrors, ethical and moral dilemmas, and abandonment by the UNHQ and the international community, he asked to be relieved as he rightly assessed that he was becoming a liability to his command. It was now the time to hand over to someone else for the next phase in the life of that sad country.

Astonishingly, the Belgian Army decided to court-martial Colonel Luc Marchal, Dallaire's right-hand man in Kigali, for the death of the ten Belgian soldiers. Was it his government's way of covering up their own woeful inadequacy in the face of the massacres in withdrawing their troops and then trying to persuade the other nations to do the same? The case went to trial but was thrown out on the grounds that casualties will happen in military operations and political leaders must realise it and accept proper responsibility. Nonetheless, Dallaire's view was clear. They were trying to get at him through his subordinate. It was he that they thought the real culprit. The Belgian senate incomprehensibly had the idea that he should never have put the soldiers in harm's way. Clearly, no senator had ever been in an army on active service. For a time, Dallaire admits, he became a convenient scapegoat for everything that had gone wrong in Rwanda.

Dallaire has been rightly honoured by his own country and the world for the outstanding work he did in Rwanda. Lesser men would have folded in the early days of the operation. How many times would it have been tempting to pull out his team, with the wholehearted agreement of New York, or given in to the inadequacies of the UN? How many times did he have to fight his corner for what he knew was right in the face of the perfidy and intransigence of developed nations? How many times did he have to fight for the bare essentials of food, water, vehicles, radios and fuel for his command? As a man of deep integrity, he felt it his moral duty to stay and help, even if the impact of his actions was small. For him, the toll was heavy; he felt guilty that he had not succeeded in persuading the UN to do better. Like many commanders, he suffered the guilt of the death of his soldiers. Attendance at the International Criminal Tribunal for Rwanda where he faced again people like the malevolent Bagosora, caused the traumatic stress to catch up with him to the near destruction of his life.

In December 1999, a fifty-nine-page report (S/1999/1257) was forwarded to the United Nations Security Council. It concluded that the UN had failed to prevent, and then stop, a genocide of 800,000 Rwandans in one hundred days between April and July 1994. It made fourteen recommendations. Failure by the governments of Belgium, France, the United States, the United Kingdom and the UN Secretariat was made very clear. It was one of the more disgraceful episodes in the annals of the UN.

This final chapter is about a man who was not actually a scapegoat, but was a victim, nevertheless, of the total ineptitude and weakness of the international community that failed to support him. It selected him and gave him the task. It did not provide him, however, with the authority to do that task or the materiel and force levels to accomplish it. It was the culprit and that is where the blame lay.

EPILOGUE

So, what makes a scapegoat? In some cases, Carey for example, it is very clear. For others, did they bring misfortune on themselves? One could hardly accuse McVay of that. Indeed, his crew would never have supported him so fully if they thought so. Smyth, on the other hand, was an ill man and might have behaved differently if he had been 100 per cent fit. Longstreet, latterly, did not help himself but was an easy target for sour Southern disaffection. Poor Corporal Short, unable to defend himself – was he really a mutineer, even by the standards of the time? Warren was clearly not the best general around on the day, but, nevertheless, did not deserve Buller – who did? Byng, inadequately supported from the top and poorly advised, fell victim, in effect, to judicial murder. Dreyfus, an amazing survivor of not only Devil's Island but also two courts martial and the persecution of a paranoid and powerful politico-military faction, emerges as a man with an admirable moral courage of his own. Was George Taylor really fixed by his British battalion commanders or was he the *Danegeld* Cassels paid to the Americans for their materiel support? Sad Bevan surely did not deserve a general like Erskine, but should he have moved earlier? Then, in a sense, the last three – Dupleix, Elazar and Dallaire – were not scapegoats in that other individuals directly benefited, but their governments, or in Dallaire's case the United Nations, initially tried to slide away from culpability and avoid responsibility. However, they were equally victims of military injustice by being dropped, neglected and unsupported when it mattered.

Few, if any, of these accounts had happy endings, and even when they did, the weight of injustice that had been done to the individual continued to cloud the rest of his life. A critic will say that some brought part of what happened on themselves but, in the main, they were men subjected to immense pressures yet condemned and blamed by the very people who should have sustained them. Sadly, this is not a story that ends here.

SOURCES

Unless it is a very detailed and complicated book, I have always found footnotes interfere with the flow, so I hope readers will forgive me for not putting them in. I have therefore listed below the sources by chapter. I have tried, where possible, to gather primary sources, but where these have not been available, I have sought permission for use of secondary sources. WO, ADM and CAB are National Archive documents. I am very sensitive to copyright and if I have inadvertently trodden on toes somewhere, please accept my apologies, and revised accreditation will appear in subsequent editions.

I am indebted to the British Library, the National Archives at Kew, the National Army Museum, the Imperial War Museum, the Liddell Hart Centre for Military Archives at King's College London and the Library of the Royal Borough of Kensington & Chelsea.

Introduction
Butterfield, Professor Sir Herbert, *George III, Lord North and the People 1779–80*: (California: Russell & Russell, 1949)
Conrad, Joseph, *An Outcast of the Islands* (1896)
Dixon, Norman, *On the Psychology of Military Incompetence* (London: Pimlico, 1994)
Fraser, George MacDonald, *Quartered Safe Out Here* (London: Harper Collins, 1993)

Chapter 1: Captain Jahleel Brenton Carey
WO 32/7735 Zulu War: Diary of operations by 2nd Division under Major General E. Newdigate 26 April to 24 May, with reconnaissance reports, including one by Prince Imperial L. Napoleon
WO 71/343 Carey, J. B., Offence: Misbehaviour before the enemy. Case arising from the death of the Prince Imperial in the Zulu War
WO 162/198 Copies of correspondence relating to the conduct of Lt J. B. Carey and the death of the Prince Imperial

Featherstone, Donald, *Captain Carey's Blunder* (London: Leo Cooper, 1973)
Greaves FRGS, Dr Adrian, 'The Prince Imperial: A Psychological Perspective', *Anglo-Zulu War Historical Society Journal*, No. 7, June 2000.
Jerrold, Walter, *Sir Redvers Buller* (London: Partridge, 1900)
Knight, Ian, *With His Face to the Foe* (London: History Press, 2001)
Laband, John (ed.), *Lord Chelmsford's Zululand Campaign 1878–1879* (Army Records Society, 1994)
Rubin, Professor G. R., 'The Non-confirmation of Captain Carey's Court Martial 1879', *Journal of the Society for Army Historical Research*, Vol. 79, No. 319, Autumn 2001. Extracts from this article are reproduced by kind permission of the author, Prof. G. R. Rubin, and Dr M. Nicholls, editor of the Journal. Copyright of the article remains with both Prof. Rubin and the JSAHR
Wade, Alf, 'The Prince Imperial', *Military History Journal* (South African Military History Society), Vol. 3, No. 2, Dec. 1974

Chapter 2: Captain Charles McVay

Kurzman, Dan, *Fatal Voyage: The Sinking of the USS Indianapolis* (New York: Broadway Books, 2001)

Lech, Raymond B., *The Tragic Fate of the USS Indianapolis* (New York: Cooper Square Press, 2001)

Newcomb, Richard F., *Abandon Ship!: The Death of the USS Indianapolis* (New York: Holt, 1958)

Stanton, Doug, *In Harm's Way: The Sinking of the USS Indianapolis* (New York: Henry Holt and Co., 2001)

House of Representatives Resolution dated 28 April 1999, H.J.RES.48: Expressing the sense of Congress with respect to the court-martial conviction of the late Rear Admiral Charles Butler McVay, III, and calling upon the President to award a Presidential Unit Citation to the final crew of the USS INDIANAPOLIS.

US Senate Armed Services Committee hearing report, 'The Sinking of the USS Indianapolis and the Subsequent Court-martial of Rear Admiral Charles B. McVay III', 1st session, 106th Congress, September 14, 1999

Further details of Mochitsura Hashimoto's letter dated 24 November 1999 to the Chairman, Senate Armed Services Committee can be found at www.ussindianapolis.org/hashimoto.htm.

Chapter 3: Admiral John Byng

ADM 3/64 Admiralty Board's minutes, 8 July 1755–18 Nov. 1756
ADM 2/519 Order for Byng's execution
ADM 2/1331 Admiralty orders to Byng and Hawke
ADM 51/3914 Monarch log
WO 71/22 Fowke Court Martial

Pope, Dudley, *At 12 Mr Byng Was Shot* (London: Weidenfeld & Nicolson, 1962)
Tunstall, Brian, *Admiral Byng and the Loss of Minorca* (London: Philip Allan, 1928)

For Forbes's letter, 6 Feb 1757, *see* Goldsmith, William, *Naval History of Great Britain* (1825).

Details of Alistair Burt's presentation of the petition to Parliament on 19 March 2008 can be found at www.publications.parliament.uk.

Letters from Secretary of State for Defence Des Browne were kindly supplied by Viscount Torrington.

I am extremely grateful to Viscount Torrington, Sarah Saunders-Davies and Thane Byng for their correspondence, meetings and conversations, which have proved invaluable in my research of the story. I am also grateful to Judges Roger Cooke and Ronald Bartle for their thoughtful legal judgements.

Chapter 4: Captain Alfred Dreyfus

Bredin, Jean-Denis, *The Affair: The Case of Alfred Dreyfus* (London: Sidgwick & Jackson, 1987)
Brown, Frederick, *Zola: A Life* (London: Macmillan, 1995)
Burns, Michael, *Dreyfus: A Family Affair, 1789–1945* (London: Chatto & Windus, 1992)
Lewis, David L., *Prisoners of Honour: The Dreyfus Affair* (London: Cassell, 1973)
Zola, Émile, 'J'accuse' letter in *L'Aurore*, 13 January 1898

A photograph of the Dreyfus bordereau and copy in Esterhazy's handwriting can be seen at the National Archives, reference COPY 1/442/258

Chapter 5: Lieutenant General James 'Pete' Longstreet

Eckenrode, H. J. & Conrad, Bryan, *James Longstreet: Lee's War Horse* (Chapel Hill, N.C.: University of North Carolina Press, 1986)

Freeman, Douglas, *Robert E. Lee*, Vol. 3 (New York: Charles Scribner's Sons, 1935)

Keegan, John, *The American Civil War* (London: Hutchinson, 2009)

Longstreet, Helen Dortch, *Lee and Longstreet at High Tide* (published privately, 1904)

Longstreet, James, *From Manassas to Appomattox: Memories of the Civil War in America* (New York: Barnes and Noble, 2004)

The Longstreet Chronicles, www.longstreetchronicles.org, © 2000 Brian D. Hampton

Piston, William Garrett, *Lee's Tarnished Lieutenant: James Longstreet and His Place in Southern History* (Athens, Ga.: University of Georgia Press, 1987)

Southern Historical Society Papers, Vol. 23, 14 February 1896, pp. 342–8

Thomas, Wilbur, *General James 'Pete' Longstreet, Lee's 'Old War Horse'* (West Virginia: McClain Printing Company, 1979)

Tucker, Glenn, *Lee and Longstreet at Gettysburg* (Indianapolis: Bobbs-Merrill Co., 1968)

Tucker, Glenn, *High Tide at Gettysburg* (New York: Smithmark, 1994)

United States War Department, *The War of the Rebellion: A Compilation of the Official Records of the Union and Confederate Armies*, Series I, Vol. 27, Ch. 39, Part 2 (Washington, 1889)

Wert, Jeffry D., *General James Longstreet: The Confederacy's Most Controversial Soldier* (New York: Simon & Schuster, 1994)

I am very grateful to Josh Howard, Research Historian for the Office of Archives and History, the North Carolina Department of Cultural Resources, for his care in examining the chapter.

I am also appreciative of Susan Rosenvold of the Longstreet Society's interest.

Chapter 6: Lance Corporal Robert Jesse Short

WO 71/599 Short, J. R. Offence: Attempted Mutiny. Documentation relating to the pardon was added to this file in August 2007

WO 95/4027 Étaples Base: Commandant Étaples Base: 1917 Jan.–1919 Nov. (War diary Étaples)

WO 97/5895 Attestation papers

WO 256/22 Haig diary, Sept. 1917

WO 329/697 Northumberland Fusiliers medal roll

Babington, Anthony, *For the Sake of Example: Capital Courts Martial 1914–20* (London: Leo Cooper, 1983)

Corns, Cathryn & Hughes-Wilson, John, *Blindfold and Alone: British Military Executions in the Great War* (London: Cassell, 2002)

Corrigan, Gordon, *Mud, Blood and Poppycock* (London: Cassell, 2003)

Gill, Douglas & Dallas, Gloden, *The Unknown Army* (London: Verso, 1985)

Holmes, Richard, *Tommy: The British Soldier on the Western Front 1914–1918* (London: Harper Collins, 2004)

Laffin, John, *British Butchers & Bunglers of World War One* (Glos: Sutton Publishing Ltd, 1988)

Lawrence, James, *Mutiny: In the British and Commonwealth Forces, 1791–1956* (London: Buchan Enright, 1987)

Putkowski, Julian & Sykes, Julian, *Shot at Dawn* (London: Leo Cooper, 1989)

The letter from the MOD dated 30 November 2009 was addressed to the author, ref. TO/04634/2009.

I am very grateful for the exchange of emails I have had with Julian Putkowski in researching this chapter.

Chapter 7: Major General Jackie Smyth

CAB 106/176 Correspondence between the official historian and Brigadier J. G. Smyth with comments on the draft official history *The War Against Japan*, Vol. II, Ch. IV, the Bilin River action and the disaster at Sittang Bridge

WO 203/5709 Operations in Burma 1941 Dec. to 1942 Mar.: report by Lieut-General T. J. Hutton

Liddell Hart Centre for Military Archives, King's College London: the Lt Gen Sir Thomas Hutton papers 3/1/2, 4, 6, 8, 3/13, 4/11, 17, 18, 2/11, 13 and the Field Marshal Earl Wavell papers 3/1–6

Allen, Louis, *Burma: The Longest War 1941–45* (London: J. M. Dent, 1984)

DEKHO!, Journal of the Burma Star Association, Issue 160, Winter 2008

Latimer, Jon, *Burma: The Forgotten War* (London: John Murray, 2004)

Lunt, James, *A Hell of a Licking: Retreat from Burma 1941–2* (London: Collins, 1986)

Lyman, Robert, *The Generals: From Defeat to Victory, Leadership in Asia 1941–45* (London: Constable, 2008)

Randle, John, *Battle Tales from Burma* (Barnsley: Pen & Sword, 2004)

Schofield, Victoria, *Wavell: Soldier & Statesman* (London: John Murray, 2006)

Slim, Field Marshal Viscount, *Defeat into Victory* (London: Pan, 2009)

Smyth, Sir John, *Milestones* (London: Sidgwick & Jackson, 1979)

Thompson, Julian, *Forgotten Voices of Burma: The Second World War's Forgotten Conflict* (London: Ebury Press, 2009)

Woodburn Kirby, Stanley, *The War Against Japan*, Vol. 2 (London: HMSO, 1958)

I am extremely grateful to the Trustees of the Liddell Hart Centre for Military Archives for permission to reproduce quotations from material held at the archive.

Field Marshal Lord Slim's son, Colonel The Viscount Slim OBE DL FRGS, was kind enough to discuss this chapter with me.

I am also very grateful for the correspondence and discussion I have had with Brigadier John Randle over this chapter.

Chapter 8: Lieutenant General Sir Charles Warren

WO 32/7903 Boer War: Report by General Buller on conduct of operations while Commander-in-Chief S. Africa. Circumstances under which Lord Roberts was appointed to succeed General Buller by Lord Lansdowne, Secretary of State for War. Correspondence between General Buller and Lord Lansdowne

WO 32/7972 Boer War: Dispatch from General Sir R. Buller on operations from 29 Jan
    to 1 Mar., including relief of Ladysmith
WO 32/8095 Boer War: Dispatches relating to General Buller's advance across Tugela
    River and capture and evacuation of Spion Kop with intention of relieving Ladysmith
WO 32/8096 Boer War: Dispatches relating to General Buller's advance across Tugela
    River and capture and evacuation of Spion Kop with intention of relieving
    Ladysmith. Publication of dispatches
WO 32/8097 Boer War: Letter from General Sir C. Warren and remarks by General
    Buller as to circumstances of capture and abandonment of Spion Kop
WO 105/5 War Office: Lord Frederick Roberts, Commander-in-Chief (South Africa
    and England) and President of National Service League: Papers
WO 105/12 Dispatches and reports of operations in South Africa 1899–1902 by
    commander-in-chief and commanders in the field

Amery, Leo, Times History of the War in South Africa, 1899–1902
Butler, Lewis, Sir Redvers Buller (London: Smith, Elder & Co., 1909)
Castle, H. G., Spion Kop: The Second Boer War (London: Almark Publishing Co., 1976)
Coetzer, Owen, The Anglo-Boer War: The Road to Infamy, 1899–1900 (London:
    Cassell Military, 1996)
'Defender', Sir Charles Warren & Spion Kop (London: Smith, Elder & Co., 1902)
Dudley, Charles, 'Boer View of Buller' in Army Quarterly, Vol. 114, No. 3, July 1984
Farwell, Byron, The Great Boer War (London: Allen Lane, 1976)
Pakenham, Thomas, The Boer War (London: Weidenfeld & Nicolson, 1982)
Powell, Geoffrey, A Scapegoat? A life of General Sir Redvers Buller (London: Leo
    Cooper, 1994)
'Report of His Majesty's Commissioners Appointed to Inquire into the Military
    Preparations and other Matters connected with the War in South Africa' (London:
    HMSO, 1903)
Williams, Watkin W., The Life of General Sir Charles Warren (Oxford: Basil Blackwell, 1941)

Chapter 9: Brigadier George Taylor

WO 216/345 Robertson's notes, I Corps area
WO 216/728 VCIGS morale, 22 Mar. 1951
WO 216/741 Letters, Taylor to Slim
WO 281/139 War diary of Op Commando
WO 308/90 Notes on lessons learnt, 27 May 1951
Imperial War Museum 96/12/1 Collection of cuttings etc, including Taylor's
    correspondence with Slim, Horrocks and Hassett

Barclay, C. N., The First Commonwealth Division (London: Gale & Polden, 1954)
Breen, Bob, The Battle of Maryang San (Australia: Doctrine Branch, Headquarters
    Training Command, 1991)
Farrar-Hockley, Anthony, The British Part in the Korean War (London: HMSO, 1995)
Hastings, Max, The Korean War (London: Michael Joseph, 1987)
Hickey, Michael, The Korean War: The West Confronts Communism, 1950–1953
    (London: John Murray, 1999)
Macdonald, J. F. M., The Borderers in Korea (Berwick-on-Tweed, 1960)

Pike, Hew, *From the Front Line: Family Letters and Diaries* (Barnsley: Pen & Sword, 2008); see page 113 for his father's quote.

Taylor, George, *Infantry Colonel* (Self Publishing Association Ltd, 1990)

I am grateful to Beverly Hutchinson, Army Personnel Centre, Glasgow, for producing the records of Brigadier Taylor's Appeal to the Army Council.

Chapter 10: Lieutenant Colonel Charles Bevan
Archives of the National Army Museum: Bevan papers, 2001-07-1170

King's Own Royal Regiment Museum, Lancaster: Bevan letters, 1804–11

'An Incident in the Peninsula War', King's Own Royal Regiment Museum, Lancaster, www.kingsownmuseum.plus.com/chasbevan.htm

Hunter, Archie, *Wellington's Scapegoat: The Tragedy of Lieutenant Colonel Charles Bevan* (Barnsley: Leo Cooper, 2003)

Longford, Elizabeth, *Wellington: The Years of the Sword* (London: Weidenfeld & Nicolson, 1969)

Oman, Sir Charles, *The History of the Peninsular War* (Pennsylvania: Greenhill Books, 2005)

Paget, Julian, *Wellington's Peninsular War: Battles and Battlefields* (London: Leo Cooper, 1990)

Stanhope, Philip Henry (5th Earl), *Notes of Conversations with the Duke of Wellington, 1831–1851* (London: Murray, 1888)

Ward, S. G. P., 'Brennier's Escape from Almeida 1811', *Journal of the Society for Army Historical Research*, Vol. 35, 1957

Chapter 11: Marquis Joseph François Dupleix
Biddulph, John, *Dupleix* (London: F.V. White & Co. Ltd, 1910)

Edwardes, Michael, *Clive: The Heaven-Born General* (London: Hart-Davis MacGibbon, 1977)

Lawford, James P., *Clive: Proconsul of India* (London: George Allen & Unwin Ltd, 1976)

Harvey, Robert, *Clive: The Life and Death of a British Emperor* (London: Hodder & Stoughton, 1998)

Malleson, G. B., *Dupleix and the Struggle for India by the European Nations* (London: Clarendon, 1890)

Chapter 12: Lieutenant General David 'Dado' Elazar
Proceedings of the Agranat Commission, the National Commission of Inquiry established under the chairmanship of Shimon Agranat, Chief Justice of Israel's Supreme Court, on 21 November 1973

Bartov, Hanoch, *Dado, 48 Years and 20 Days: The Full Story of the Yom Kippur War and of the Man Who Led Israel's Army*, trans. by Ina Friedman (Ma'ariv Book Guild, 1981)

Dunstan, Simon, *The Yom Kippur War 1973* (Oxford: Osprey, 2003)

Herzog, Chaim, *The War of Atonement: The Inside Story of the Yom Kippur War 1973* (London: Weidenfeld & Nicolson, 1975)

Slater, Robert, *Warrior Statesman: The Life of Moshe Dayan* (London: Robson Books, 1992)

Hanoch Bartov, apart from writing an outstanding book on Dado Elazar, read my draft, helped with some inaccuracies, and approved the final version. I was also grateful to Yair, Elazar's son, for our exchange of emails, and my conversation with Abraham Ben-Joseph.

Chapter 13: Lieutenant General Roméo Dallaire

Dallaire, Roméo, *Shake Hands with the Devil: The Failure of Humanity in Rwanda* (London: Arrow Books, 2004)
Dowden, Richard, *Africa: Altered States, Ordinary Miracles* (London: Portobello Books, 2008)
Melvern, Linda, *Conspiracy to Murder: The Rwandan Genocide* (London: Verso, 2004)
Wallis, Andrew, *Silent Accomplice: The Untold Story of France's Role in the Rwandan Genocide* (London: I. B. Tauris & Co Ltd, 2006)
UN Security Council report S/1999/1257, 16 December 1999, www.securitycouncil report.org
UN General Assembly Convention on the Prevention and Punishment of the Crime of Genocide, effective from January 1951 (Resolution 260 (III)).

I am most grateful to Senator Dallaire for taking the time to read, and approve, the draft of this chapter.

PICTURE CREDITS
Plate **I** John Weedy, www.iln.org.uk; **II** © Chris Hellier/Corbis; **III** Courtesy of Commandant, Royal Military Academy Sandhurst; **IV** San Diego Air & Space Museum, via Wikimedia Commons; **V** © Bettmann/CORBIS; **VI** UIG via Getty Images; **VII** Time & Life Pictures/Getty Images; **VIII** Courtesy of the Hon. Robert Byng; **IX** Courtesy of the Hon. Robert Byng; **X** From the National Park Service, with thanks to Susan Rosenvold of the Longstreet Society; **XI** US Library of Congress, Prints & Photographs Division, LC-DIG-cwpb-06235 DLC; **XII** With thanks to the Commonwealth War Graves Commission; **XII** The National Archives, ref. WO71/599; **XIV** Courtesy of Dr Sir John Smyth Bt; **XV** Portrait by Herbert Rose Barraud of London, via Wikimedia Commons; **XVI** Getty Images; **XVII** Photo by F. G. Hassett, published in *The Battle of Maryang San*, Headquarters Training Command, Commonwealth of Australia (Australian Army), 1991; **XVIII** Courtesy of Leonie Seely; **XIX** Painting by Dawn Waring, published in *Wellington's Regiments* by Ian Fletcher (Stroud: The History Press, 1994); **XX** Dick Tennant; **XXI** Reconstruction by James Collins from an original photograph by Mark Thompson; **XXII** Courtesy of Yair Elazar; **XXIII** © Stapleton Collection/Corbis; **XXIV** Courtesy of Roméo Dallaire.

The map on **p. 121** is from The Great War Archive, University of Oxford (www.oucs. ox.ac.uk/ww1lit/gwa); © John Blackburn. All other maps drawn by Barbara Taylor based on original maps from: **p. 99**: Hal Jespersen, www.cwmaps.com; **p. 136**: *The War Against Japan*, Vol. 2 by Stanley Woodburn Kirby (London: HMSO, 1958); **p. 175**: HM Stationery Office, 1903; **p. 165**: From original contemporary maps; **p. 189**: 'The Battle of Maryang San', Doctrine Branch, HQ Training Command, Naval PO BALMORAL NSW 2091; **p. 225**: *Wellington's Scapegoat* by Archie Hunter (Barnsley: Leo Cooper, 2003), p. 139, and contemporary Portuguese map; **p. 238** and **p. 250**: *Dupleix* by John Biddulph (London: F.V. White & Co. Ltd, 1910) and *Clive: Proconsul of India* by James P. Lawford, (London: George Allen & Unwin Ltd, 1976), p. 38.

INDEX